Send Me a Pair of Old Boots
& Kiss My Little Girls

Send Me a Pair of Old Boots & Kiss My Little Girls

The Civil War Letters of
Richard and Mary Watkins, 1861–1865

Jeff Toalson

iUniverse, Inc.
New York   Bloomington

Send Me a Pair of Old Boots & Kiss My Little Girls
The Civil War Letters of Richard and Mary Watkins, 1861-1865

iUniverse books may be ordered through booksellers or by contacting:

iUniverse
1663 Liberty Drive
Bloomington, IN 47403
www.iuniverse.com
1-800-Authors (1-800-288-4677)

Because of the dynamic nature of the Internet, any Web addresses or links contained in this book may have changed since publication and may no longer be valid. The views expressed in this work are solely those of the author and do not necessarily reflect the views of the publisher, and the publisher hereby disclaims any responsibility for them.

ISBN: 978-1-4401-1047-4 (pbk)
ISBN: 978-1-4401-1046-7 (ebk)

Printed in the United States of America

iUniverse rev. date: 10/7/2010

To my wife

Jan Sandstrom Toalson

Jan, I would want a "million of letters" from you.

The Butternut Series:
Dedicated to preserving the true history
of the ordinary Confederate soldiers and civilians, by using their
voices, which are so eloquently recorded in their diaries, letters and
journals.

Books by Jeff Toalson

Butternut Series

No Soap, No Pay, Diarrhea, Dysentery & Desertion
A Composite Diary of the Last 16 Months of the Confederacy from 1864 to
1865

"Send me a pair of old boots & kiss my little girls."
The Civil War Letters of Richard and Mary Watkins
1861 to 1865

Contents

Introduction

Collections of Confederate correspondence between a husband and wife are rare. Many students of history of the period cannot name a single collection. In fact, barely a handful of collections exist. The letters of Richard H. Watkins and Mary P. Watkins of Prince Edward County, Virginia, are stunning in their volume, scope and content. Their letters begin June 27, 1861 and end October 4, 1864. Virtually the entire span of the War Between the States is covered by their correspondence.

The correspondence is about equally split between Richard and Mary and totals just over 300 letters written, mostly in ink, on all varieties and colors of paper. Most of the ink has stood up well to the past 140 plus years and is quite legible. Richard saved Mary's letters in his haversack and periodically sent bundles of letters back home when one of the soldiers, in the Prince Edward Troop, was going home on furlough. Mary saved all of Richard's letters in a trunk and placed the bundles of returned letters with them for safe keeping. Then an even more remarkable event occurred when their children saved not only the soldier's letters, but also the letters of the farm wife, and donated the entire grouping to the Virginia Historical Society.

When I was researching and editing *No Soap, No Pay, Diarrhea, Dysentery & Desertion*, I found a wonderful group of letters from Sgt. Nathaniel V. Watkins, of the 34th Virginia Infantry, in the collection of the Swem Library, at the College of William and Mary, in Williamsburg, Virginia. In the collection was one 1864 letter from Captain Richard Watkins to his younger brother Nathaniel.

Richard's humor, his phrasing, his writing style and his warmth were remarkable. After publishing the book I started wondering if there were more letters from Richard hiding somewhere. Finding over 300 letters, and a writer of equal quality in Mary, was beyond my wildest dreams.

Richard Henry Watkins was born on June 4, 1825 in Prince Edward County, Virginia. Mary Purnell Dupuy, also of Prince Edward County, was born on June 23, 1839. The 1850 census shows Richard as a 24 year old lawyer with $200 worth of real estate. On August 24, 1858, Richard and Mary married. He was 33 and she was 19. Richard's occupation is listed as a lawyer/farmer on the 1860 census. They live in the Moore's Ordinary Post Office district and have real estate with a valuation of $10,000 and personal property (mostly slaves) of $25,000. Richard is 35, Mary is 21 and they have a daughter Emily who is one. Mr. John Daniel is their overseer and he has $5000 of his own slaves shown on the census report. Those slaves are probably also working on the Watkins property.

Following the secession of Virginia, Richard and many of his neighbors enlist in Company K (The Prince Edward Dragoons) of what would become the 3rd Virginia Cavalry. Richard begins his life as a private but his education quickly moves him to the Commissary Department as a Quartermaster; first for his Company and then for the Regiment. In April of 1862 he is promoted to Lieutenant. In October of 1862, after Sharpsburg, he is promoted to Captain. He will be wounded in 1862 near Aldie, Virginia and in late 1864 at Tom's Brook in the Shenandoah Valley of Virginia. His letters give marvelous details and accounts of Yorktown, Williamsburg, Seven Pines, Sharpsburg, Fredericksburg, Chancellorsville, Gettysburg, Bristoe Station, Buckstown, Averell's Raid, Spotsylvania, Cold Harbor, Trevilian Station, Yellow Tavern, Haw's Shop, Petersburg, and campaigning with General Early in the Shenandoah Valley. In addition, his letters speak of camp life, disease, weather, food, boredom, picket duty, the lack of forage for the horses, a longing to see Mary, and a continuing hope that the war will soon end and that they will be together again. Richard always asks Mary for information regarding their farm and to tell him all about their little girls. How his letters have been neglected is a mystery.

Mary sends us all the news from Meherrin, Farmville and Prince Edward County. Her letters are filled with details of planting and harvesting the crops, making clothing for soldiers, the impressment of crops, raids by Union cavalry, stories about their little girls, the challenges of keeping an overseer, the devaluation of Confederate currency, the difficulty procuring salt and sugar, paying taxes and crop tithes, and hopes that Richard will soon get a furlough to come visit. Disease is rampant in the county and Mary writes of typhoid, typhus, measles and whooping cough. Her letters are the equal of Richard's. Perhaps they are of even greater value since so few accounts by Confederate farm wives are available, especially those that span the entire conflict.

Richard and Mary have left us a tapestry. These letters have journeyed from haversack to trunk to archival folders and finally, after more than 140 years, to you. Enjoy.

Editor's Notes

The vast majority of the letters in this book are from the Richard H. Watkins papers in the manuscript collection of the Virginia Historical Society. Rather than footnote each letter, I will footnote the first letter of each year grouping since Richard and Mary's letters are in folders by year. I will provide footnotes and documentation for all other letters, documents, and pertinent information.

It is my belief that the documents lose their historical flavor and feeling if the spelling, punctuation, and wording is modified. In many cases, because of the scarcity of paper, there are no paragraphs as written. You will be reading it as they wrote it. I will not be creating paragraphs.

Both Richard and Mary had unusual habits for using both periods and capital letters. This type of sentence structure is normal: *Mr Holt has planted the wheat and on saturday he will sow oats. J A Baker has come home wounded.* They will seldom capitalize a day of the week and only sometimes will Sunday be capitalized. Periods are used at the end of a sentence but irregularly in other situations.

Quite often our writers will spell a person's name or a place incorrectly. I will put the correct spelling in brackets. *Genl J E B Stewert [Stuart] is our cavalry commander. We are now at Emmetsville [Emmitsburg], Maryland.*

Certain abbreviations are used on a regular basis: Yr Aff [Your Affectionate], tob [tobacco], Genl [General], &c [etc], and CoHo

& CH [Courthouse] are the most common. You will see consistent misspellings of recognizable words and phrases and these will not be changed: Troope, Sargeant, pursueing, staid [stayed], sabre, negroe, defence, casmated, comparitively, hurridly, skulker, tendincy, and befel, are key examples. Also there will be terms such as *prizing the tob* and *labelia tea* which I will explain in editor's notes at the end of the letter where the term first appears.

Those readers who are familiar with my editing style know that I use ... to indicate that I have left out text before or after other text. ... *I have been waiting to send this letter by Archer Haskins ... and Archer must wait until he can have him a suit of winter clothes wove ... I reckon ... I will send it to Richmond as you directed ... Good bye.*

I have tried to stay true to the style of the writers and have sometimes wished that my computer would quit trying to correct what I am typing. It will automatically turn befel to befell and saturday to Saturday. It is necessary to go back and "correct" the computer.

It is my pleasure to offer you the remarkable letters of Richard and Mary Watkins.

Principal Characters

Richard Watkins
Mary Watkins

Emily (Emmie)	b. 1859	d. 1939*
Mildred (Minnie)	b. 1861	d. 1901
Mary P.	b. 1863	d. 1870*
Virginia	b. 1868	d. 1870*
Asa	b. 1873	d. 1932

Mildred S. Watkins (Richard's mother) – referred to in the letters as "Mother."
Pattie Watkins (Richard's sister living with mother as a care taker)

Nathaniel Watkins (Richard's brother living in Granville Cty., North Carolina)
Nannie Waktins

> Charlie
> Mildred (Minnie)
> un-named daughter

Emily Howe Dupuy (Mary's mother) – referred to in the letters as "Mama."

Maria L.	b. 1841	Mary's sister
Eliza L. (Lavalette)	b. 1843	Mary's sister
Nannie L.	b. 1845	Mary's sister
Lucinda H. (Lucy)	b. 1846	Mary's sister

Sue Watkins Redd (Richard's sister – will reside at times at the Dupuy home.)

(ed: All correspondence and files stop in 1939 relating to Emily. There is a letter from family in Indiana dated 10-15-1870 with condolences on the passing of Virginia. It could be assumed that Virginia passed first and that the second letter relating the death of little Mary P. had not arrived. We do know that their deaths were less than two weeks apart.)

RICHARD AND MARY WATKINS (CIRCA 1890)

Courtesy of Richard Dupuy Watkins

RICHARD AND MARY WATKINS WEDDING PICTURE (1858)

Courtesy of Richard Dupuy Watkins

Emily "Mama" Howe Dupuy (Circa 1860)
Mother of Mary D. Watkins

Courtesy of Richard Dupuy Watkins

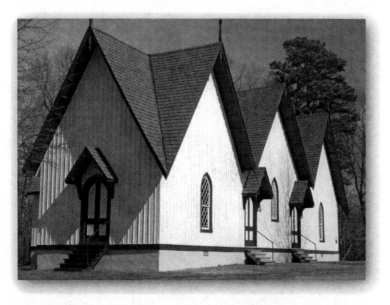

BRIERY PRESBYTERIAN CHURCH - FRONT VIEW
PRINCE EDWARD COUNTY, VIRGINIA

BRIERY PRESBYTERIAN CHURCH - SIDE VIEW
CHURCH DEDICATED TO GOD IN 1858

Photos by Jan Toalson

Sabre of Captain Richard H. Watkins - handle detail

Courtesy of Richard Dupuy Watkins

Envelope to Captain Richard Watkins from Mary
with Moore's Ordinary penciled in the upper corner
actual size 6" x 3 1/2"

Author's collection

EMILY "EMMIE" WATKINS (CIRCA 1878)

Courtesy of Richard Dupuy Watkins

ASA DUPUY WATKINS
(CIRCA 1920)

Courtesy of Richard Dupuy Watkins

EMILY "EMMIE" WATKINS DUPUY
(CIRCA 1925)

Courtesy of Richard Dupuy Watkins

WATKINS HEADSTONE
WESTVIEW CEMETERY, FARMVILLE, VIRGINIA

Photo by Jan Toalson

Formation of the 3rd Virginia Cavalry

When Virginia seceded, in May of 1861, companies of artillery, cavalry and infantry began to muster throughout the state. Some of these units had existed as militia companies from earlier times and many were literally created from scratch. In the weeks during May and June the eleven companies that would serve in the 3rd Virginia Cavalry were formed and mustered in for one year of service:

Co A   Mecklenburg Dragoons (Boydton Cavalry) Mecklenburg County
Mustered in 5-14-61 with 121 men on the 1861 rolls

Co B   Old Dominion Dragoons   Hampton & Newport News
Mustered in 5-14-61 with an initial 80 men

Co C   Black Walnut Dragoons   Halifax County
Mustered in 5-20-61 with an initial 84 men

Co D   Charles City Troop   Charles City County
Mustered in 5-18-61 with 84 men on the 1861 rolls

Co E   Nottoway Troop   Nottoway County
Mustered in 5-27-61 with 58 men enlisted in 1861

Co F   New Kent Cavalry   New Kent County
Mustered in 6-28-61 with an initial 63 men

Co G   Cumberland Light Dragoons   Cumberland County
Mustered in 5-14-61 with 88 men mustered in 1861

Co H   Catawba Troop   Halifax County
Mustered in 5-30-61 with 75 men in 1861

Co I   *James City Cavalry*   *James City County*
        Mustered in 6-24-61 with 57 men enlisted in 1861
        Transferred to 5ᵗʰ Virginia Cavalry on May 1, 1862

Co I   Dinwiddie Cavalry   Dinwiddie County
        Mustered in 5-29-61 with an initial 79 men

Co K   Prince Edward Dragoons   Prince Edward County
        Mustered in 6-24-61 with 58 men on the 1861 rolls

The 3ʳᵈ Virginia Cavalry is cross section of troops from the Peninsula, the Appomattox River basin and the southside counties of Halifax and Mecklenburg. In total, 1724 men will serve in the unit during the conflict. As is the custom in the 1860's, each company elected its own officers.

On July 1, 1861 they are officially transferred to the Confederate service and designated as the 2ⁿᵈ Virginia Cavalry. The companies are ordered to various locations for training, instruction and drill. The Mecklenburg, Cumberland and Prince Edward Companies are sent to Ashland, Virginia. On October 31, 1861 they are redesignated as the 3ʳᵈ Virginia Cavalry.

The Confederate government orders a re-organization effective April 26, 1862. John T. Thornton of Company K is elected the Lt. Colonel for the regiment in the April 26 election. He had been the initial Captain of Company K. Peyton R. Berkely, Richard H. Watkins and finally John H. Knight, successively, will be Captains of the Prince Edward Dragoons during the war. 1

CAMP ASHLAND
June 27 to August 26, 1861

In late June of 1861 the Prince Edward Troop is ordered to Ashland, Virginia, for organization and training. They arrive in Ashland on June 29th and commence what will be two months of drilling and boredom. Richard, with his education, is quickly appointed Quartermaster for Company K. On July 1st he writes a marvelous letter to Mary detailing the daily duties of the Quartermaster. Three days later he is promoted to Assistant Quartermaster for the Regiment. This will earn him more pay and also relieves him of drill and guard duty. In late July, while in Richmond on Regimental business, he will encounter President Jefferson Davis who "appeared care worn and pale." Richard's letters describe the ease of early camp life. He constantly asks questions about the crops and the farm and begins his trademark closing note to "kiss my little girls."

Mary keeps Richard current with events on the farm and with what little Emmie and Minnie are doing. She does not like living alone at Oldham with the girls so she moves to Linden to live with her mother and several sisters. There is considerable bad news about local soldiers in the battle of Cheat River in western Virginia. Typhoid fever is prevalent in Prince Edward County and several folks have died and others are sick. In her farm updates, she tells Richard that "the corn crops are very fine."

Both the Union and the Confederacy are still working to assemble and create their armies and to organize governmental departments and command structures to fight a war. The state of Tennessee secedes on June 8th, and on June 11th West Virginia secedes from Virginia in a convention in Wheeling. The United States government recognizes that secession.

Two early significant victories are won by Confederate forces at Manassas, Virginia, on July 21st and at Wilson's Creek, Missouri, on August 10th. Both cause fear and confusion in the North as Confederate forces are just south of Washington City and are also moving northward into central Missouri. Some people think the war will be short lived.

On July 24th the Confederate government authorized a second issue of currency in the amount of $20,000,000. The initial printing of some $2,000,000 was authorized on March 9th and had been printed in New York City. Most of the second issue is printed in Richmond, Virginia. [1]

Letter from Private Richard Watkins to Mary Watkins

Richmond
June 27th 1861

My Darling Wife

We reached Richmond last night after Dark & Excepting the fatigue and the heat our trip was in all respects a most delightful one. The citizens of Cumberland & Powhatan received us most cordially, [   ] and cheered all along the road, until our men became hoarse from responding. They had heard of us coming and 'twould surprise you to learn that ice water and a great many nice drinks &ct were meeting us all along the road. And I am satisfied that you can form no idea of the enthusiastic greeting which we received on reaching Manchester.

Last night after riding 30 miles and being greatly fatigued we reached our stables, fed, watered, and curried our horses, walked them about a mile to a large tobacco factory, carrying our baggage. Laid on beds with straw down upon the factory floor and slept. Retired at half after twelve and arose at day break. All hands getting on finely. Couldn't get any place to have our rations cooked & this morning after the stable exercises the Capt gave us permission to breakfast at the Hotels. I have finished my breakfast, [   ] Cousin Barrett (good old fellow) and am writing in his [   ]. I have no time to write more. Please say to Cousin Robert Smith to have my tobacco sent as [   ] as possible to McKinney & Dupuy. They tell me that tob[acco] is selling very well indeed in good qualities. Please send to me in Ashland Care of Capt Thornton & Care of McKinney & Dupuy Richmond a small trunk packed with shirts drawers & socks & collars a goodly number of them just such as I have. Kiss my little girls for me & give love to all.
Your own
Richard 2

(ed: Richard signs all of his letters with the abbreviation Rrd and since I really have no way to easily type that abbreviation I will just spell it out as Richard. He will also use tob, quite often, as his abbreviation for tobacco.)

- - - - -

Letter from Private Richard Watkins to Mary Watkins

Ashland
June 29th 61

My Darling child

Here I am. We reached here yesterday afternoon. The Charlotte Troop and the [   ] Halifax Troop had left the day before. But we were kindly recd by the Lunenburg & Cumberland Troops. The Lunenburg Troop had a good dinner in readiness and have treated us with marked kindness. I will after we get fixed I will write again & give a detailed account of our manner of living. I met with the Meherrins in Richmond. They are doing well. Our troopers are all well & very cheerful. I think they have the right spirit. Yesterday Capt Thornton appointed me Quartermaster of his Company. Am kept very busy all day but have no duties to perform at night. Think that after keeping house during the war for 60 men I will be able to relieve you entirely of housekeeping when I return. We are getting on finely, but do not appear altogether as neat as we sometimes appear at home. Would write more but have not the time. Have bought me some stationary and will write to you frequently. Orlando Smith & Taylor Johns were specially kind to me last night. I slept with Taylor. We have just had a heavy rain which will relieve us of the dust. My quartermaster duties exempt me from drill and when the dust is very thick will sometimes probably take [   ] of it. Mean to drill whenever I can. Much love to all. Kiss my little girls.
Your own
Richard

- - - - -

Letter from Mary Watkins to Private Richard Watkins

Home July 1st 1861

My dear Husband

I shall send your trunk off tomorrow morning and though it is right late at night I must write you a few lines to send along with it. I wish you were here to talk to me and pet me some. You don't know how much I miss you. It hardly seems like home over here without you, I am all the time listening for your step and hoping that you will come in after while. Willie is staying with me tonight but she has gone to bed and is fast asleep. I wonder what you are doing now, sleeping soundly and sweetly I hope. I am so glad you don't have to stand guard at night.

I have been rummaging the house and office over today looking for a small trunk but can't find any that will do. I hope the one I send will not incommode you much but I am afraid it will take up too much of your tent room. Mama has been over this evening and brought a pillow, four or five bottles of blackberry bounce and some ginger cakes to put in the trunk, but I am afraid I shall have to leave out the bounce, there is so much room in the trunk that I can't put it in securely. My ink is so thick I can hardly write and I believe my eyes are getting heavy too. So I must say goodnight.

Tuesday morning
Mama has come over to breakfast: she was so much afraid I would not send your trunk off in time, but it had gone before she got here. Nannie has been right unwell for several days and we began to feel right uneasy about her she took a violent cold, bathing a week or two ago and hasn't been well since. Aunt Milly has been laid up for several days but I don't think there is much the matter with her, Purnall has a pain in his breast too this morning. Tilman came back the day you left, half starved and with a mighty bad cold he said.

I am going to move over to Ma's in a day or two though I think I could stay here very well. I will put the key to your trunk in this letter. Write as often as you can to
Your aff
Mary

(ed: Richard and Mary Watkins call their home place "Oldham.")

- - - - -

Letter from Private Richard Watkins to Mary Watkins

Ashland
July 1, 1861

My Precious Wife,

We are getting on finely all well & cheerful. Yesterday (Sunday) I attended church and heard a good sermon from old Jesse Armstead. Suppose you recd my letter of Saturday telling of my appointment to the office of Quartermaster & Commissary for our Company. My duties are to arise at 4o'clock in the morning & attend roll call. Immediately after that with my own hand, I measure out corn for 59 horses, after that I measure hay by taking it up by the armfulls for the same number, then take breakfast, then go on foot to head quarters – nearly half mile off taking with me 5 or 6 men and get provisions for the men. bacon or beef, bread (Bakery) coffee sugar, beans or rice, salt vinegar soap & candles. These are carried in bags on the mens shoulders to camp on reaching which I take them bag by bag around to the doors of the several tents and measure out provisions to the men for the day. This brings me to 12o'clock (our days counting from 12o'clock to 12 of the next day) At 12 I begin again to measure out corn & hay for the horses, then eat dinner. After dinner I make out my requisitions for provisions and get them signed by the Captain and take them to head quarters taking with me men to load a wagon with corn & hay for the horses, then go to the post office then return & deal out provisions for the horses, then eat supper then attend prayers (this commenced last night I being

8

requested to conduct them) After prayers I attend roll call and then spread my overcoat on some planks throw my bed without straw upon that (the authorities have promised us straw but don't get it) and cover with my blanket and sleep soundly exempt from all guard duties till morning. –

My messmates are Alick Crable, Charley Redd, Jno Redd, Lee Redd, Truman Redd, Charles Crawley, Fayettte Scott, (Meredith, Bragg & Williams of Farmville) & 2 others whose names do not just now occur to me. We have two good tents & 2 stalls, are very snugly fixed now & begin to feel at home. Wish you could come to see us. It has rained nearly all the time that we have been here. The place ought to still be called Slash Cottage. Mr. H. Wall of Meherrin has just come in. He comes on a visit to the [   ] Company. I must close in order to send this letter by him. I have recd no letter at all since leaving home and was much gratified at hearing by Mr Wall that you were all well. I requested that you send me a small trunk full of my underclothes, shirts, drawers, collars, socks & also a pair of black cloth pants. I find that a quartermaster who dresses really commands the respect of the higher officers. Also a pair of old boots. Love to all. I love you my darling.
Yr Own
Richard

Direct yr letters to care Capt Jno T. Thornton Ashland

- - - - -

Letter from Maria Dupuy to Private Richard Watkins

Linden
July 1st / 61

Dear Brother

If I had been home I should have written to you several days ago, as I know you will be anxious to hear . . . that we think of you very often, and miss you ever so much. . . .

I wish you could see Minnie now with short dresses on. She is almost as sweet as Emmie – Your Mother and Pattie spent a day with sister Mary last week. Mrs. W[atkins] thought Minnie was beautiful . . .

Mr. Bob Smith says he is going down to Richmond last of this week and means to go out to Ashland to see you all – He is afraid you will be ordered off somewhere and he wants to see you in Camp. . . .

I expect Sister Mary has finished her letter and I must slip in my note altho' it is scarcely worth reading – I am going downstairs soon and kiss Emmie and Minnie for you. Good bye.
Your aff Sister
Maria 3

- - - - -

Letter from Pattie Watkins to Private Richard Watkins

Mt Pleasant
July 4ᵗʰ 1861

My Dear Brother

I will write you a few lines this 4ᵗʰ of July . . . I received a letter from Brother Nat a few days ago. He writes that his Gov will accept of no more volunteer companies until he has established a standing army of 10,000, say N. Carolina has 35,000 volunteers now ready for the field. He had heard that the P. E. Troop has joined Gov. Wise & said if it had he would go straight & join it. He is now at home trying to straighten matters, said he had been in camp two or three weeks but the company had split up. Nannie & the children are well & he has a fine crop . . . all join me in love to you
Your own loving Sister
Pattie 4

(ed: Nathaniel is living in Granville Cty., North Carolina and is trying to join either a North Carolina unit or perhaps a Virginia unit. The P. E.

Troop is one from Prince Edward County, Va. Things are very confusing in the early months of the secession. Everyone thinks the war will be over quickly and that only a few troops will be needed.)

(ed: Pattie Watkins, Richard's sister, is staying on the family farm and caring for their mother. Mrs. Mildred S. Watkin's homestead or plantation is called Mount Pleasant.)

- - - - -

Letter from Private Richard Watkins to Mary Watkins

Camp Ashland
July 4th 1861

My Dear Dear Mary

I thank you beyond measure for your sweet little letters recd yesterday. You are indeed dearer to me than ever. My trunk came along with the letters promptly forwarded by Cousin Barrett and contained just such articles as I especially needed on this the 4th of July. I have been told this morning by Capt Ballard who is Quartermaster at Head Quarters that I will today be promoted from the place of Quartermaster for the Company to that of Assistant Quartermaster at Head Quarters. This appointment will exempt me from all Camp duties, from guard duties & from drill also 40 cnt per day additional pay. My duties are to deal out rations to the different companies here. And as there remain now only three the Lunenburg, Virginia Rangers and our Troope. My duties will probably be light. Since we came five companies have recd marching orders viz: the Amelia, Mecklinburg, Henrico, Cumberland & one other – I expect to resign my office when our company leaves and go with them. Upon my recommendation Charley Redd has recd the appointment of quartermaster of our Troope – We are all getting along finely. Lee Redd, Truman [Redd] & Ned Scott have just come in having stood guard 8 hours each out of the last 24. They look tired but make no complaint. Our officers & men have received many compliments since we came for good behavior & gentlemanly bearing. Indeed ourselves being judges we are a fine set of fellows. I went through both drills yesterday in addition to my regular duties and so far from being broken down felt as if I had just taken a pleasant evening ride. When I wrote before it was raining constantly and I thought <u>Slash Cottage</u> proper name for the place but since the dust begins to rise think that <u>Ashland</u> or Ashesland would perhaps be better. – Am obliged to close just here for want of time. Good by my dear dear wife. Kiss my little girls again & again for me and be assured that I will come home as early as possible.

Good bye Much love to all

Your own

Richard

- - - - -

Letter from Mary Watkins to Private Richard Watkins

Linden July 8th 1861

My dear dear Husband

I am so much obliged to you for writing me so often, I know if you are as glad to get my letters as I am yours, I ought to write every few days. I staid at home a fortnight without you but was getting rather tired of it, and at the end of that time was right glad to come back to Mama's. I am going over again this morning for an hour or two, and then up to the depot, hoping to get a letter from you. Minnie has learned to eat right well, and I can leave her now for several hours at a time. Ma says I am thinner than ever and she starved Minnie to it, and made her drink half a cup of milk yesterday. I think it is right strange Minnie never has sucked her thumb since the morning you left. I try to make her do it sometimes but she has forgotten how altogether. Emmie is really getting right-fat and well and isn't half so bad as she was. She sits in the porch almost – all day playing with her doll babies. She is a funny child. . . . She says I must send you this flower and tell you "How ty Emmie." I have my same old room upstairs and I like it a great deal better than the one downstairs.

Minnie and Edna and I sleep up here and we have real good quiet times. . . .

Cousin Joe seems to be very busy, he gallops by our house, every day or two going to see Tom Haskins some of Dr. Wotten's family or George Dixon. I reckon he was needed at home, though I was right-much provoked at his staying behind. Mr Bagby brought me a letter to read, friday, from his Cousin William Dixon who is stationed at Laurel Hill. He says there is no such good luck as a fight out in that direction. They eat ten cows and thirty barrels of corn a day he says, besides plenty of sugar and coffee.

The girls are very busy making soldiers clothes. Sister Sue got a box of them from Richmond and sent four pair of pants here to be made. Mother sent for your letters the other day and said she wanted to hear from you so bad that I sent them to her. She is mighty good and kind to me and I love her very much. . . . A letter came for you from Farmville Friday and Mama thinks I had better send it to you though I hate to trouble you with business matters.

I wish you would keep the place of assistant Quarter-Master but you know best and I am willing for you to go when and where your duty calls you. Sister Maria received a letter from Mr. Anderson last week and seems in better spirits since. I must close now my dear husband hoping you are well and happy I remain

Your affectionate wife
Mary

(ed: Mary is moving back to Mama's house. That would be the Dupuy farm home which they call Linden. Also living at Mama's are Cousin Ann Dupuy; Mary's sisters Maria, Lavallette, Nannie and Lucy; and her sister-in-law Susan Watkins. The farm managers or overseers stay at the other homesteads managing the slaves and the production of crops and cattle.)

(ed: To keep us alert the writers refer to everyone as "sister" and there is Mama, Mother, Mrs. W, and Mom. In the above paragraph Mama is Mrs. Dupuy (Mary's mother) and Mother refers to Mrs. Watkins (Richard's mother). However, other than Mama the others are tossed around quite liberally and are more confusing than "sister.")

(ed: The Confederacy has a shortage of manufacturing facilities and, already in 1861, to meet uniform demands, piece work is being sent out to the communities. Sister Sue has received material and has recruited the other "sisters" to help her sew pants.)

- - - - -

Letter from Private Richard Watkins to Mary Watkins

Camp Ashland
July 8th 1861

My very Dear Mary

Capt Ballard is sick this morning and the duties of the Commissary Department devolve on me and yet I must steal a little time to write you a hurried letter for I love you with my whole heart and think of you more than I do all else beside, the war, the Commissary department & all other things included. Yesterday (Sunday) our duties were light, roll call at 4 then breakfast then whilst the men were engaged sweeping up the yard & cleaning out the tents I dealt out the days rations of bread & bacon and joined them at dress parade at 8 o'clock. After that we were allowed to attend church. I heard a war sermon from a Mr McDowell (Methodist). A very amusing and entertaining sermon. . . .

Our men all well. ie none seriously sick, some few complain a little. My health is good. I feel I have nothing to complain of & a great deal to be thankful for. My duties are very light compared with those of any other member of the Troope, the officers not excepted. I hope Capt Ballard is not seriously sick as I expect if nothing happens to get a furlough next week and stay a few days with you. Many things however may happen to prevent and you must not expect me till I come.

The main difficulty that I contend with, indeed the only one is at my meals, I do not use coffee & therefore my throat gets pretty dry sometimes. However we occasionally get buttermilk and then I make the most of it. Your cakes were very acceptable. I sent the Captain a large plate full of them and the rest we consumed very speedily. Our fare is very good for soldiers ... and it will take me a little while to become accustomed to it ... Much love & many thanks to Sister Maria for her letter. Must try to write to her next. But find it almost impossible to begin a letter to any body but yourself. Recd a letter from Patty yesterday ... When you write call up Mr Bagby and tell all that is going on at home. Has my wheat been stacked? Has the tob been piled up? The corn laid by etc. & how do the other crops look. Tell him to thresh the wheat as soon as possible and deliver it. And tell me about Mothers crop & Uncle Joe's & Mr Geo Redds etc. Write often and long letters. . . .

My duties press upon me & I must close. Love to all. I will write again soon, this is a poor letter, hastily written. Kiss my Dear girls for me and good bye my dear dear Mary
Your own
Richard

(ed: Mr. Bagby is the overseer at Richard and Mary's farm and Mary will pass him instructions and solicit answers regarding Richards farming inquiries. Richard did get his furlough which began on July 8 and ended on July 20.)

- - - - -

Letter from Private Richard Watkins to Mary Watkins

Camp Ashland
Saturday July 20th 61

My Mary P.

We are still at Ashland. Nothing especially interesting in my trip from home except that about 400 soldiers went into Richmond on the same train with us. Consequently I could not take my box on and it has not reached me as yet. Feel really disappointed with regard to it for I am sure the contents would prove a great treat to our mess. – Charley and I went out to the Fair Grounds [Richmond] Thursday evening to witness the dress parade were standing quietly looking on at a parcel of Texians engaged in erecting their tents, when a gentleman apparently of middle age dressed in a plain suit of grey, rode up on a fine gray horse. He appeared to be a little taller than I am, quite spare, with features like those of Hillery Richardson of Farmville. A large round-faced jolly looking fellow who . . . was busily at work with the Texians, suddenly quit his work and seizing him by the hand said, "How are you this evening President Davis?" "Thank you I am well Wigfall & have come to see what arms your men are needing." . . . The President appeared care worn and pale: the contrast between the appearance of the two men is quite as stricking as that between their characters.

We could gather very little news concerning the fight at Rich Mountain and heard nothing of the Central Guard. Heard while there that a great fight was going on at Manassas . . . Friday morning the cars were all in requisition for the soldiers going to Manassas and no passenger train came to Ashland but after some persuasion we were suffered to get on a freight train & reached here in good time, two hours before our leave of absence expired. Found the boys all well and glad to see us. I am again perfectly well no cold no sore throat & no cough. Slept last night in a tent and rain poured in torrents . . . I am writing this letter at the Commissary Desk at Head Qtrs and fear . . . that our Superior Officers are making a poor preparation for the Sabbath for a large barrel of whiskey has just been rolled in. . . . I wish you could visit Ashland. I do wish you could see the Mississippi Troope drill. Oh it is beautiful. They move like machinery. The men and horses are remarkably fine looking . . . .

Just here was interrupted by a call from Capt Ballard to go to the store room & assist him in dealing out rations for five days, in order to keep from working on Sunday. Am now pretty tired measuring flour & meal & weighing coffee & sugar rice etc – Whilst so engaged a train passed & left my box at the gate. So it is here and I hope to have good eating at camp tomorrow while the Superior officers are drinking their whiskey . . .

The train brought the paper also & as all is excitement I must close. Much love, much love to all. Kisses to my dear children. Good bye – Yr own

Richard

- - - - -

Letter from Mary Watkins to Private Richard Watkins

Sunday July 21ˢᵗ 1861

Dear Mr. Watkins

Archer Haskins promised to carry a letter to you tomorrow morning and though it is Sunday I must write a few lines. . . . Archer told me that you had to stay a whole day in Richmond and I was so sorry you didn't stay here with me. And you had to stay several hours at the Depot too, the day you went down. Very well sir, for being in such a hurry to leave me. It is rumored that your troop has been ordered to Staunton but I don't much believe it . . . Mr Bagby told me yesterday that the Militia has been called out in the county too. So you see we are in a bad box all around.

. . . Sister Maria has been very blue ever since she heard of that fight at Manassas and will wait impatiently for further tidings. Mr Ewing received a letter from Henry yesterday. He is a prisoner but says he is very well treated and expects to be exchanged in a few days. I wish you could see a parody of Lincoln's message published in Friday's Whig. It was first rate. I almost believe it is (as it purports to be) Lincolns original message. It sounds so much like him. He said Seward wrote the other one. Goodbye for the present my dear husband, I hope you will come home again before you leave Ashland.

Your affectionate

Mary

- - - - -

Letter from Private Richard Watkins to Mary Watkins

Camp Ashland
July 24th 1861

My Precious Wife

. . . Oh, is it not a glorious victory which our forces at Manassas have achieved. . . . to God belongs the praise. All that I regret is that I was not there in person to share with our men their trials . . . and the honor of their brilliant victory. . . .

The health of our Troope continues good. Capt Thornton & Lieut Frank Redd have been absent this week but we get along very well & very quietly. Please send . . . thanks to Sue Redd for her glorious box. It did not reach me in the best order, was packed to loosely and in being thrown about in the cars the onions and pies became rather too intimate. About this however you need say nothing to her . . .

Please write me about poor Tom Haskins. Give my kindest regards to . . . Mr. Haskins. I do hope that he will soon recover. – Write me also about my plantation. Mr Bagby to [   ] my tob & send it to Richmond.

The militia of Prince Edward have not been called for and I think never will be. You must not listen to rumor about our being called out. Whenever that occurs I will write you. The victory at Manassas may possibly keep us here a good while for we shall not be called into service until we are needed. There are only four Troopes here now. One from South Carolina, one from Mississippi, one from New Kent & ours – My work is very light . . .

On my return I found Bob Dickinson well and therefore did not give up my place at Head Quarters.

Lee Redd has recd the appointment of Quartermaster Sargeant and fills it very well. My mess are all fattening and seem to enjoy good eating when they get it. And we generally manage to get it. My health is remarkably good. Monday the rain poured in torrents the whole day & night. I was in a good part of it with a pair of very indifferent boots, changed my socks at bedtime & slept in the tent & slept well. Have had no cold since I commenced sleeping in tents. Good by my dear dear wife I love you I love you I love you I love you I love you Kiss my little girls for me. Kiss them often . . .
Yr own
Richard

- - - - -

Letters from Marie E. Edmunds and Pattie Watkins to Private Richard Watkins

July 23rd 1861

My Ever Dear Brother

As I have a good opportunity, I send you a bag of cakes which is all I can do. . . . we heard yesterday through Capt Hughes that my only dear son was shot in the back of his head and when he fell he pulled his handkerchief from his pocket and laid it on the wound and asked if they were going to leave him there, he was left on the field of battle and Oh my brother to think he is dead, but I trust he is in that bright heaven above where there is no more pain . . . Cousin Henry Venable was shot in the head and instantly killed, we also heard Dr. Carrington was with the wounded and he was going to carry them to some house he was shot at Cheet River the enemy was pursueing them, Lacy was one of the wounded and J. R. Allen. . . .

From your Dear Sister
       Marie E. Edmunds

Dear Brother
       We have just got here & found all in great distress. Left all well at home & your folks were well but Mr. Redd will tell you all. Your own Sister
Pattie 5

- - - - -

Letter from Mary Watkins to Private Richard Watkins

Linden
July 25th 1861

My Dear Husband

It seems so long since I heard from you, though I believe it has been only four days . . .

We had sad tidings from the central guard Saturday. Henry Venable killed and Henry Edmunds left mortally wounded on the field of battle. I felt as if I wanted to go right straight to him and try to do something for him. I can't believe that it is so bad, his company were in such a hurry to get away, I don't recon they looked to see how badly he was wounded. . . . Oh dear! what a dreadful thing war is, I am just beginning to realize it.

Sister Maria says I won't have time to get to the Depot if I don't hurry, so good bye my darling husband, I want to see you so bad. Your own
Mary

(ed: The Central Guard is Company I of the 23rd Virginia Infantry. Many members of the Guard are residents of Prince Edward County.)

- - - - -

Letter from Pattie Watkins to Private Richard Watkins

Mt Pleasant
July 27th 1861

My Dear Brother

I write to let you know that Hal Edmunds arrived at home yesterday safe & well. He had a slight wound on the ear. . . . Mrs. Richardson came up & brought word that Hal had gotten home . . .he asked [his fellow soldiers] if they were going to leave him there but they had no way to take him along & were running for their lives & didn't answer him at all. He says he laid there about half an hour & then the enemy came up & took away everything he had but one of the officers furnished him with money to take him home. I forgot to say he is a prisoner on parole. He said that Dr. William Carrington was taken prisoner & requested to be permitted to bury H. Venable off by himself but they would not allow it. They buried all in the same grave. H. Venable was shot in the forehead. . . . It was at Cheat River that he was wounded. John Booker writes that he was sick & was not in the fight – He says . . . they have gotten safely to Monterey where they found Albert Todd with their tents & a new suit of uniforms. . . . Drury Lacy was wounded and left on the road at a farmhouse . . .

Mollie carried a box to the Depot to send you by Mr. Redd but got there too late. We want to see you mightily. All send love.
Your own Loving Sister
Pattie 6

(ed: So Hal Edmunds was not killed as his mother feared in the July 23 letter. He was only wounded in the ear and from some other items in the letter it appears that he fell behind and was captured more from marching exhaustion than from his wound. Early in the war prisoners were paroled and in the parole they gave their word not to take up arms again within a specified number of months. They would return home but were honor bound to be a prisoner of war and not return to their unit until the parole lapsed.)

_ _ _ _ _

Letter from Private Richard Watkins to Mary Watkins

Camp Ashland
July 27th 1861

My own Dear Mary

I have only time this morning to write you that I am well very well and most sincerely hope that you are all as well at home. We have had a very pleasant visit from Mr Geo Redd & Capt Smith (my pen very bad) and Mr Jno A. Scott. It makes me feel as if I were very near home when such home-staying gentlemen visit us. Mr Williams who married Miss Drucilla Redd is now with us. Our friends keep us well supplied with eatables and really Camp life in itself is not to hard after all. But being absent from you so much, aye there's the rub. Wish Old Abe would quit his foolishness and his meanness. Tis such a curse even upon his own people to have such a Ruler. However as for me I mean to take things coolly and see the old fellow out no matter how long his war lasts ie provided my life lasts equally as long. I am overjoyed at hearing that Hal Edmunds & Branch Worsham have reached home in safety and deeply pained at the death of Henry Venable. . . . I love you my dear wife.
Your own
Richard

_ _ _ _ _

Letter from Private Richard Watkins to Mary Watkins

Camp Ashland
Aug 1, 1861.

My own Dear Mary.

I do want to see you so bad . . . Can't you leave Emmie and Minnie with Mother and come to see me. There is a real nice Hotel here and I will pay all expenses and try my best to entertain you and make your time pass pleasantly and will try my best not to get in the Guardhouse . . . will try to get permission to go at least as far as Richmond with you on your return. I want to hear . . . all about Emmie. What she has said and done and where she has been and how she looks and whether she grows. Tell me about Minnie. Has she cut any teeth. Does she crawl? Has she improved. Does she eat . . . Has Bagby finished prizing the tobacco etc etc Has he threshed the wheat etc etc . . . The cars have just passed and I hope they bring me a letter from you . . .

I hope that our victory at Manassas will result in much good to our cause. I think it will probably secure our recognition by the European Powers. God grant that it may be the means of restoring peace to our country. Liberty is indeed precious when it has to be purchased at such a cost. . . .

Would write more but it's growing late and Capt Ballard has some work for me. Write me often my darling . . . I have no enemies except the Yankees – and am very willing to make friends with them if they will let us alone, and give us our rights and liberties. Until they do . . . expect to remain a private soldier in the Army of the Confederate States. Good bye. I love you & ever will.
Your own
Richard

- - - - -

Letter from Mary Watkins to Private Richard Watkins

Saturday night Aug 3rd 1861

Minnie is asleep and I am all alone in my room thinking of you and wondering what you are doing just at this time . . . I have just been reading your letter . . . for the fourth time. . . I should love dearly to go and see you while you are at Ashland but I don't think I could leave Minnie long enough . . .

. . . Dr. Owen . . . thinks Aunt Milly has the heart disease and will hardly get well. He gave her a little calomel and put on a blister. She says she don't suffer the least bit of pain, only feels tired and weak. . . .

Everybody in the house is asleep but me and I am very tired and must bid you good night.
Your own,
Mary

(*ed: In an August 5th addendum to the above letter Mary noted that Aunt Milly died the night of August 4th and "Minnie has no teeth and can not crawl yet, but she is just as sweet and bright as she can be."*)

- - - - -

Letter from Private Richard Watkins to Mary Watkins

Camp Ashland
Aug 5th 1861

My Darling girl,

Have only about 5 minutes to write . . . If you think at any time that any of the negroes need a physician do not hesitate at all to call in one. And let him be just the one that you like best or find most convenient. I thank you so much for writing so much about my plantation. Please tell Mr Bagby to finish prizing and send the tob to Messrs McKinney & Dupuy. We have no marching orders yet. . . . as soon as possible would like for you to send me a fatigue jacket of grey flannel . . .
Love to all,
Richard

(*ed: When you prize your tobacco you pack it in hogsheads, seal them tight, and store to sell at a later date vs. cutting and selling immediately.*) 7

- - - - -

Letter from Private Richard Watkins to Mary Watkins

Camp Ashland
Aug 8th 1861

You are entirely too good to me my own very dear Mary. . . . I have had a great deal of writing to do this week in making up our monthly report. I do nearly everything connected with the Commissary Department. Captain Ballard is away at least one half of the time. He treats me with marked kindness though and seems willing to put himself to inconvenience to render me favors. Told me a few days ago that if I wanted to go to Richmond at anytime he could always find some excuse for sending me. I declined accepting his offer not thinking it right to go unless there was really some necessity for it, for whenever he sends me, my expenses are paid by the Confederate States.

. . . They say that immense numbers of troops are daily arriving at Richmond. Oh if this war is continued 12 months longer what a terrible war it will be . . .

Was very sad to hear of Aunt Milly's death. She was a good servant and altho not as intelligent as some, was much more attentive and trustworthy than others. . . .

Goodby again my dear one. Kiss my children for me and give much love to all.
Your own
Richard

- - - - -

Letter from Mary Watkins to Private Richard Watkins

Linden
Aug 9th 1861

My dear husband

I had hardly commenced writing before Emmie and Minnie began to cry and I had to give them their supper and put them to bed, then I had to eat my supper and after that I had some work that was obliged to be done and here it is 11 oclock and my letter just begun. I suppose after the prelude you do not expect a long letter and will not therefore be disappointed if you do not get one.

. . . I saw in today's paper an obituary of Joe Morton Scott. He died of Typhoid fever, after eleven days of sickness. Poor fellow, away from home and friends. I believe I had rather be killed in battle. Hillery Richardson is dead too. Dick McCormick was in the battle at Manassas and is now in Lynchburg sick with Typhoid fever.

. . . Well it is past 12 oclock . . . so good night.
From your own
Mary

- - - - -

Letter from Mary Watkins to Private Richard Watkins

Linden August 13th, 1861

My dear Mr. Watkins

. . . I have busied . . . fixing a box for you. I am really ashamed of myself for not having sent one before. . . . We put in some vegetables and hope they will keep fresh until you get them. I wish I could send you a great box of ice with a plenty of cool, fresh milk in it.

I received your letter today and was very much obliged to you for writing . . . I am very well and am fat. . . . Minnie can eat tolerably well now and is a great noisy mischievious thing. Emmie is cutting her eye teeth and doesn't seem to be well. She has very little appetite and coughs right badly . . .

Pattie Booker died very suddenly of typhoid fever last week. We heard Saturday morning that she was very sick . . . Her friends have little to comfort them in her death, as she was delirious most of the time . . . Cousin Joe has the fever now . . .

Mr. Bagby has commenced thrashing out wheat at last. He got Mr. Carrviles at the Depot to make the missing part to the straw carrier and put it down Monday morning. Mr. Baker finished thrashing his last week. The corn crops are very fine in all this country and the tobacco I believe is tolerable.

Ma and sister Maria dined at Mr. Redds Sunday. Mother is better and sister Sue is looking very well and has the prospect of becoming a Mother again . . . I am right tired and sleepy . . . Good night and pleasant dreams to you.
Your loving
Mary

ps: Be sure and give Mr. Meredith a biscuit for me and sister Maria says give Archer one for her.
M

- - - - -

Letter from Private Richard Watkins to Mary Watkins

Camp Ashland
Aug 17th 1861

My very Dear Mary

I thank you so much for the box . . . Twould gratify you to see how much the contents were enjoyed by my mess-mates and myself. . . .

Our quarters consist of a row of white tents fronting South with a row of stables but opposite facing North. I am lying down in one of the tents on the bed of my room-mates Charles Crawley, Rich Dalby & Fayette Scott which bed consists of a large pile of straw covered with blankets – on one side of the bed is a watermelon, a pair of holsters, a pair of coarse government shoes, a pair of gov-gray pants (the Government furnished us a full suit of coarse grey clothes & a pair of pegged brogans), a sabre, a pair of spurs, a pair of thin shoes . . . At the foot of the bed . . . is a large gun box turned on it's side & filled with clothes, sabers etc. On the gun box is a candle-stick, two testaments, a little mirror, a bottle of ink, a pair of buckskin gloves . . . a clean calico shirt . . . & a pair of dark green breeches. . . .

. . . Are daily expecting orders to leave Ashland, but none have come yet. . . . Tell Mrs Charley Redd that her husband has been elected Corporal and fills the office with distinguished ability . . .

Good bye I love you. Oh, I do want to see you so bad – I love you so much. Kiss E & M for Papa.
Your own
Richard

- - - - -

Letter from Mary Watkins to Private Richard Watkins

Linden Aug 19th 1861

Dear Mr. Watkins

Your last letter was dated Aug 8th and I began to think you have forgotten that you have a wife and children somewhere in these regions . . . We all wonder every day why you don't write oftener . . I thought you were a "grand rascal."

Pattie was here Thursday, she had just received a box of work from Richmond and left us four jackets to make. They are for Alabama soldiers and it is the prettiest uniform I have ever seen. Black cloth faced with blue with Alabama brass buttons. . . . Mama has helped us all though and I reckon we will finish today.

Mr. Bagby finished thrashing wheat last Wednesday and then hauled Cousin Robert Smiths over and thrashed it. He thinks our wheat will turn out about 250 bushels. They are prizing the two last hogsheads of tobacco making nineteen in all. The hogs are improving very fast though eleven shoats and pigs died . . .

Emmie has been a great deal better the last few days, eats heartily and is a much better tempered child when she is well. . . . I did not intend writing you half as much as this but have finished my sheet without knowing it. Good bye.
Your own
Mary

– – – – –

Letter from Private Richard Watkins to Mary Watkins

Camp Ashland
Aug 21st 1861

Oh yes: Miss Purnall you can talk very large when you know I am away off here and my hands are tied by military discipline. Never mind Madam just wait till I get home and call me a "grand rascal" if you dare. . . . Oh you are too good, I love you too much . . . It is 9 o'clock at night. Taps have been sounded by the Bugle and the Sergeant has ordered all light to be extinguished. . . . Charley Redd and I have taken a piece of candle, an inkstand, pen & paper, two boards and two camp stool and have hid ourselves in the forage room to write to our darling sweethearts at home.

I believe that next to me Charley loves his wife the best of all the men in Camp. His eyes frequently are filled with tears almost to overflowing when he hears from home. And so it is with me. . . . in addition to my duties at the Commissary Department I drill twice a day with the men and have concluded not to urge Capt. Thornton to give me another furlough until some of the men return. . .

Am delighted to hear that Emmie is well again and that all things are getting on so pleasantly at home. Kiss her & tell her that Papa says howdy Emmie. I was walking along the railroad this evening on my way from Camp to HdQtrs and met two little girls very neatly dressed and one of them about the size of Emmie walked up to me and put out her hand and said howdy soldier. How you do. . . . and now it is getting too late for me to write more . . . remember that I love you with my whole heart . . . Good night my dearest. Sweet sleep and pleasant dreams.
Yr own
Richard

- - - - -

Letter from Private Richard Watkins to Mary Watkins

Camp Ashland
Aug 23^d 1861

Well Darling our Orders have come. Not exactly marching orders either but to get ready to march as early as possible. And to what point do you guess? To Johnson's Regiment between Yorktown and Fortress Monroe . . . to act in conjunction with Mcgruder's [Gen. John B. Magruder] forces. . . . we go with the New Kent Troop every member of which is well acquainted with the country with all the roads & by paths. So you may expect us soon to pay our respects to Gen. Wool. . . . Our company is well drilled and well officered and tolerably armed . . .

Please tell Mr. Bagby to continue to send my tob to Richmond as fast as possible if any remains on hand. . . .

I will come to see you just as soon and as often as possible . . . I love you above all else in the world. Kisses to my dear children & love to all.
Yr own
Richard

(ed: In an Aug 25th letter to Mary – "I eat heartily breakfast, dinner and supper. My breakfast frequently consists of a piece of ash cake and some fried or boiled bacon. I have not yet tasted coffee. Our dinner generally right good. We buy corn and with potatoes and sometimes tomatoes but whatever it may be I eat heartily and then generally lie down and take a nap. For supper we often have buttermilk and generally butter. And I eat heartily of bread & butter and drink a large tin cup of buttermilk.")

- - - - -

Letter from Mary Watkins to Private Richard Watkins

Linden
Aug 26th 1861

My dear husband

I received the expected letter Monday and an unexpected on Thursday . . . I promise to take back all that I said about you. . . . It is three years day before yesterday since we were married. How many unforeseen things happen in three years. The 26th of August, three years ago, we were in Washington . . . now Washington is cut off from us, the whole country involved in war, you in the Army and I at home with two children . . .

Yesterday Jim Cliborne came and asked for Nelly. He brought a note from his master and I told him he could have her. I thought they had as well get married they have been engaged so long. Edna makes an excellent nurse, a great deal better than Nelly ever was, and Minnie and Emmie are both very fond of her.

Mr. Bagby told me to write you about some axes he says there is only one good one on the place. Shall I order them from Richmond? He wants to know whether he should fallow all of the oat land for wheat. He does not think it will bring good wheat . . . Horace Booker (told me that) your tobacco . . . was the best crop he has seen anywhere this year.

. . . Emmie is as cunning as she can be. When I tell her to make a mouth she screws up her little nose and makes the funniest mouth. Emmie calls it making ugly nose. . . .

Your affectionate wife

Mary

(ed: Richard got a short leave before the command is transferred to Yorktown and is able to visit Mary and the girls for a few days.)

- - - - -

YORKTOWN
September 12, 1861 to May 2, 1862

Mary's letters in the fall and winter detail bringing in the crops, killing hogs, making lard, prizing tobacco, and making winter clothing for the negroes. Sister Maria Dupuy writes details of the Mason and Slidell Affair. Typhoid fever strikes again in January.

Richard dispatches a wonderful grouping of letters detailing activity around Yorktown and as winter approaches he tells Mary that, "our company voted unanimously to spend the winter at home." Richard will amuse us with spellings of the names of General J. E. B. Stewart and General John McGruder until he learns that they are spelled Stuart and Magruder. In his letters we learn that the 3rd Virginia Cavalry is already having trouble keeping their horses well fed and serviceable. This is a problem that will plague the cavalry for the entire war. Richard hopes that the Mason and Slidell Affair will cause "England and the United States to get into a war." In late April of 1862 Richard is elected 2nd Lieutenant of Company K and two days later is promoted to 1st Lieutenant.

In February, a Union general named U. S. Grant captures Forts Henry and Donelson in western Tennessee. This opens the way for Union gunboats to navigate up the Cumberland and Tennessee rivers. On February 25th Nashville falls. In a matter of weeks major parts of Tennessee are lost for the remainder of the war. Union victories continue at Pea Ridge in Arkansas; New Madrid, Island #10, and New Orleans on the Mississippi River; and on April 7th, 1862, General Grant wins a major victory at Shiloh. Back in Virginia, General Johnston abandons Yorktown and retreats toward Richmond. The world seems to have turned on the young Confederacy.

The capture of Santa Fe by Confederate forces cannot offset all the Union success. Then on March 28th the Confederate forces are defeated, near Santa Fe, in the battle of Glorieta Pass. Money cannot be printed fast enough to fund the Confederate government. A third series of $210,000,000 is authorized in September of 1861 and on April 17th, 1862, $5,000,000 in $1 and $2 bills and another $165,000,000 in interest bearing notes is approved. In September of 1861 the Confederate dollar is worth 95 cents to the U. S. dollar. The first signs of inflation are slipping into the picture. 1

The thoughts for a quick conclusion to the war are fading fast.

Letter from Private Richard Watkins to Mary Watkins

Adam's Ranch
Sep 12 1861

My darling Mary

I reached Richmond in safety Monday and on Tuesday morning at 8 o'clock took the cars on the Richmond and York River RR for Yorktown. Reached the terminus of the railroad at West Point and learned to our surprise that the boat would not leave till the next day. . . . The next day (Sep 11) we reached Yorktown about 9 o'clock and hired a waggon to bring us to this place. . . . Capt. Thornton's Company and the Mecklenburg Troop had gone off on a scouting expedition and would probably be absent for several days. Lieut. Redd, Sergeant Knight and about 6 privates left to guard the camp. . . .

We are 8 miles below Yorktown but I hear that today we will be moved back one mile . . . to be more convenient to water. Yorktown is a small village and looks dilapidated. Most of the troops have been moved out of it. The Yankees . . . do not venture more than 3 miles from Fortress Monroe. Our pickets are almost in sight of the fort.

Must close now . . . Good night . . . I love you I love you
Much love to all
Richard

- - - - -

Letter from Private Richard Watkins to Mary Watkins

Camp Phillips
near Adams Ranch
Sep 17th 1861

My own Dear Mary –

. . . all is quiet and dull . . . Our duties are very light except that we have to bring water for the distance of nearly a mile and do our own cooking, the servants having all gone with the majority (of the troops near Bethel Church). Ned Scott and I cooked breakfast this morning and it was pronounced by all hands as a first rate breakfast. It consisted of hot flour hoe cakes, some nice fried meat, some cold ham and very good coffee. Since coming here I have commenced drinking coffee and find no inconvenience from it.

. . . I feel it was a great piece of negligence in me in not getting the measurements of the negroes shoes, but I was thinking about you and that is my only excuse. . . . get Cousin Barrett who has a good deal of my money in hand to buy them i.e. if they cannot be conveniently made by Old Jacob out of my leather at Daltons. I will also send you now a sight draft of McKinney & Dupuy for $ which you can fill with any amount that you want and the bank at Farmville will give you the money. Write to me. Adieu My Darling I love you so much.

Yr own

Richard

- - - - -

Letter from Private Richard Watkins to Mary Watkins

Camp Phillips
Sep 24th 1861

My Darling Mary –

. . . Today Ned Scott, James Baker and I rode down to the half-way house to see our fellow troopers. Their situation is in a pretty country, very level and fertile and in full view of the Pecosan [Poquoson] River which is but an arm of the sea, quite broad and about a mile or two long. We rode down to the river, found the tide very high, the water clear, salt water of course, and saw the greatest quantity of fish of all sizes, shoals and schools of them. Not far from the bank was a man in a small boat gathering oysters . . .

We had invitations from everybody, officers and men, to dine with them each mess telling us what they were going to have for dinner, Some said fish oysters sweet potatoes, others chicken stew and peas etc. I accepted Dr. Berkeleys invitation and had peas, sweet potatoes, stewed tomatoes, & fried bacon and very nice biscuit. Ned dined with Charley Redd and our old mess. They had chicken stew, stewed tomatoes, potatoes, peas and something else which I have forgotten....

Oh I do wish I could see you and be with you and talk with you ...
Good bye ...
Yr Own
Richard

- - - - -

Letter from Private Richard Watkins to Mary Watkins

Half-way house
near Yorktown Oct 2 '61

Darling Child –

... Yesterday evening our company voted unanimously to spend the winter at home and enlist again for next summer and the war department will be petitioned accordingly. For the present we are doing mighty well here....

I hope Nannie is well again and that Mother & all continue well. What is Mr. Bagby doing at home. Is he ... cutting and curing [the tobacco]. If so please write me how many houses has he cut and how many are cured. Write me a plantations letter again ... Tell me about the hogs, how many, and about the sheep and the cattle and horses.. .. write especially about the negroes their winter clothing etc...

I love you so much I want to eat you up just now.
Your own
Richard

(ed: The tobacco is cut and hung in the tobacco houses to dry. Richard wants to know how many of his tobacco houses are full and how many are cured and ready to sell.)

- - - - -

Letter from Private Richard Watkins to Eliza Dupuy

Half-way house
Oct 4th 1861

My Sweet Sister Lettie

. . . I feel very thankful that you told me so much about my dear family and very grateful that my Mary was well and cheerful and my little girls were fat & happy. I have not for a moment expected to hear anything else. . . .

In my letter to Mary sent herewith dated the 2nd and detained a day in order that it might be sent by Mr Dickinson out of the Peninsula I told her of my being on Pickett at a place called Sawyer's Swamp near by where Vidette Carter was taken prisoner. . . . But am in the loft of an old stone house with a small piece of borrowed candle and a plank and have to hurry up to go on guard and stand sentinel tonight – would you believe that that brother of yours . . . goes down into a swamp in the morning at 10 oclock stays all day & at night lies down on an oil cloth & covers with a blanket, having his overcoat, coat & fatigue shirt on sleeps until eleven oclock at night then gets up and stands sentinel till morning . . . then returns at 12. rests that day & night & the next day & night & then on the day after is put on Camp Guard. Stand 3 hours during the day and from 7 oclock to 11 at night and from 3 to 7 next morning and then rest 24 hours and goes on pickett again as before. And yet his health and spirits continue very good. . . .

. . . Write to me again dear Lettie . . . and tell Mary that I love her more than all the world . . .

Yr Aff bro
Richard

(ed: A vidette or vedette is a mounted sentinel stationed in advance of the normal outposts or picket lines.)

- - - - -

Letter from Private Richard Watkins to Mary Watkins

Halfway House
Oct 15 1861

My own Dear Mary –

I wish you could realize how happy your letters make me. . . . let me hear how my Mary is, and how she feels, and how she looks, and what she is thinking, and what she is doing, and what she is going to do . . . It was said of old Cyrus Chambers a lunatic who lived near Farmville that he wished one day for a million of dollars and on being asked what he wanted with so much he said that he wanted to take one half of it and buy whiskey. And what with the other Cyrus? "Well, I think I would buy more whiskey." Thus with me darling I wish I could get a million letters. . . .

And now good night my Darling. With my whole heart I love you.
Your own
Richard

- - - - -

Letter from Mary Watkins to Private Richard Watkins

Linden
Oct 15th 1861

My own dear husband

. . . Emmie is right well again. She and I sleep in the nursery and Minnie sleeps on the couch in Ma's room. I am going to get Mrs. Dixon to weave the negroes clothes Miss. Sally Stokes has so much work engaged & was afraid it would be late in the winter before I got them done.

Oct 16th I have been over house today and brought over all the wool, a barrel of apples, some ducks, and Minnie's cradle. They have cut all the tobacco, seven houses full, and finished curing six of them. Have pulled all the fodder and will finish cutting tobacco tomorrow. I am very much afraid we will be scarce of meat another year. Mr. Bagby says there will only be 30 hogs to put up this fall and some of them very small. . . . The cattle are not looking very well too. I am very much afraid that they will get the distemper. Capt. Smith has lost nearly all of his cows with it. I wish you could settle that account with Libby & Son for lime it is about twenty-eight dollars. I have not drawn on McKinney & Dupuy for any money and hope I shall not have to do it for sometime yet.

I have had to whip Emmie several times lately and she thinks it is very hard that Minnie can cry for anything and behave badly and not get a whipping when she can't. . . . I don't know what I shall do for envelopes. There are none at the Depot nor in Farmville and I have directed my last one to you. . . .

Give my love to all . . . Good bye
Your loving
Mary

- - - - -

Letter from Private Richard Watkins to Mary Watkins

Half way House
Oct 18th 1861

My Precious Wife

... I went out on vidette 10 miles from Camp down on Messox Point which projects out into the Chesapeake Bay at the mouth of the Back River. Tis quite a lonesome place right down in the marsh on the sea-beach. . . . From that point we have a fine view of the Bay our main object being to watch the passing vessels and report if any turn their courses into Back River or begin to land soldiers on the beach. These vessels ply between Baltimore and Fortress Monroe. Just across the river the country is entirely in the possession of the Yankees. . . . one soldier deserted . . . and delivered himself up to me. He belonged to Company C of the 16th Massachusetts Regiment was born and raised near Boston. his name is Hartwell . . . He has been sent on to Genl. McGruder being the 4th deserter who has been sent from our camp. . . .

The news in the papers last night especially the European was very encouraging to us of the South. If you have the *Examiner* of that date please read the Article from the *London Review*. It is decidedly the best which I have seen concerning the war. I hope it will be read in the North but expect that it will be surpressed.

... Give love to everybody. And I know I will ever love you with my whole heart. Good bye.
Your own
Richard

(ed: Both sides referred to deserting as "going up" or "delivering themselves up.")

- - - - -

Letter from Private Richard Watkins to Mary Watkins

Half way House
Oct 26th 1861

We are here again my own dear Mary and every thing is quiet. My little cot sits snugly in the same corner by the fire-place; by it's side my trunk, in the corner my gun and sabre, on the nail above my

haversack with comb and brush. Nothing is heard of the enemy and no indication of battle. The 1ˢᵗ N. C. Regiment is below us. Our vidette duties light and our men very cheerful . . .
Good bye Yr own
Richard

(ed: Sabre is the British variation of saber.)

- - - - -

Letter from Private Richard Watkins to Mary Watkins

Camp Bethel
Oct 31 1861

Darling Child

Tis a beautiful bright evening. Everything is quiet about Camp. The enemy afar off at least I reckon so and although times are very hard I thought I would be willing to pay five cents for the privilege of telling you that I am very well and that I love you with every bit of my heart and want to see you so bad I do not know what to do. I have a great mind to run away and go to see you anyhow. I think tis right cruel of Genl. McGruder not to let me go sometimes.

No news at all except that the N C 1ˢᵗ Regiment leaves us today their term of service having expired and the 8ᵗʰ Alabama takes their place at Bethel. Good bye my darling girl. Oh I do love you. Write to me soon and tell me all about yourself.
Yr Own
Richard

- - - - -

Letter from Mary Watkins to Private Richard Watkins

Linden
Nov 7ᵗʰ 1861

Dear Mr Watkins

It is such a pleasant, beautiful morning and I keep thinking about you so I believe I will write to you again. I sent a letter to you day before yesterday . . . I think of you so often these cold days and wish you could come in and sit by a great fire with me. I am afraid you will suffer with cold this winter you are naturally such a chilly body. . . .

Emmie is well again and is a real good child when she is not sick. My cold is considerably better too and I think it will be well in a few days. Sister Maria is expecting a letter today and I am going to ride to the Depot hoping that I may get one too. . . . You may look out for a big box of cake shortly. . . . Minnie trys very hard to talk, she can say "very well" "Papa" and "bye bye" and can scold like anything if you don't do to suit her. Emmie is perfectly devoted to her, will do almost anything for "Little Hitter Minnie" as she calls her. . . Emmie is calling for me to come to bed so good night and pleasant dreams to you.
Your own
Mary

- - - - -

Letter from Private Richard Watkins to Mary Watkins

Camp Bethel
Nov 10th 1861

Darling Child:

I write a short letter this morning because I have a good opportunity to send it. Ned Jeffreys has rheumatism & goes home to recruit. . . . Yesterday evening Genl. McGruder came down with about 500 cavalry & several thousand infantry with the intention I learn of going below the pickets today to gather all of the corn, cattle etc. but a heavy rain came during the night and . . . the ground was too wet this morning for such operations . .

As to plantation affairs Please tell them to deliver the wheat as speedily as possible. I always keep money in the hands of McKinney and Dupuy for you and mean to do so as long as the war continues. They have now five hundred dollars subject to your orders and I hope you will not hesitate to draw on them . . .

Good bye my dear Yr own

Richard

- - - - -

Letter from Private Richard Watkins to Mary Watkins

Half-way House

Nov 13th 1861

My own Dear Mary

Since my last letter . . . Genl McGruder has been steadily engaged with several regiments of infantry and one of cavalry gathering corn and forage, cattle etc from the country between us and the Yankees. They go . . . every morning . . . and load 75 or 100 wagons and send them back and they are unloaded, and the contents stored away, by the troop left in reserve. . . . A few days ago some of the Cumberland Troop were fired at across Back River by the cowardly Yankees lying there in ambush . . . Today one of the Georgia regiments mistaking their own Major and attendants for Yankees . . . fired and killed him.

. . . It is now getting late and the wagons are coming in and I must close. . . . Give love to everybody. . . . especially my dear little daughters.

Yr own

Richard

- - - - -

Letter from Mary Watkins to Private Richard Watkins

Linden

Nov 16th 1861

My dear Husband

I have intended every day this week to write to you . . . Minnie has been right unwell for several days, she has a dreadful cold and had right hot fevers for awhile. Her gums are a good deal swollen and I think she will have some more teeth in a few days. Mama has a bad cold too and is right sick today. Mother and Pattie were here Monday. Mother looks very fat and well and cheerful. She says I must tell you not to write to me so often and to write to her sometimes.

We got leather . . . last week and Uncle Jacob is here now making shoes. We will not have quite sole leather enough and Cousin Robert Smith advised that we should try the wooden sole. . . . Cousin Robert has concluded to employ Mr. Bagby again. There is no one else . . .

. . . Frank had a pain in his side and breast and a dreadful cold. Mr. Bagby had put on a mustard plaster (John Daniels old remedy) but that did not cure him . . . I thought a spoonful of Ipecac in molasses would not hurt him so I tried it and he has gone out to work. . . .

They have sowed 116 bushels of wheat. Hand gathered 150 barrel of corn and are now more than half done they say. 300 barrels will be a pretty good crop . . . will it not? Mr Bagby says he can't find short corn enough to feed to the hogs and has to give them good long ears. The hogs are improving some we have 41 in the pen . . . There are 104 pieces of meat in the smoke house . . .

Emmie says howdye to you and says I must tell you to bring her a bird, a cat, dog cow and calf. She is very much exercised on the subject of dogs of late . . .
All send love. Your loving
Mary

- - - - -

Letter from Private Richard Watkins to Mary Watkins

Camp near Bartlett's
Nov 17th 1861

My Darling Mary

... On the morning I last wrote you I was again sent as vidette to Sawyers Swamp and again a cold northeast rain came on me ... on returning to our Camp which was then near Bethel I found to my surprise that the Troop had been moved above the Half Way house to Bartletts farm and some said we were going into winter quarters there ... Bartlett was a wealthy farmer who had left his fine house and large commodious stables & out houses and gone over to the Yankees. ... on reaching the place ... the dwelling house was turned into a hospital and the stable into a corn house by order of Genl. McGruder and our troop in tents on a cold bleak hill side right upon the banks of the Pecosan River. ... I forgot to tell you too that in addition to my other trials when I reached the Camp my haversack containing all of your letters was gone. ... [that] which I prized more highly than all else, could not be found ... Charley Redd came riding up and told me that he had my haversack and had it in his trunk. And now Darling the letters are all again in my side pocket along with the nice letter that came last ...
Good bye my own Darling and I must close ...
Love & Kisses
Yr own
Richard

- - - - -

Letter from Private Richard Watkins to Mary Watkins

Half way house
Nov 23d 1861

My Darling Mary:

This is Saturday night – six days have passed since I last wrote you. This should not have happened but on Wednesday evening the time which I had fixed on for writing I was taken quite sick from imprudent eating. Had to retire early and before nine o'clock had a violent attack of cholera morbus accompanied with a severe chill. Was really sick until midnight when a dose of laudanum afforded me relief but a fever succeeded the chills and I had to remain in my bed for 24 hours. It is all over now Darling and I am again well . . .

This morning I was detailed as forager for the day and have been busy loading our wagon with wood & corn . . . Am delighted that you take so much interest . . . in the welfare of the negroes. Hope that they will not give you trouble and that the time will not be long ere I can relieve you of all such care. Was very glad to hear we have such an abundant crop of corn. Please say to Mr. Bagby that it must not be used wastefully and yet that my hogs must be made very fat before they are killed. . . . I will try to get a furlough . . . before long. Just as soon as this foraging is over and Mr. McGruder and the Peninsula get quiet.

. . . No war news here of any interest. Last night heavy firing to the west of us, but it proves to be the firing at some of our pickets by a Yankee vessel on the James and nobody hurt.

Oh I want to see you so bad it almost makes me right sick. . . . I do not feel satisfied unless I write you two letters every week. And wish always that I could write more. . . .
Yr own
Richard

- - - - -

Letter from Private Richard Watkins to Mary Watkins

Half Way House
Nov 26th 1861

My own Dear Mary

... We were called out by Col. Winston to go on a scout ... and to remove a family from near New Market Bridge. This was the Bridge over Back River near Hampton which was burnt by the Yankees to make safe their retreat. The Dinwiddie Cavalry, the 8th Alabama Regiment and a detachment of the Richmond Howitzers was with us. The Cavalry was mostly sent out in small squads as videttes to watch the different roads so as to prevent surprise. The detachment of Howitzers and the rest of the Cavalry with a company of riflemen were sent down to the Bridge whilst the 8th Alabama were loading the wagons with the family and there furniture.

Nov 27th Charley Redd goes home today on a furlough of 20 days in order to have tumor cut off of the side of his head. It was but very small when he entered the service but is enlarging and the Surgeon has advised him to go to Dr. Mettauer and have an operation performed. We hope that it will not be a serious matter. . . . I went straight to Dr. Berkeley who in the absence of Col. Thornton is our Commander and asked . . . for 12 days leave of absence . . . five or six were before me but he approved it and let me take my chances . . . I could assign no reason except that I wanted to visit my family & home. My health is very good . . . As Charley is going home I will send this letter by him and he will tell you all the rest of the news. . . . I love you and how much I want to see you. Much love as usual & many kisses to my precious little girls.
Yr own
Richard

- - - - -

Letter from Private Richard Watkins to Mary Watkins

Half-way House
Dec 1st 1861

My own Dear Mary

You will have heard before this reaches you of the sad affliction which has come upon us. Ned Scott who has endeared himself to us as much as any member of the Troop . . . has been suddenly and unexpectedly killed by the enemy. He was acting as a temporary vidette for a small foraging party, was stationed along with Charley Flournoy and three others near some thick pines to watch a road when the enemy fired from ambush . . . and shot him through the body killing him instantly. Charley Flournoys horse was shot under him and he and the rest very narrowly escaped. . . . It afforded us great gratification to have Mr. Wharey [minister] with us at such a time.

. . . This accident will lead our commander to exercise greater vigilance and may be the means of preserving the lives of a great many . . . Mr. Wharey is about to address us a few remarks this (Sunday) morning before his body leaves and therefore I cannot write more . . .
Much love
Yr own
Richard

PS Please thank Patty for a pair of gloves & letter . . .

(ed: Private Edwin "Ned" Scott is listed on the roll of Co. K with the following notation alongside: "killed on picket near Newport News.") 2

- - - - -

Letter from Mary Watkins to Private Richard Watkins

Linden Dec 4th 1861

My very dear Husband

Your last letter was received by John Flournoy and oh! what sad tidings . . . I don't believe I was ever so shocked in my life. . . . I feel so thankful it was not you . . . Poor fellow! Cut down so suddenly . . . Pattie was with us yesterday and went with us to the funeral in the evening. . .

I think so much about you these cold nights. Have you clothes enough! Patty is knitting you a Vizor to keep your head, ears and throat warm while you are standing guard. I think it is just the thing for a cold, snowy night, if it does not obstruct your hearing . . . Frank Scott said there was some probability of your getting a furlough week after next. It makes me so happy . . .

Just five years ago tonight Sister Sue, Cousin Poe and I were sitting up with Emmie [Mary's younger sister] the night before she died. Oh the agony of those nights! May I never have to endure such again. . . .

Emmie and Minnie are right well now . . . The fire is nearly out and I must follow its example so good night. Dec 5th Sister Maria and I are going to ride over home in the wagon and then she is going to ride Fancy to the Depot as I must send my letter by her. A letter came here to you from Mr. Robinson, something about law tax. I don't remember exactly what . . . all send love to you. Good bye.
Your affectionate
Mary

(ed: John J. Flournoy is also a private in Co. K and was detailed to escort Private Ned Scott's remains back to Farmville for burial. John, no doubt, brought mail from Co. K members back to several friends & families in Farmville in addition to Mary Watkins.)

(ed: The Depot at Moore's Ordinary [Meherrin] served as the post office for the area. Two main postal lines ran out of Farmville using Depots for local distribution. This mail route left Farmville with stops at Moore's Ordinary, Lunenburg Court House, and Yatesville.) 3

- - - - -

Letter from Private Richard Watkins to Mary Watkins

Half way House
Dec 7th 1861

My Darling Child

... Our Company still in tents but I, Robt. Dickinson and Mel Arvin by special permission sleep in a small room in a house near by. Our room has no fire-place but tis warmer than a tent and not so damp ... I am writing now in Lieut. Redd's tent. He is lying in a pile of straw with his bed clothes over him, complaining of a slight pain in his side ... the weather is so cold that we all have to sleep with our clothes on. I do not think that I have taken mine off except for the purpose of changing my underclothes for two months excepting perhaps once or twice (two exceptions in one sentence!!).

Oh darling I so want to get home so bad. Am trying my best to get a furlough for 12 days to commence on the 15th ... and hope that I may succeed. ... I need a pair of coarse heavy oversocks. Can you not make Neely knit them and send them by Frank Scott or Charley Redd. ... Goodnight my Darling precious wife – I long to be with you.
Yr own
Richard

Dec 8th Our troop has just been ordered to Gloucester Point which is just over the river from Yorktown. I have been detailed to remain with the baggage and go tomorrow ...

(ed: The orders were cancelled and the command stayed in camp near "Half way House.")

- - - - -

Letter from Mary Watkins to Private Richard Watkins

Linden Dec 11th 1861

My dear Husband

... Mama and I rode over home in the wagon one day last week and fixed up about two hundred pounds of lard to send to Richmond. *[see Appendix 3]* We spent the day over there, eat dinner in the kitchen and walked home. Mr. Baker the new overseer had just come. Mr. Bagby at first refused to give up the place but Cousin Robert Smith came over and settled the difficulty.

Mr. Baker says he wishes you would come home and show him where to put the tobacco crop next year. And I wish you would come home for a great many reasons. Mr. Bagby killed the beef just before he went away. It was not very fat but it was so old . . . it would not get fat.

... Mrs. Dixon was here yesterday and she says she has woven five hundred yards of cloth this fall. Mama is pulling in a piece now and I am learning to warp. . . . I am going to the Depot presently to carry this letter and then I have to go to Mrs. Dixon's to pay her for my weaving. . . . Good bye my darling husband.
Your own
Mary

- - - - -

Letter from Private Richard Watkins to Mary Watkins

Half way House
December 17th 1861

My very Dear Mary

We have again moved back to this place and are once more in comfortable houses. Today was my time for vidette but my horse is so sick that he is certainly unfit for service. Has taken a violent cold, and has pneumonia or something resembling it. I fear very much that he will die and a better horse for the service I have not seen. . . . furloughs are not granted now, but I hope they will be granted again ere long. Just as soon as I possibly can I will come to see you. . . . Good bye My darling precious one.

Yr own
Richard

(ed: *In a Dec 13th note from Half way house Richard told Mary, "I do not need anything excepting a pair of very thick, very coarse, very strong pantaloons. My government pants having nearly worn out and my others too thin to wear."*)

- - - - -

Letter from Maria Dupuy to Private Richard Watkins

Linden
Dec 19th 1861

Dear Brother

I have intended for a long time to write you a good long letter telling you all the home and Neighborhood news. . . . This evening Sis Mary received your letter and I was provoked to hear that you had written me a letter and then concluded not to send it, that I resolved to sit down and give you a piece of my mind forthwith . . .

We have been perfectly jubilant this evening because England has taken some notice of the Mason and Slidell affair. . . . Willie says she thought that peace had been declared. I ran into the house so frantic with joy. I am afraid though that I expect too much of England but I can't help being wicked enough to think that I would be glad if she would declare war against the United States.

You don't know how disappointed we were last Tuesday that you did not come home. You wrote Sister M that you had applied for a furlough to commence the 15th . . . Emmie would run in every few minutes and ask if Papa had come . . .

The hogs at your house were killed to day and Sis Mary is going over tomorrow to attend to the lard. Mamma has been in the grease all

the week and is going to help Sister M – Last week she sold upwards of fifty dollars worth of butter and lard. Thats doing pretty well for a young housekeeper isn't it. . . . Sister Mary, Ma and all the rest send oceans of love to you – Remember me kindly to my friends in the troop and believe me as ever,
Your affectionate
Sister Maria 4

(*ed: On November 8th crewmen from the* **USS San Jacinto** *boarded the British ship* **Trent** *and removed Mr. Mason and Mr. Slidell who were representatives of the Confederate government bound for England and France. This was a major insult by the United States. Great Britain was outraged at the actions of Captain Wilkes in boarding a British ship in international waters and removing passengers. The opposite action, when the British were boarding and removing sailors from U. S. ships, had been one of the key factors in starting the War of 1812.)* 5

- - - - -

Letter from Private Richard Watkins to Mary Watkins

Camp Shields near Yorktown
Dec 20th 1861

My Darling Mary

My last letter told you of our . . . winter quarters at the Half-way House . . . but that very night orders came for us to report the next day at Yorktown and we are in tents again but protected from the weather by very thick pines so that we are . . . as comfortable as we have been for several months . . . our vidette duties are very light and we no longer form the advance guard of the army. . . . My hopes of spending Xmas in Prince Edward with my own Dear Mary P have vanished into thin air . . .

Perhaps England and the United States will get into a war and that result in the establishment of our independence. Most of our people seem jubilant over the prospects of such a war. But I should rejoice much more over peace without it. I have not that hatred towards the Yankees and never have had which would lead me to exult over their misfortunes. . . . I so earnestly hope that we may be permitted to have our own form of government and our own social institutions, and regulate our own domestic affairs . . .

Yr own

Richard

(ed: In a Dec 23ʳᵈ letter Richard advises Mary, "The officers of our regiment have petitioned Genl McGruder to send the whole regiment home this winter on account of the scarcity of forage, and there is I learn quite a good prospect of his making the order.")

- - - - -

Letter from Mary Watkins to Private Richard Watkins

Linden Dec 25ᵗʰ 1861

My dear dear Husband

A merry Christmas to you . . . though I am afraid you have very little to make it a very merry one. . . .

We killed hogs last Thursday and I have been attending to the lard etc. Mama went over and helped me one day . . . We only killed 18 hogs and I thought they were right poor but they averaged 158 and Mama says that's doing very well. . . . We are very scarce of salt. I wrote for some several weeks ago and Cousin Barrett wrote me *[see Appendix 3]* that it was $25 a sack and I thought it best to wait awhile before buying . . .

Minnie is pulling my sleeve and looking very wishfully at me. Poor little thing I reckon she thinks I neglect her lately. I go away any time and leave her all day. Mama sends her love . . .

Your own, Mary

- - - - -

Letter from Private Richard Watkins to Mary Watkins

Camp Shields
Dec 28th 1861

My very Dear Mary

We are still here within two miles of Yorktown doing comparatively nothing. Just waiting, waiting. Xmas is almost gone, spent as pleasantly as we could ... there is a camp rumor afloat ... to send us home ... to spend the balance of the winter with our families, for lack of forage for our horses and to recruit the Regiment ... Tis too good to be believed and yet I will rejoice ... if it proves true. ... But Darling I am about crazy to see you ... I like to hear of you romping with the children and riding over home and I like to hear everything you do and think and say. ...
Good bye My precious one
Yr own
Richard

- - - - -

Letter from Private Richard Watkins to Mary Watkins

Camp near Yorktown
Janry 6th 1862

My own Dear Mary

I thank you very much for your last ... If you direct [mail] to Cavalry Camp near Yorktown care of Capt Jno Thornton it will be sufficient. Yours was a real business letter and gave me exactly the information which I have been wishing for. I know you are the best wife in the world. ... I thank you for acting as you did about the Woolton land. You acted right. ... It will not be possible to get any guano this year [for fertilizer] ... no probability of any till the blockade is broken up. ... I notice in the papers that salt is selling cheap in Lynchburg. ... Please tell Mr. Baker to take especial care of the young orchard indeed of the whole orchard. . . . Tell him not to expose the negroes in bad weather & to strip tobacco as fast as possible. . . . I was very glad to hear the hogs weighed so well . . . times quite cool & lonesome but we are all pretty well. Darling in looking over my eight pairs of socks yesterday I found that everyone has a hole in it. Intended sending them home . . . but forgot. Can you send me two or three very coarse pair by the first opportunity? . . .

Give love & kisses Minnies birthday on the 19th of this month wish I could be at home then. How are Emmie & Minnie. Still growing & fattening? Good bye
Yr own
Richard 6

(ed: Guano is dung from sea birds and bats. It is an excellent fertilizer.)

- - - - -

Letter from Mary Watkins to Private Richard Watkins

Linden Jan 6th 1862

Dear Mr Watkins

I suppose Mr Charles Redd will leave for Yorktown tomorrow so I must have a letter ready to send . . . We have a box ready . . . which I hope will reach you in good order. I wish the box was larger am afraid we can't get all of the things in it but it is the only box in the house that was at all suitable. . . . Uncle Shepherd says he sent a "sweet cake" and Mammy Jenny a loaf of light bread. Liny made the biscuit she was very much amused at the idea of your making biscuit . . . and would like to know if they are any better than hers.

. . . I haven't seen anything of the man with your socks has he come home yet?

Mrs W

PS ... If it continues as cold a few days longer I think we may be sure of a full ice house. ... Mama had the rest of the hogs killed today. I don't know what we are to do for salt when we kill ours. Shall I give $25 a sack for it? ...

(ed: On Jan 13th Mary wrote Richard, "I expect the Militia will be called out soon and we will be without an overseer ... Cousin Robert Smith wrote to Lynchburg for some salt for us last week ... Salt seems to be more precious than sugar in this neighborhood. ... I am glad your horse is getting better.")

- - - - -

Letter from Private Richard Watkins to Mary Watkins

Camp Shields
Janry 8th 1862

My Precious Mary

I was delighted with the spirit in which your last was written ... I begin to feel almost entirely dependent on you for happiness ... I realize now and more the value of a good wife and rejoice constantly that you are my partner for life. ... I did not sit down to write you a love letter but to answer your questions about hiring the negroes. ...

... Tell Patty that I cannot afford to pay hire for Jim and Nancy [slaves] and hope that she can get Bro Wm or somebody else to take them. Mr. Baker must get along as well as he can with my own negroes. I will of course pay hire for the time they have been in my service this year. ... Nancy's family is too large for us anyhow. Please get Mr. Baker to tell you how much plowing he has done ... Also ask him how many hogs shoats etc how many sheep & lambs & how many cattle. .. and how much tobacco stripped.

Have I not descended from the sentimental to the practical . . .
Commence telling you how much I love you and find myself a few
moments later writing about cattle & hogs.

. . . Just here it was announced that the mail has come bringing a
letter for me from Nat. Will enclose it along with this . . . Good
night
Your own
Richard

- - - - -

Letter from Private Richard Watkins to Mary Watkins

Camp Shields
Janry 14th 1862

My Precious One

You ought to be here a little while this morning just to see how
soldiers live . . . Snow rain and hail are falling and the ground already
covered with the mixture about three inches deep. We still in tents
with our little fires built at their door: all around the fires melting
snow & mud through which we are chased by the smoke . . . Day
before yesterday Charley Redd & I were sent as videttes to a point
of the York River about 8 miles from here. The day was remarkably
pleasant and the night one of the most beautiful that I have ever seen.
. . . York River is about as large as the Potomac. And our business was
to sit and watch the River to see whether any fleet was approaching.
We could see the River for about 14 miles, YorkTown & Gloucester
Point were in plain view and orders were being given by signal
lights from Yorktown to different points on the River the greater
part of the night. . . . At one time the Operator in Yorktown told
the signal master just below us that his negro boy had gone down
the River after terrapins and had remained so long he was fearful
he was sick . . . But this sight [signal lights] did not compare in
beauty to another that we saw which was the phosphorescent lights
of the sea water. This was something which I heard of before but had

never witnessed. The River seemed to have hundreds & thousands of lightning bugs & glow worms down under the water and along the beach were streams and balls of fire. It was indeed beautiful. The night was very mild so that we could enjoy the night . . . to our satisfaction. . . . We were relieved by other videttes at eleven o'clock yesterday & returned to Camp found Mac Venable here. . . . he could not stand our smoking fires was afraid he would lose his eyes. . . . and I here take occassion to tender to you and to Mother and to Sisters Maria Lavallette & Nannie and to Mammy Jenny & Liny & Uncle Shepherd and to any & every other person who contributed to the box . . . my sincerest thanks. A soldier never peeped into a better box and if I could gather up all the thanks which I have recd from my messmates & other members of the Troop for a share of the contents I reckon they would fill the box again and if I should pour in my thanks to you all I know the box would turn over. . . . I love you with all of my heart . . . my horse is well again and but for the bad weather would soon be as fat as ever – Mr Wharey continues with us [preaching] and seemed to enjoy the box as much as any of us.

And now farewell my precious one. I will come to see you as soon as I can and love you always.
Your own
Richard

(ed: Mammy Jenny, Liny & Uncle Shepherd, who were also mentioned in Mary's letter of Jan 6th, are slaves, but from these two letters it is difficult to determine who owns them.)

- - - - -

Letter from Mary Watkins to Private Richard Watkins

Linden Jan 21st 1862

My dear Husband

I wrote to you yesterday but write again today just to tell you how kind Providence has favored us. I was really troubled about salt . . .

this morning while we were at breakfast Brother William came in to tell me that Mr Redd was going to send up to Cousin William Morton's for salt and would get some for us too if I wanted it, of course I wanted it . . . Then in an hour the mail came from Cousin Barrett saying he had purchased 2 bags of salt for us at $4 a bag. I think it is the best way now to trust Providence for everything and I know we shall not suffer if we do. . . . Bro William seems very concerned about the militia . . . others are just trying to scare people . . . I can't believe the President intends taking every man over seventeen and under forty five. . . .

Mama sent the money to pay our taxes by Mr. Baker yesterday to court. It was $84 and some cents . . . Now that I have salt I can afford to sell some bacon and pay her. . . .

Jan 24th Raining, snowing and hailing this morning. I never saw such weather . . . I pity you and your poor horses today. I am afraid Henry [Richard's horse] will take another pneumonia this weather unless sheltered. I don't expect you or the Yankees either will do much more this winter. . . . Cousin Purnall is right sick with Typhoid fever. He has lost several servants with it. I never heard of so much fever as there has been this winter though none in our immediate neighborhood. All send love to you.
Your own
Mary

(ed: The initial Confederate draft will cover men from 18 to 35. In September of 1862 it will be expanded from 18 to 45. As the need for manpower becomes more desperate in 1864 and 1865 it will expand to 17 to 50 and finally 16 to 55.) 7

(ed: Mary and the family get a nice surprise when Richard shows up on furlough after this letter is mailed and spends the last week of January at home.)

(ed: A relief fund for needy (indigent) soldier's families is established in 1862 by the Prince Edward County Court. Men are appointed as

administrators in each district. Mr. George Redd is in charge of the "Courthouse" district for 1862. Monies allocated: Farmville - $1064.36; Courthouse - $735.13; Sandy River - $915.53; Prospect - $829.84; Spring Creek - $825.33. Later in the war a crop tithe (tax) of 10% would be collected to feed these families. Crops would be delivered to locations designated by the Court.) 8

- - - - -

Letter from Mary Watkins to Private Richard Watkins

Linden Feb 6th 1862

My dear Husband

I am just going to write you a short letter to send by Mr. John Redd. ... I felt very sad and lonesome the morning [probably February 1st] you left. I wandered all over the house ... and at last I went upstairs in our room and sat and cried awhile ... I am very much afraid you will take cold going back into a tent in this weather ... Minnie has been crying all day to get out doors. . . . I guess I had better stop ... Goodnight.
Your affectionate
Mary

- - - - -

Letter from Private Richard Watkins to Mary Watkins

Camp Shields
Febry 9th 1862

My Precious Darling

Here I am in Camp again and wanting to see you just as bad as ever and loving you just as much and more. My furlough was entirely too short. . . . would you believe it there are eighteen now at home and two more going tomorrow. Since coming to Camp I have been on a 25 mile pickett once and feel very well indeed. . . . I did not see

Cousin Barrett in Richmond, so you will please fill the draft with any amount you want, enough to pay Mother and all the little debts . . . and the bank in Farmville will give you the money for it. . . . Give a great deal of love to Mother for my nice box. It would do you good to see how we all enjoy it. . . . I don't know that I shall re-enlist. I must stay with you more next year than I have this. That is certain. Am willing to enlist as a private if they will give me officer furloughs, but otherwise I am not unless the necessities are very pressing. What do you think about all this. Write to me and tell me. Oh I wish you could see the roads over which I had to ride 25 miles to my vidette station. If all the roads at Manassas and Bowling Green are of like character there is not much possibility of any advance of the enemy for a long time. . . .

Good by Darling . . . Kiss Emmie & Minnie for Papa

Yr own

Richard

- - - - -

Letter from Mary Watkins to Private Richard Watkins

Linden Feb. 15th 1862

Dear Mr Watkins

I received your second letter this morning. It was hailing hard . . . I was afraid that going back to camp in such bad weather would make you take cold and it was a great comfort to me to hear that you were well.

Emmie has been quite sick for several days and we sent for the Doctor this morning. She has a very high fever and has entirely lost her appetite . . . there were ulcers on her throat . . . and one side of her neck was considerably swollen. . . . Cousin Joe says it is nothing serious . . .

Tuesday Feb 18th

Intended finishing this letter to send Monday but have been sick ever since Saturday and was unable to sit up . . . Emmie . . . is considerably better today though her throat, mouth, tongue and lips are still covered with ulcers. She is running about now playing with her doll babies . . . I feel considerably better this morning. . . .

I am going to send this to the depot now and can not write any more. Do not be uneasy about me or Emmie either we are getting well just as fast as we can. Good bye.
Your loving
Mary

– – – – –

Letter from Private Richard Watkins to Mary Watkins

Camp Shields
Febry 16 1862

My own dear Mary:

. . . Time hangs more heavily now than when we were activily engaged in scouts and skirmishing in the Fall. The ground around the Camp is covered with a mixture of snow and mud and our daily occupation is simply to provide for our horses and then render ourselves as comfortable as possible. As usual my thoughts are all the time running back to you and to home. . . . Febry 17 Monday – Heard a rumor that we have discomfited the Yankees at Fort Donelson and that they were retreating before our forces. Hope it may be true. The weather yesterday so cold that Mr Wharey did not preach. . . .

Good bye my precious darling write to me.
Yr own
Richard

– – – – –

Letter from Private Richard Watkins to Mary Watkins

Camp Shields
Febry 20ᵗʰ 1862

My Precious Mary:

The papers of yesterday bring us sad news indeed. Our reverses in Tennessee have been very great and will probably prolong the war many years by giving encouragement to the Yankees. I still do not, cannot doubt as to the final result. . . . Justice and right must in this Enlightened age ultimately prevail and we long to be a free and happy people. . . .

The evening mail modifies the news of the Donelson disaster very materially substituting 1500 prisoners in the place of 15,000 and stating furthermore that our Generals Buckner, Pillow & Floyd have all escaped. I hope that in the end our loss may not prove even so great as 1500. . . . Everything is still quiet on the Peninsula, no appearance of an approaching fight. . . . May God in his infinite mercy preserve the lives and health of my dear little family. Farewell my precious one. Much love to all. Yr own Richard

(ed: In a 2-23 note to Mary, "The weather down here has been very bad lately, raining nearly every day and mud without bottom.")

- - - - -

Maria Dupuy to Private Richard Watkins

Linden
Feb 24ᵗʰ / 62

Dear Brother

I believe I am indebted to you for a letter received about Xmas and as Sister Mary isn't well I will act as her amanuensis. . . . She has been suffering for several days with a very sore mouth just such as I had last Spring. . . . Minnie is a real little Lady now . . . she begins to walk a little and will soon be trotting all over the home.

Mr John Baker came over this evening to tell us that he had joined the troop [Co K, 3rd Virginia Cavalry] and expects to leave Saturday. Our Mr. Baker will hardly join a company unless drafted and he had promised to go over to your house every day and attend to things.

Tilman [slave] has been very sick for several weeks and Dr. Owen thinks he has a disease of the heart. – he is staying here at present – the rest of the servants are well I believe.

. . . Tuesday morning – Sister Mary's mouth is rather better this morning. . . . All send love to you.
Very affectionately
Your Sister
          Maria 9

– – – – –

Letter from Maria Dupuy to Private Richard Watkins

Linden
Feb 26th 1862

Dear Brother

I sent a letter to you yesterday but Sister Mary keeps quite sick and seems rather low spirited and Mama thinks if you can get a furlough and come home it will cheer her up and do her more good than any thing else.

She sits up the greater part of the time but suffers a good deal with her mouth and throat.

The rest of the family are well –
Your affectionate

Sister

Maria 10

(ed: On the 28th, Maria sent yet another letter telling Richard to disregard this letter because Mary was doing much better.)

- - - - -

Letter from Mary Watkins to Private Richard Watkins

Linden March 2nd 1862

My dear Husband

. . . Hal Edmunds spent Saturday here and I am very sorry I did not have a letter ready to send by him. He starts back today . . . he says he has fallen off three pounds since he came home. I saw in the papers yesterday that Fitzhugh Lee has had a skirmish with the enemy near Culpepper CH and captured a good many. I hope none of you were hurt though I feel right anxious to hear from you. . . . March came in beautifully clear and I hope we will have some pleasant weather now. I am so tired of rain and snow and bad roads. . . . I sent to Farmville . . . and drew \$400 out of the bank. . . . Mr Lockett sent me four bales of cotton at \$8 per bale but I was glad to get it at any price. Have not had the shirting for the negroes wove yet because I could not get the warp and now I don't know that I can get any body to weave it. . . . Have just been making a pair of shoes for Emmie and am going to put the soles on them as soon as I can get a last. . . . Emmie knows 12 [letters] and Minnie nearly as many. Minnie learns rather quicker than Emmie. I sent 8 bushels of Irish potatoes to Richmond last week and got about \$40 for them. Cousin Barrett sent me some stamps in a letter and I am going to send some to you. . . . They do not keep them at our Post Office. . . .
Your
Mary

- - - - -

Letter from Private Richard Watkins to Mary Watkins

Young's Mill
March 16th 1862

My own Dear Mary

The Courier is about to leave for Yorktown but I must write to you a few lines. We are all in fine health and spirits. The morning is beautiful and we have just recd a dispatch from Genl. Magruder that Price and Pike had united their forces in Arkansas and driven the enemy back from that state. Everything quiet down here and no prospect of a fight.... Mr. Asa Dickinson promised me that he would introduce a bill to exempt the overseer of widows and volunteers. I do not know whether he has or not. I have not re-enlisted yet and will not for the present. Only 15 of our troop have as yet re-enlisted. Yesterday we received 15 recruits, among them Mr. Jno Baker. Good bye my darling Mary I want to see you so bad.....
Yr own
Richard

(ed: In a 3-17 letter from Mary, "Mr Baker is the happiest looking man this morning that I have seen for a long time [he was exempted yesterday] says he feels like going to work now.")

- - - - -

Letter from Private Richard Watkins to Mary Watkins

Young's Mill
March 23d 1862

My own Dear Mary –

I wrote you a few days ago from this place but fearing that my letters may not reach you with the same regularity as formerly inasmuch as we are farther from Yorktown have concluded to write again . . . Nothing new has transpired . . . everything quiet . . . I hope that the

months of April May & June will soon pass and then if circumstances will possibly allow I mean to remain with my Mary awhile. I hope that the Southern Confederacy can dispense with my services a little while ... The weather too has been very damp and cold, but we hope soon to have pleasant weather and better times. You wrote that Ma was sick with a cold. Please write me about her again in your next. ... I love you with all my heart ... Give love & kisses – and write very often to
Yr own
Richard

- - - - -

Letter from Mary Watkins to Private Richard Watkins

Linden March 24th 1862

My dear Husband

... Mama is getting better, walks about a little though her mouth is still very sore and she looks pale ... I don't think I ever remember her keeping her bed so long in my life. Mother has been quite sick too .. . she has spit a great deal of blood.... I had some vegetables planted in the garden for the servants too, cabbages, lettuce and tomatoes. I left some English pea to be sown for seed too.... Mama believes I am beginning to fatten some.... They have taken down all of the tobacco and are sowing oats.... Mama is going to plant a very small crop of tobacco this year. Our sheep are looking very badly and only 8 lambs yet. Mama has over 50.... Write as often as you can to your loving
Mary

(ed: It does get confusing but "Mama" is Mary's mother and "Mother" is Richard's mother and although not in this letter, "Mamma" and "Mammy" refer to slaves.)

- - - - -

Letter from Private Richard Watkins to Mary Watkins

69

Young's Mill
March 27th 1862

My Dear Dear Mary

Your nice little letter of the 24th reached me yesterday. . . . You must take care and not walk too far . . . it is quite as bad to take too much exercise as too little. . . . It is cold down here but my health is very good indeed. Yesterday we had a Regimental Inspection. . . .

Have never heard whether Nat [Watkins] has returned to Gloucester or not. Somebody told me that he had enlisted in a company over there. Please write me about it in your next letter as I want to go over to see him. . . . Got bad news again through the papers yesterday of the defeat of Stonewall Jackson near Winchester with a loss of 200 men. Hope the Central Guards are not among the lost. . . . Please tell Mr. Baker not to give so much attention to my place as to neglect Mothers. His first duty is to her and it will make me very unhappy to find that he is neglecting her business. . . .

Believe I forgot when in Richmond to take the *Examiner* as I promised, but am very glad now that I did, because it has turned against the administration and I think from no other cause than that the President would not appoint Floyd Secretary of War. I am heartily glad that he did not appoint him for although a good general yet I do not consider him a good man nor can I believe that he acted right at Fort Donelson. I still have confidence in Jeff Davis and in the justice of our cause . . .

Good bye my own dear one
Yr own
Richard

*(ed: The **Richmond Examiner**, for most of the war, was an anti-administration newspaper.) 11*

- - - - -

Letter from Private Richard Watkins to Mary Watkins

Young's Mill
March 28th 1862

My Darling Mary

I wrote you a day or two ago . . . I have only to add that yesterday the enemy advanced and drove in our Pickets and gave Genl Magruder a skeer! Of course we were at once ordered to fly around all over the Peninsula . . . he telegraphed for reinforcements and we began to think we were about to have a general engagement. . . . But this morning the enemy have returned to Newport News and we are again in our quarters and all is quiet. . . . Our troop are in fine health and spirits . . .
Yr own
Richard

- - - - -

Letter from Mary Watkins to Private Richard Watkins

Linden March 28th 1862

My dear Mr. Watkins

Thank you for the two good letters which I received this week . . . I went over home tuesday Mr. Baker was planting potatoes in the garden. We have quite a large patch. All of the back of the garden where he had them last year and behind the grape vines up to the hot bed. We have a good many seeds left and I think we had better have another patch in the new orchard. I think we ought to raise everything we can to eat this year. They have about finished sowing oats. Sister Maria made a right nice pot of soap yesterday . . . wish I could send a cake of it.

We are right uneasy about Nannie. About a week ago she was in the wood room picking up chips and Ward not seeing her threw an armful of wood through the window right on her head. She came in almost fainting and said I believe Ward has almost killed me. . . . she suffers a good deal with headaches . . . and gets right low spirited.

Linny was at work the day I was at home and looks better. Tilman gets worse I think. He has fallen off and looks very pale. . . . I have not time to write more. . . . Goodbye
Your own
Mary

- - - - -

Letter from Private Richard Watkins to Mary Watkins

Young's Mill
Apr 1 1862

My own Dear Mary

Your letters always come in the very best time . . . I know you are the best wife in the world. I love you too much and yet I do not feel that I love you enough. . . . Nearly every day we hear rumors that the Yankees are advancing . . . We may have fighting here this spring and summer . . . Our fortifications are getting to be very strong . . . I thank you much for the larger potatoe patch which you had planted. It was exactly what I wanted done, the very best use which you could have made of the gardens. Darling I had to borrow the paper envelope, all our baggage was sent back to Lebanon some time ago . . . Hope to have my paper soon and will write again. Yr own Richard

(ed: In a letter dated April 2nd, Mary wrote, "The children are well and Minnie as bad as ever squalling at the top of her voice. . . . several of the Meherrin Grays were missing after the battle near Winchester and they don't know whether killed or taken prisoner. . . . Nat Venable was killed.")

- - - - -

Letter from Mary Watkins to Private Richard Watkins

Apr 6th 1862
Linden

My dear Husband

It is such a beautiful quiet Sunday evening. Mama and all the children are out doors . . . There was no preaching at Mt. Pleasant today and Bob [horse] was too lame to take us to Briery. . . . Mother is not as well as when I was there and had the Doctor to see her twice last week. She has no appetite and a dreadful cough . . . We have not heard from Bro Nat since he left Richmond he wrote Mother then that he had joined some artillery company on the Peninsula but did not say what one. . . . Tilman is failing every day. We don't think he can live many days longer. It is a great effort for him to eat now and he does not sleep at all unless he is under the influence of laudanum. . . .

Minnie was right sick last night was vomiting all night and has thrown up several times this morning. Mama says she will have to take calomel but I dread that so much I have been putting it off as long as I can. She is asleep now . . . Good bye. I must go see to Minnie.
Yours affectionately
Mary

(ed: Calomel is mercury chloride. When used as a purgative it is normally a white, tasteless compound. It can also be used externally in a powder or paste form. Sometimes massive necrosis and tissue loss can occur with excess dosages. This is referred to as mercurial gangrene. Doses of 5 to 10 grains, 320 – 640 milligrams, were quite common. In 1984, the smallest dosage of mercury chloride reported to cause death was 500 milligrams.)
12

- - - - -

Letter from Mary Watkins to Private Richard Watkins

Linden
Apr 11 1862

Dear Mr Watkins

We have had nothing but rain, rain, rain since I last wrote ... Tilman died very suddenly last Monday. Harriet was helping him sit up and he fell back and died. Mama and Mrs. Geo Redd sent their hands over to our house for two days and have all of our tobacco stripped out. Mr Baker goes over every day and I think it is quite necessary.... Tom is very careless with the stock and he frequently finds the cattle in the wheat. We lost a young cow this week through carelessness .. . There was a right heavy frost last night and we are afraid the frost is killing....
Good bye, Your own
Mary

(ed: In letters sent to Mary on April 9th and 11th Richard noted, "the enemy advance, infantry lines skirmishing, and the Troop is now in a rear guard area near Lebanon Church. The lines are about a mile apart and in some cases a few hundred yards. Very little fighting and some skirmishing every day.")

– – – – –

Letter from Private Richard Watkins to Mary Watkins

Camp near Lebanon Church
Apr 15th 1862

My darling Mary

Twas so good of you to write me again so soon . . . We are still patiently awaiting an attack from the enemy. When we were ordered to the rear of our Army and the enemy advanced . . . I expected a great battle . . . nothing of especial interest occurs . . . and we have nothing at all to do . . . Forgot to tell you that the Prince George Troop is near us now. Saw Dr. Dupuy a few days ago . . . and had a pleasant talk. His brother William is in the Nottoway Troop . . . Will always tell you all whether good or bad news – Give much love to all. I'm delighted that they are well again & write to me every day Darling.

Yr own,

Richard

- - - - -

Letter from Pattie Watkins to Private Richard Watkins

Mt Pleasant
April 15th /62

My Dear Brother

I went down to see your wife and children a few days ago, & thinking perhaps you would like to hear about them, concluded I would write you a few lines. Mary was just about starting to walk over home & as I had to go to the Depot I carried her over & left her & she walked back, she looked very cheerful & happy. Minnie looked a little thin but she & Emmie were both well & were glad to see me I carried Emmie some flowers & as soon as she got them she said, "I will send Papa some flowers." . . .

. . . Brother Nat wrote that he was as well fixed as he could be without a wife & children said he was going to write to you & said that you must go see him when you get a chance he would go to see you if he knew where to find you. He is at Gloucester Point in the King & Queen Artillery Capt. John R Bagby. . . .

All join me in love to you.
Your own Sister
Pattie

(ed: Gloucester Point is on the north bank of the York River directly across from Yorktown. So, while they are just a few miles from each other, depending on where Richard is camped, they have a very wide river separating them.)

- - - - -

Letter from Private Richard Watkins to Mary Watkins

Camp near Lebanon Church
April 18th 1862

My Precious Mary

Since my last written about 3 or 4 days ago nothing of especial interest has happened except a sharp engagement on the 16th . . . at Dam No 1 on our line of defense. . . . From the most reliable information our loss was about 25 killed and about 70 wounded. After fighting more than an hour the enemy were repulsed . . . with quite a heavy loss. . . . Col. McKinney (Cousin Barrett's nephew) was killed while leading his regiment . . . We have been very strongly reinforced . . . and if Genl McClellan reaches Richmond by this route his picked men will have to do some very pretty fighting. Darling I see by a Proclamation of Gov Letcher that as soon as our time is out we will be immediately drafted as militia and put right back into service again. I am sorry indeed that this is so . . . The condition of our country is such as to require every man in the field who can bear arms. . . . I still think of joining the artillery with Nat. Since my last letter about one half of our company has been sick I among the rest from exposure and the irregular & poor fare but yesterday I took a large opium & ipecac pill and today some crème of tartar and feel nearly well again. . . . Supper is announced and tis most too late to write more today, will not seal my letter tonight and add to it tomorrow if I can . . . So good night my dear dear precious one. . . .
Yr own
Richard

- - - - -

Letter from Mary Watkins to Private Richard Watkins

Linden April 20th 1862

My dear Husband

The children are sleeping quietly and I sitting up stairs by the the fire very snug and cozy this rainy Sunday night. Everything is so comfortable around me that I can not help thinking about you . . . my poor soldier who is probably lying out in the rain without even a tent to shelter him. It makes me feel so badly . . . I received a letter from you yesterday but it was written eight days ago . . . I expect the Yankees, now that they have got Fredericksburg will approach Richmond from that direction and you will not have much more to do on the Peninsular. O! dear how I wish this miserable war was over. Two refugees staid here last night from Leesburg Louden [Loudoun] County . . . they give a terrible account of the state of things about Leesburg. . . . I must go to bed now for I must get up very early tomorrow morning and make out our tax bill to send to court. I forgot all about it until Mama reminded me of it this evening. . . .

All send love. Your affectionate
Mary

- - - - -

Letter from Private Richard Watkins to Mary Watkins

Camp near Lebanon Church
April 22nd 1862

My Dear Dear Mary

No further news from here . . . Perfectly quiet. We have nothing to do . . . We have had a great deal of rain but since bringing a few of our tents have been comparitively comfortable. I recd a few days ago a letter from Pattie dated 15th April bringing me the welcome intelligence that you and our little children were well and Ma much more comfortable and that you appeared to be cheerful and happy. Am not surprised that my health improved after that. . . . the days fly rapidly away and our Southern Confederacy is strengthening itself by organizing a better army and I begin to hope that a long peace will be restored and our independence established. I hope that the visit of the French Minister to Richmond is significant of good. . . . Our Capt is so much averse to our leaving Camp lest we should not be found ready when called that I have not yet had an opportunity to visit Nat . . . Andrew Venable seeing my scarcity of paper very kindly presented a half quire and so I must write a little more.

Would you like to know something of our line of defence. . . . There are some redoubts between Fort Magruder and Yorktown which have been thrown up since I passed there. North of Ft. Magruder sat the head of Warwick [River] in a swamp, then comes Wynne's Mill pond, then strong fortifications at the mill, a large pond between this & Dam No 1. another between that & Dam no 2. another between that & Lee's Mill. after passing which the river widens & deepens rapidly. Heavy guns are mounted at each of the points named above and entrenchments along the whole extend from Fort Magruder to a point far below Lee's Mill. Warwick River a mile wide at its mouth is blockaded so as to prevent the enemy's gunboats from entering it. Mulberry Island or Mulberry Point (it only being an island at high tide) is strongly fortified and casmated i e made bombproof. Our little Troop have been stationed all the while in a field near Lee's Mill which is called the center of the line, a little in our rear in Lee's dwelling house is Genl. Magruder who is using that as his headquarters for the present. It is a large & quite pretty brick house surrounded by green wheat fields all of which were nicely enclosed three weeks ago and promised a fine crop this summer, but the fences have all been burnt up, wagons & artillery and cavalry have passed over & over them until they are almost completely destroyed.

I have written you a good many letters since coming here but fear they have not reached you. . . . Our life here is too monotonous at present and our channels of information so completely cut off that our letters cannot be interesting. It would not surprise me at all if he [Union General McClellan] should draw off his army and make his attack elsewhere. He may rest satisfied though that he cannot reach Richmond without a sever struggle. It cannot be taken as Nashville was.

Good bye darling write to me soon & give much love to all
Yr own
Richard

(ed: A quire is 1/20 of a 500 sheet ream. A quire is sold as 24 sheets even though the actual math would provide 25 sheets. So, Andrew gave Richard 12 sheets of paper which would be a half quire.) 13

- - - - -

Letter from Private Richard Watkins to Mary Watkins

Camp near Lebanon Church
Apr 23rd 1862

My Darling Mary

. . . I have written you a number of letters but the mails have been so irregular that it is quite doubtful whether you have recd them. Wrote you quite a long one yesterday. But Robt. Dickinson has just recd the appointment of 2nd Lieutenant in the Provisional Army. Is ordered forthwith to report at Richmond . . . We have had no skirmishing today for the first time since the advance of the enemy. . . .

I am so glad that my children are your children and are being brought up by you. May God in his infinite mercy long spare your life & health & their lives & health & render all of you happy . . . in this life & that which is to come is my constant prayer. Good bye, my precious darling.
Yr own
Richard

- - - - -

Letter from Maria Dupuy to Private Richard Watkins

Linden
April 24th 1862

Dear Brother

... I wish so much that you could be at home with us this beautiful spring weather. It seems to me that I never saw everything about home look quite so pretty as it does now – The wheat field on the hill in front of the house is so green and the cherry and peach trees have bloomed so beautifully and we have such pleasant weather. Oh I do wish you were here....

Emmie sends some flowers to Papa which she got with her own little hands and she sends a kiss too ...
Your affectionate
Sister
            Maria 14

- - - - -

Letter from 2nd Lt. Richard Watkins to Mary Watkins

Camp near Lebanon Church
April 25th 1862

My Darling Mary

I have time to write you only a few lines today to tell you of events which have just transpired. This morning an order came from Genl. Johnston who is now in command here that our Regiment of cavalry was to be reorganized today by the election of officers in each company under the conscription bill – I had determined not to re-enlist and being over 35 years of age flattered myself that I could return quietly home ... but it seems the members ... determined to give me the office of first or second lieutenant. *[see Appendix 4]*

Several of them came to me and entreated me to remain with them and take one of these offices. I told them . . . in no event would I run against Dr. Berkeley for the office of 1ˢᵗ Lieut . . . When the election took place I think I received every vote for that office except two. And am therefore 2ⁿᵈ Lieutenant of the Company enlisted for two years more should the war continue that long. This office gives me a good salary, gives me a chance of getting furloughs more frequently . . . and keeps me at . . . the post of duty. . . . Besides this the thought occurred to me that if I return home . . . I would probably be soon drafted with the militia and sent into the field again. I hope darling this step will meet your approval. Would certainly have consulted with you about it if I had had the time. Everything still remains quiet here . . . Soon . . . I will apply for a furlough & come home to get ready for my office. Your letter of the 16ᵗʰ has just reached me . . . tell Mother & the girls that Lieut Watkins sends his love to them. Good bye

Yr own, Richard

- - - - -

Letter from 1ˢᵗ Lt. Richard Watkins to Mary Watkins

Camp near Lebanon Church
Apr 27ᵗʰ 1862

My own Dear Dear Mary:

Lieut Redd . . . has recd this morning an honorable discharge from the army and goes home forthwith. . . . Capt. Thornton has been promoted to the place of Lieut Colonel of the Regiment and this morning I have been promoted again from 2ⁿᵈ to 1ˢᵗ Lieutenant of the Troop. Dr. Berkeley is the Captain. Mr Wharey I am sorry to say leaves this morning also his time having expired. . . . Heard from Mr Anderson this morning He is with the 18ᵗʰ Va not far from us and is well. . . . Emmit Woolton is in our camp now and is very well. . . . Genl Johnston has stopped us from sending letters from the Peninsular by mail, but has not stopped the return mails. . . . the duties of a Lieutenant are of a more pleasant character than those

of a private. Would write more but have not time now. Goodbye my Darling. Give much love to all.
Yr own
Richard

(ed: A 1ˢᵗ Lieutenant is a full Lieutenant as opposed to a junior Lieutenant. Hereafter Richard's rank will just be shown as Lieutenant.)

- - - - -

Letter from Mary Watkins to Private Richard Watkins

Linden Apr. 28ᵗʰ 1862

Dear Mr Watkins

I have received three letters from you within a week . . . I felt very badly when I heard you were sick and don't know what I should have done if you had not written again soon and told me you were better. . . . Sister Maria wrote the last of the week and I thought it was not worthwhile for me to write too.

. . . I am very glad Cousin Andrew is with you and hope if you re-enlist it will be in the Company with him. The papers say you can't change from one branch of the service to another and I am & I was going to say I am right glad of it – but . . . you know which will suit you best . . .

Minnie has just brought me a burnt finger for me to kiss. A kiss cures all of her aches and pains. . . . She and Emmie have both had very sore eyes. Emmie thinks it is very strange that she can't open her eyes in the morning. . . .

Mr. Baker has tobacco stalks put around the trees in the new orchard and he says they took very well. I went all over the new house about a fortnight ago and did not see any signs of the waters coming in. . . . Two of the gutters were broken down by the snow . . . Three of the shoats and one yearling died in the wet spell last week. . . . Mr Matt

Dance saw old Mr. Ramey our refugee from Leesburg at Lunenburg C.H. saturday, said he found him in a peck of trouble. He had sent forty negroes on to Lunenburg before him and when he reached there every man but one had run away.

I asked Emmy just now what I must tell you She says tell him Minnie's asleep and I have got her doll "baby." She runs to the door and window very often to see if you are coming and asks me, "don't you reckon my Papa's most home now." ...
Yours,
Mary

(ed: It will be a few more days till Richard's letter of April 25th, informing her that he is an officer in Co. K of the 3rd Virginia Cavalry, arrives in Farmville.)

- - - - -

Letter from Mary Watkins to Lt. Richard Watkins

Linden May 2nd 1862

My dear dear Husband

I was not much surprised at the contents of your letter dated Apr 25th. Indeed I rather expected that you would re-enlist, though I hoped as you were over thirty five and had served one year in the Army you could ... come stay with me another year. As you thought it was your duty to reenlist of course it was right for you to do so... . I am very glad you remain in the same company where you have so many friends ... Don't be troubled any more about it....

I really was right much disheartened when I heard that New Orleans was in the power of the enemy. When they had been saying all along how well fortified it was and that they had quite a little navy of Ironclad gunboats equal to the *Virginia*. I don't see how it could have happened. I expect Yellow Fever will dislodge the Yankees next summer though if they are so rash as to hold it till then. I dread to see anything in the papers about Yorktown being impregnable for the next thing I expect to hear is that it is taken.

I am very much interested in drawing lately, have brought my drawing book and draw some every day.
Good bye your
Mary

(ed: Yellow fever is an acute infectious disease, mostly found in subtropical areas, transmitted by a mosquito and is characterized by jaundice and dark colored vomit resulting from hemorrhages.) 15

- - - - -

WILLIAMSBURG and SEVEN PINES
May 11 to June 11, 1862

The month of May has brought more bad news for the Confederacy. Norfolk falls, the Norfolk Navy Yard is evacuated, and the CSS *Virginia* is blown up to avoid her falling into Union hands. Corinth, Mississippi, is abandoned in late May. On the final day of May, General Johnston attacks General McClellan at Seven Pines just east of Richmond. Johnston is wounded and General Robert E. Lee takes command. A young general named Stonewall Jackson is bewildering a group of Union generals in the Shenandoah Valley of Virginia as he marches and countermarches some 300 miles, fights four battles and many small engagements, defeating and occupying some 60,000 Union troops.

Richard's letters describe the retreat from Yorktown to Richmond and the rear guard actions by Co. K and the 3rd Virginia Cavalry. Richard is detailed to the wharfs at King's Mill, on the James River, to evacuate wounded to Richmond via river transport. 2,900 soldiers, which include soldiers from the 3rd Virginia, are gathered at King's Mill for evacuation. The 3rd Virginia provides rear guard duties on the march from Williamsburg to Richmond. During the battle of Seven Pines the cavalrymen serve behind the lines to collect stragglers and skulkers. Richard describes the shameful behavior of these soldiers.

In Prince Edward County the farmers are planting potatoes, distemper is killing hogs at Linden, several locals have died, and the Farmville General Hospital is seeking local homes to lodge ambulatory patients. Spring is the time for planting tobacco and Mary reports that both oat and wheat crops are coming up well. Mary tells Richard of the local men wounded on the Peninsula and of two relatives wounded in the battle of Shiloh. Sister Maria is collecting monies to help build another Confederate ironclad gunboat.

The fortunes of war place Co. K of the 3rd Virginia Cavalry and the King and Queen Heavy Artillery of the 4th Battalion Virginia Heavy Artillery within 300 yards of each other after the battle at Seven Pines. Richard and his brother Nathaniel get to visit with each other almost every evening.

Letter from Lt. Richard Watkins to Mary Watkins

Charles City County
May 11 1862

My own Dear Mary

I have only time to write a very few lines this morning by a gentleman going to Richmond. It is the very first opportunity I have had since we commenced our retreat from Yorktown nearly a fortnight ago. I have undergone very great privations and exposure and passed through a fiercely fought battle but God in his infinite mercy still spared my life and health. . . . I have been able to perform my whole duty on this perilous retreat. Have remained with the troop all the time in the extreme rear of the army. . . . We are now on the Chicahominy [Chickahominy River] near the Long Bridge about twenty miles of Richmond. No members of our troop has been killed. for although we were on the battlefield the whole of Monday in view of the contending forces with bombs bursting . . . and minnie balls in great abundance passing over our heads yet we were not called into direct action . . . On last Friday week before the rear guard of the army took up its march I was ordered to Kings Mill Wharf on the James [River] in charge of all the sick of our Regiment. There I witnessed one of the saddest scenes ever witnessed in the army. Twenty nine hundred sick men were lying on the cold wet ground awaiting the boats. I had forty or fifty under my charge which I succeeded in getting off very soon but my orders were to remain . . . and I had to stay till Sunday. . . . On Sunday I left for Williamsburg in company with detachments from various companies who had been sent to the Wharf to forward Commissary stores. When within a few miles of Williamsburg an aid of Genl Stewart [Genl. J. E. B. Stuart] came by at full speed saying that his entire command has been cut off including our regiment . . . fortunately before going far we met the General and all were safe. The next day the battle commenced in earnest about daybreak and raged until nearly sundown . . . The next day we commenced our march again and have been right closely pursued . . . It can hardly be called a pursuit for we travel only 3 or

4 miles a day and the enemy very often in sight . . . I must close for want of more time. . . . Oh I do want to see you too bad. . . . since the battle Andrew Venable has been separated from me having been detailed with others to go in advance & get provisions . . . Good bye my precious one. Give much very much love to all.
Yr
Richard

(*ed: When Richard mentions that the troop is in the extreme rear of the army he means that Co. K is part of the "rear guard" covering the withdrawal of Confederate forces toward Williamsburg and then on toward Richmond.*)

- - - - -

Letter from Lt. Richard Watkins to Mary Watkins

New Kent
May 14th 1862

My darling Mary

I am away out here in the woods hardly know where riding around every day watching the Yankees & sleeping out in the pines at night sometimes eating two meals a day sometimes only one never three. Sometimes setting on my horse all day at other times one half of the night, always moving with no means of writing letters and no regular courier or post office. My health is first rate my darling and I am longing to see you more and more every day. Am first lieutenant as you seemed at a loss to know how to address me and by the by I am on a certain occasion was much more at a loss how to address you. Your darling letter by Mr Spencer was recd and I thank you ever so much. Please write again when ever you can send it by any one coming down. I have no time to write more tonight. It is late and I must be in my saddle at 3 ½ - will send this by John Knights boy and hope it will reach you. will always write when I can get a chance. Andrew sends love and says he is taking good care of me. Love and kisses to all Good bye my precious one

Yr
Richard

(ed: This letter was not in ink and not in Richards normal neat writing style. It was in pencil and hastily scrawled in uneven lines.)

(ed: I would estimate that only 30% of their letters were mailed. The rest were carried by soldiers and civilians going back and forth between Prince Edward County and the 3rd Virginia Cavalry. As you have noted, and will note on an increasing basis, parties were constantly going back to Prince Edward County with broken down horses and returning with fresh mounts. Mary's envelopes all show a Moore's Ordinary return address.)

- - - - -

Letter from Pattie Watkins to Nannie Watkins

Mt Pleasant
May 14th 1862

My dear Sister

... We felt so anxious about our dear ones in the army ... that I had no heart to write but we heard Sunday from Dick through Charley Redd & heard that he was well. ... Yesterday your letter & one from Brother [Nathaniel] came together ... He was at Hanover C. H. all well, thought that they would all come to Richmond ...

So many around here were wounded on the Peninsula & near Staunton, one body was brought home Sunday & buried in this neighborhood ... and the same day Tom Hines brought home his son who died with fever several weeks ago. Branch Spencer is home wounded & Emmet Woolton is wounded and at home. His father is very low and not expected to live with consumption. And there are a great many more ...

Pattie Watkins 1

- - - - -

Letter from Mary Watkins to Lt. Richard Watkins

Linden, May 16th 1862

My dear Husband

I wrote you by Capt. Miller who was to have returned to his regiment at Gloucester Point last week and promised to get to see you and deliver the letter . . . but I suppose he hasn't seen you as you left Yorktown . . . I went over home Tuesday and spent the day, had the beds sunned, the house swept out, the blankets and woolen clothes put away. The wheat is looking very well and the potatoes in the garden are up and we have a fine chance of them. Mr. Baker had another patch planted last week and I let Mama have several buckets that were left. We have not quite finished planting corn had to wait to have some ditching done before we could finish. . . . The folks were hauling out manure. Mr. Wharey spent Sunday night with us and talks about going back to the army. . . . Sister Maria has collected a hundred dollars for the gunboat . . . Mama received a letter from Cousin George Dupuy yesterday begging her to take him and his young wife as boarders. He is just from Kentucky and was married the day Nashville was taken. . . . We are all very well. Good bye my dearest. I want to see you so bad and love you so much
Your own
Mary

(ed: Mr. Wharey must miss serving as chaplain with the 3ʳᵈ Virginia Cavalry. Mr. Wharey is normally the minister at Briery Presbyterian Church. Sister Maria is involved in raising monies to help build a gunboat for the Confederate navy just as others are involved in sewing uniforms, socks, and underclothes for the soldiers.)

(ed: The shortage of salt has become critical in Prince Edward County. The local board has appointed Charles D. Anderson & Richard B. Thackston as agents, this month, to contract to purchase, transport & distribute salt

at the direction of the Court. The intent is to provide a supply for citizens, at a non speculative price, using county funds.) 2

- - - - -

Letter from Lt. Richard Watkins to Mary Watkins

Camp near Bottom's Bridge
May 20th 1862

My own dear Mary,

We are again within fifteen miles of Richmond. Still in the rear of the Army watching the movements of the enemy, almost always in sight of them. We sleep in the woods with our horses saddled, and remain in the ranks all day from daylight till dark. . . . a majority or at least half of the troop are on sick leave. . . . am quite sure that some of them are well enough to be here. . . . I think that McClellan has shown plainly that he is not a great general. He suffered our army to retire right before his face along a narrow peninsular with both rivers in his possession and a larger force than ours and now at the end of the retreat we find that the retreating army has taken more prisoners than the pursuing and has repulsed them at every attack. . . . I hope that ere long I will meet you again though I cannot tell when it will be. . . . I am ashamed to say that Charley Redd . . . [is] trying to get a substitute. It is a shame. . . . Please write to me at once & send to Richmond – Lieut. RHW Company K 3rd Regt Cavalry Va Volunteers. Love to all
Yr own
Richard

(ed: A person is allowed to hire a substitute to take their place in the service. A contract is signed between the two individuals. The substitute must be presented to the command and be accepted by the commanding officer as a fit and dependable replacement before the contract in binding on all parties.)

- - - - -

Letter from Mary Watkins to Lt. Richard Watkins

Linden May 27ᵗʰ 1862

I received two good letters from you this morning . . . How I wish I had gone with Mrs Elbert Redd to Richmond, but I hope the war will be over soon and then I can be with you all the time. We had green peas and strawberries for dinner yesterday and I wanted to send you some so bad. . . . Dr Woolton died last night. I have not heard any of the particulars . . . Cousin Asa and Johnny Dupuy were wounded at the battle of Shiloh. Cousin Asa very badly wounded in the head, he lost some of his brains and has been paralyzed for two days when we heard . . . I am going to send this note and one of your blankets by Mr. Sublette tomorrow. . . . I am going to ride over to Mr Redds and carry your letter for Mother to read . . . Fancy is saddled and waiting for me so good bye
Your own
Mary

*(ed: Mary did not take the children along to the Redd's because there is an outbreak of measles over there. Mary had dropped Richard a note on May 22ⁿᵈ with the news that "Mama has lost thirteen hogs with distemper and several others are sick." Also she penned, "John Womack died in the hospital in Richmond this week . . . This is the fourth grown son Mrs Womack has lost. David is the only one left now. . . . I saw in the **Whig** that little Johnnie Waller was dangerously wounded in the battle of Williamsburg. He was only fourteen years old . . .")*

- - - - -

Letter from Lt. Richard Watkins to Mary Watkins

5 miles below Richmond
May 30ᵗʰ 1862

My own dear Mary

Your very welcome letters of 3 May & 21 May were handed me today ... thank you ... I am now sitting right down in the middle of the road in the midst of a swamp. The enemy about a mile below us ... yesterday our company on pickett took five prisoners. It seems right strange that Nat on foot should have retreated at the rate of 20 miles a day and we on horseback have hardly averaged four. We often march only a mile a day ... holding our horses by the bridles. They have been saddled the whole time of our retreat ... We have hard work with very little food but the men (those who remain) are in good spirits. ... I lost no clothes at all ... I had only one blanket with me and on the battlefield at Williamsburg in the midst of a hard rain gave that to a poor wounded soldier. ... Andrew and I sleep together very comfortably we have one oil cloth blanket, one woolen blanket & two overcoats. Would be glad if you could send me one of my blankets if you have a chance ... By the by you ought not to show my love letters to Ma ... Kiss my dear children for me & give love to all and to Ma especially every chance you have
Good bye Yr own
Richard

(ed: Sgt. Nathaniel Watkins and the King and Queen Artillery were forced to abandon their works at Gloucester Point, losing their heavy artillery, and flee on foot toward Richmond. Without artillery, they were used as infantrymen in the battle of Seven Pines.)

- - - - -

Letter from Lt. Richard Watkins to Mary Watkins

Battlefield near Richmond [Seven Pines]
Sunday June 1 1862

My dear dear Mary

I write simply to let you know I am well. Our company in the rear of the Army doing the most disagreeable of all work, catching stragglers from the Army and sending them back. Yesterday afternoon for five hours a fierce battle was fought mainly with musketry, a large number of killed and wounded on both sides ... Our men forced the enemy back, took two batteries, all their tents, camp equipage, ammunition and still hold their position, some sharp fighting this morning & preparedness for a great deal more. ... I write on paper taken from a Yankee portfolio ... Charley Flournoy has just brought in a very good India rubber cloth which he took from one of the enemy tents. Nearly all of our Troop have supplied themselves with them. One has a fine saddle, another a portfolio filled with paper, another a large quantity of coffee and a good number of excellent guns and a large quantity of ammunition also taken. We cannot tell though what will be the final result. Genl Johnston is wounded ... Poor Charley Redd ... yesterday brought out a worthless substitute. Capt Berkeley ... refused to take him and properly too. Oh tis a shame not a single Redd is now with the company all sick without exception – Have heard nothing from Nat. Genl Rhodes brigade has been in the fight but I do not know whether Nat is the infantry or heavy artillery since our retreat. If in the infantry he had in all probability been in the engagement. ... Darling the battle has not ended ... You must not be too much concerned about me Remember that God still rules and that he dwells over all things ... Mr Dickinson is about to leave and I must close to send this by him to Richmond.

Goodbye dear one

Yr own

Richard

(ed: This time when Richard mentions working in the rear he is now behind the CSA lines instead of between the main CSA forces and the Union forces. General Johnston has chosen to attack General McClellan at Seven Pines and halt his drive on Richmond. Fate has intervened with the wounding of General Johnston and President Jefferson Davis appoints General Robert E. Lee as the new commander of the army.)

- - - - -

Letter from Lt. Richard Watkins to Mary Watkins

Near Richmond

June 3rd 1862

My darling Mary

I wrote you last Sunday just after the fearful battle, was then near the battlefield stopping stragglers and sending them back to the ranks. Most of our regiment were engaged in gathering up arms left on the battlefield and one company with others in the disagreeable business which I have mentioned. It is shameful and at the same time amusing to hear the various excuses given by men for leaving their companies. One man had cramps in his feet, another said he was a raw recruit and had not been drilled enough to know how to fight, some were lying in the shade unable to walk but when told that our army might fall back they left to walk rapidly to the rear. Our Troop on the whole though are brave and determined . . . Fortunately for me I have not been required to go over the battlefield either here or at Williamsburg after the fighting was over. . . . I knew I would suffer greatly at the sight of the dead & wounded . . . Nearly all of our troop went from curiosity and they tell of such painful scenes. . . . Reckon you will like the cavalry better than ever when you hear that we are always held in reserve . . . They are as Genl Magruder remarked the eyes and ears of the Army. . . . changing the subject I saw Nat this morning he has been right sick and was unable to be on the battlefield . . . he looks better than I expected to find him, is a little reduced in flesh but not more so than the majority of our soldiers. His company was in the hottest of the battle, charged the enemy battery and after taking one turned the guns upon them and gave them five rounds before they could get out of sight. . . . Out of 58 in the company 5 were killed and 28 wounded. Everything is quiet today . . . Every letter appears to me to be your best. Oh how shall I ever repay you for them. . . . I love you more and more. And now must close in order to get this off today. Good bye dear one. Much love to all. I long to see you.
Yr own
Richard

(ed: Weapons are collected on the battlefield after every engagement. They are forwarded to various CSA arsenals where they are repaired and

refurbished for return to the supply system. Captured Union weapons, in addition to weapons purchased overseas and run through the blockade, are the major sources of small arms for the Confederacy. Manufacturing capacity of CSA arsenals is totally inadequate to meet the demand for rifles and pistols.)

- - - - -

Letter from Mary Watkins to Lt. Richard Watkins

Linden June 3rd 1862

My dear Husband

It is raining and I can not help thinking about the "poor soldiers" so I have concluded to let my thoughts flow on in the same channel and write to my dear soldier. Sister Maria and Nannie are making bed quilts for the soldiers, Mama making up bread for the soldiers, Lavallette carding lint for the soldiers and all talking at once about the soldiers, so Lou and I have stolen a candle and run off in the parlor to get out of the bustle that we, at least one of us, may write to some of the soldiers. . . . I have heard a great many people wondering why so many of the Prince Edward Troop were at home at this time . . .

Mr. Mat Dance came here to day to see if Mama could take any wounded soldiers, he and Mr. Haskins are going down tomorrow to bring up some. Mama thought as there were only ladies here we could not nurse them very well. I went to see Mother last Tuesday. Mr Redd and Emma sick with measles . . .

Emmie and Minnie were very much pleased with the candy you sent them. I believe Emmie has told every body on the land about it. I took Emmie to Mr Pleasant with me last Sunday there was only Prayer meeting. She behaved very well indeed.

Went over home early this morning . . . We have a very good crop of wheat and oats, heading out finely. . . . They were planting tobacco today . . . Will shear sheep tomorrow . . . My ground peas that I had planted in the garden have all come up . . . Our bees swarmed nine times and then went off. They were hived several times but would not stay. . . .

Good night dear Mr Watkins I hope you are not sleeping out in the rain tonight. June 4th I have not forgotten that this is your birthday . . . Are you thirty six or thirty seven today? . . . I wish I had a nice birthday present to send you . . . I . . . send my best wishes that you may spend many more happy birthdays at home. . . .
Your loving
Mary

(ed: To free up room in the hospital wards, once a patient did not need regular nursing and was ambulatory, they would try to transfer them to local homes. The patient would then check in with the hospital on a weekly or monthly basis till they were discharged.)

(ed: The Farmville General Hospital was established in 1862. It would serve mostly convalescents & chronic care cases to free up space in the Richmond hospitals. Farmville had a capacity of 1200 – 1500 beds. Dr. H. D. Taliaferro was in charge with Mr. R. W. Marye serving as his Quartermaster. The hospital had 3 divisions. Two were in converted tobacco warehouses and Division 3 was in new quarters built on the north side of the Southside Railroad.) 3

- - - - -

Letter from Lt. Richard Watkins to Mary Watkins

Richmond
June 5th 1862

My own dear Mary

We are now only one mile from Richmond . . . actually resting but still without tents and yesterday (my birthday) I arose with my clothes very damp, my blanket wet, with the prospect of . . . sitting about on stumps . . . taking the rain. . . . I had a real treat and what do you suppose it was . . . A letter right fresh from your own hand written on my birthday and received on the evening of the same day. Really I almost felt as if I were with you and could hear your voice. Well our Col gave me leave this morning to get my horse shod [in Richmond] . . . and while that is being done I have stolen off to Cousin Barretts office . . . upon reference to his books I find that McKinney & Dupuy are owing me Four Hundred and Thirteen dollars. This is in their hand subject to your orders at any time. . . . Cousin Barrett told me if you will send my old trunk to him he will keep it for me and I can then get clean clothes at least once a week. Please send in it my silk shirts, my blue flannel shirt, a half dozen pair of yarn socks, the best of my flannel drawers and a half dozen white cotton shirts . . . I cannot be too grateful . . .

I cannot write more at present. Was exceeding sorry to hear of Dr. Woolton's death . . . I sent your letters by Mr. Haskins along with the candy. . . . you mentioned the candy but said nothing of the letters. . . . I would give anything for a furlough but cannot expect one until the fate of Richmond has been decided. . . . Again good bye. Many kisses for the little girls . . .
Yr own
Richard

(ed: Mary's birthday is coming up on June 21 and she will be 23.)

- - - - -

Letter from Mary Watkins to Lt. Richard Watkins

Linden June 10th 1862

My dear Husband

I am only going to write you a short letter on business today. Mr Baker wants to know if you had not better hire David White for a while to prize your tobacco. He says there is such a large crop on hand and they are so behind hand he don't know how he can spare

Tom to do it. . . . I am afraid if you all don't stop fighting we will not make bread this year. We don't have two clear days in a week and we begin to think that the firing of so many guns is the cause of so much rain. . . . Tom Haskins said . . . the whole army was half starved and all that the sick soldiers needed was something to eat. . . . Must stop now and go to work.

Yours aff

Mary

(ed: Mary is afraid if the fighting does not stop that she and Richard will not see each other to share any meals for the rest of the year.)

- - - - -

Letter from Sgt. Nathaniel Watkins to Nannie Watkins

Camp near Drury's Bluff
June 11, 1862

My dear wife

. . . We have been taken out of the Chickahominy swamps and the main body of the army and are on the bluffs of the James River. . . . The greatest objection to moving from our old resting place yesterday, was that Bro Dicks Regt was camped about 300 yds from us & we had been allowed to be together a good deal . . .

NVW 4

- - - - -

Richmond
June 17 to August 21, 1862

The men of Co. K are sick and the horses are broken down. The same is true for the rest of the 3rd Virginia. Richard writes on June 25th, "Two thirds of the regiment is sick." From June 26th through July 1st, while the Army of Northern Virginia is fighting the Union forces in the Seven Days battles, Co. K is on sick call, in the hospitals and back in Prince Edward getting fresh horses.

On July 6th Richard's horse fails. Richard, also in poor health, reports to Chimborazo Hospital for evaluation. A few days later, with no improvement, he gets a furlough for three weeks to recover from disease in his lungs.

Mary has very little good news to pass on from Prince Edward County. A bad storm has flattened the oats, both Emmie and Minnie have colds, she fears 1862 may bring famine and suggests that selling their farm might be their best move. The wheat is OK with some 200 shocks and the tobacco is right fine. Some animals have distemper and there is scarlet fever in the county.

Memphis, a major hub for trade on the Mississippi, falls to Union forces. On June 17th General Braxton Bragg replaces General Beauregard in command of Confederate forces in Tennessee and Mississippi. President Lincoln calls for 300,000 three year volunteers to bolster the Union ranks. The Copperhead movement, composed of Southern sympathizers, is gaining strength in Indiana and Ohio.

The removal of General McClellan, and his Union army, from the gates of Richmond by the Army of Northern Virginia has boosted morale, both military and civilian. In the process, an army has found a leader and the leader has found his three key generals in Stonewall Jackson and James Longstreet for his infantry and J. E. B. Stuart for his cavalry. What they started here during the Seven Days, and what they will accomplish in the next year, will become legendary in the annals of Confederate military history.

Letter from Pattie Watkins to Nannie Watkins

Mt. Pleasant
June 17ᵗʰ 1862

My Dear Sister

. . . Mollie sent us a letter from Brother Dick Sunday he had seen Brother Nat. I will write you what he wrote about him. He says, "I saw Nat this morning he has been right sick & was unable to be on the battlefield is better though now & will soon be with his company again. He looks better than I expected to find him, is a little reduced in flesh but not more so than the majority of our soldiers. His company was in the hottest of the battle, charged the enemys battery & after taking one turned the guns upon them & gave them five rounds before they could get out of sight. Mr. Sam Brooker's son made a very narrow escape a minnie ball passing through his cap near his head. . . . Out of 58 in the company 5 were killed & 28 wounded." Brother Dick writes that his company were kept in the rear of the Army to drive in stragglers said it was a very disagreeable business. He has kept very well though the troop is reduced by sickness from 76 to 25. . . . Brother Dick said they were at Richmond now resting & it is the first time the saddle has been off of his horse since the middle of May.
Pattie 1

- - - - -

Letter from Lt. Richard Watkins to Mary Watkins

Camp near Richmond
June 25ᵗʰ 1862

My Precious Mary

Yesterday I got permission . . . to visit Richmond. Found my trunk at Cousin Barretts full of nice clean clothes and cakes. Twas a real treat I tell you . . .

There has been quite a sharp engagement on the line today, but our regiment has not been called out . . . We can hear the firing of artillery . . . Rumors are afloat that Old Stonewall Jackson is here but I know nothing of the truth of them. If he is here I believe we will whip the Yankees . . . Am afraid that I will never be fit for anything if this war continues much longer. . . . It is really a task . . . the monotony of camp life. My health is excellent but our tents are full of sick men. Two thirds of the regiment is sick . . . Nearly all of the sickness now is intermittent or bilious fever. Not as bad as typhoid but still very bad. . . .

Much love. Good bye dear one.
Yr own
Richard

(ed: Bilious means pertaining to or characterized by gastric distress caused by sluggishness of the liver or gall bladder.) 2

- - - - -

Letter from Mary Watkins to Lt. Richard Watkins

Before Sunrise June 28th 1862

Dear Mr Watkins

. . . Mama and I went over home Wednesday . . . We melted the lard over and put it in buckets ready to send off. I rode over in the wagon again the next day, nailed it up and sent it to the Depot. . . . Mama and I have been consulting on the propriety of sending you cherries, concluded that they would not be fit to eat . . . I have pickled some though and am going to send you some in a box next week. . . . We have a very good wheat and oat crop though the oats are beginning to rust. . . .

I have not heard a word from Mother and Pattie this week hope to see them at church tomorrow. Sister Maria's flowers look very thirsty and as she is away I believe I will go and water them . . .
Your own,
Mary

(ed: Rust is a fungus that can attack several of the grain crops and cause great damage. "A parasitic fungi of the order Uredinales that are injurious to a wide variety of plants and are characterized by reddish or brownish spots on leaves, stems, and other parts.") 3

- - - - -

Letter from Emily Howe Dupuy to Lt. Richard Watkins

Prince Edward Co
July 5th 1862

My dear Son

We have felt great solicitude about you during the past week, but have heard up to last Tuesday . . . that You & your company were all safe. God grant that the same care & protection may be vouchsafed to you to the end of this dreadful war.

All our sympathies have been greatly excited by hearing of the terrible carnage of our brave soldiers, which has sent desolation and mourning into so many families of our land. This must have been a dear bought victory to our Arms. May its results be of sufficient importance to compensate for the loss in some measure. Now let us forget the war and talk a little of other things. Your little family are quite well. Mary is in good health & devotes herself more & more to the children. She has begun in earnest to discipline both & even Minnie begins to stand in awe of the Locust switch. . . . The crops on your farm . . . are good, about on average I should judge. Wheat first rate crop, fallowed oats already cut, & not rusted your oats looking vastly better than ours tho somewhat rusted in spots. . . .

Cousin Polly . . . told us Mr. Tom Venable had heard from his son lately. He was in Fort Deleware & had been kindly furnished with money & clothing by Mr. Comfort. As Mary is writing to you I will enclose these few lines in her Envelope.
Your affectionate Mother
E H Dupuy 4

(ed: Fort Delaware is a prison camp on Pea Patch Island, in the Delaware River, a few miles downriver from Wilmington, near Delaware City.)

(ed: Emily also mentions that it has been a difficult growing season with heavy rains and significant dry periods. One of the neighbors has suggested that Richard should harvest some of his tobacco now but should not pull men from tending the other crops to accomplish the task.)

- - - - -

Letter from Lt. Richard Watkins to Mary Watkins

Camp near Richmond
Sunday July 6th 1862

My Dear Dear Mary

On our late reconnoisince through Charles City and New Kent my horse broke down and when the regiment was ordered out yesterday they left me in Camp and I shall be compelled to buy another horse . . . unless mine should recover rapidly. . . . I would like for it to be done soon because it is not very comfortable to an officer to remain in camp in such times. . . . Dr. Walker in Richmond . . . offered to take my horse and fatten him for me if I could send him to his house. Would prefer sending him home . . . I consider him a valuable horse and all that he needs is rest and generous diet.

Our regiment is still suffering much sickness and our company almost as much as any. . . . My health is most excellent . . . looked in "mirror" . . . was really surprised to find what a great coarse looking man I had become. . . . am getting so ugly. . . . Saw Dr. Wood of

Farmville ... he had seen you and mother in Farmville and you were both looking very well. Oh, if I could only see you.

... The enemy have been driven thirty miles below Richmond ... our army is still pressing McClellan. God only knows what the result will be. ...

... I love to hear too that my children remember me and that Emmie likes to think Papa coming home. You have not written lately of Geo Redd has he recovered entirely from the measles. I have not heard from Nat since the battles around Richmond began. His company was transferred to Wise's brigade and I think are stationed at Drewry's Bluff. . . . Cousin Barrett . . . has sold your butter and lard for good prices and would return the vessels as soon as possible. Most of his time now is spent in attending to the wants of the sick and wounded in the Hospitals. ...

Good bye dear one. Write very often and always give a great deal of love to the home folks one & all. Good bye Yr own Richard

- - - - -

Letter from Lt. Richard Watkins to Mary Watkins

Camp near Richmond
July 11ᵗʰ 1862

My Darling Mary

My horse has improved a measure and I have concluded to go on today and overtake the regiment. Several days may elapse before I shall be able to write you again as I understand the regiment is constantly moving and is today starting for Middlesex County. . . . continue to direct your mail as heretofore ...

Changing the subject darling has my tobacco been prized. I understand that tobacco is selling very high with a prospect of a farther rise in prices and would like to have mine in a condition in

which it can be sold at any time. Did they ever finish planting the present crop? If so please enquire of Mr Baker as to the number of hills planted. How many stacks of wheat . . . how many stacks of oats. How much land in corn and what the appearance of it. How many hogs, sheep, cows, calves etc and their condition on the plantation . . . And now good bye my precious one . . . Yr own
Richard

- - - - -

Letter from Mary Watkins to Lt. Richard Watkins

Linden July 14ᵗʰ 1862

Dear Mr. Watkins

Enclosed you will find a letter from Cousin Purnall in regard to the horse you wished to purchase. Perhaps you could see Andrew Venable or write to him about it. . . .

There was communion at Briery yesterday and a great many people out. . . . Charlotte Wharey is very ill with Typhoid fever . . . Brother Will and Sister Kate were at church, both looking very worn . . . Mildred died a week ago . . . Fayette Scott is going back Thursday and Pattie says she will write to you by him. . . . Uncle Joe, Mr Haskins, Mr James Booker and Hillery Richardson were elected elders in Briery Saturday. Some of the ladies wanted to propose you . . . I wish you would join Briery Church.

. . . Mr Baker came in Saturday looking very dolefully, said he went over the oat field and found it lying down just as flat as if they had been cut . . . did not reckon Mama could make a stack. Ours in the same fix and Uncle Joes and everybodys . . . We had some good winter oats that have been cut. . . . I expect there will be a famine this year as well as war and pestilence. Minnie is right unwell. I reckon she is cutting her eye teeth.
Good bye Your own
Mary

- - - - -

Letter from Lt. Richard Watkins to Mary Watkins

Camp near Richmond
July 17ᵗʰ 1862

My Darling Mary

The skys are bright . . . You have written me two letters to my one.
. . . you shall not write two to my one anymore if I can help it. I
am feeling much better today . . . if you should see Dr. Eggleston
please ask him to proceed to get me [a horse] – a <u>strong</u> <u>durable</u>
<u>active</u> horse. Tolerably large. I care not how ugly if he have the above
qualities. . . . Darling five long months have passed since I saw you, it
seems to me the longest months of my life. . . . will have to seek some
situation in the Commissary or Quartermaster department which
will enable me to see you more frequently and spend a good part
of my time with you. Will make the effort as soon as circumstances
allow unless the authorities will soon grant me a good long furlough.
Just now they are more stringent than ever, granting none to those
who are well . . . I write this hurridly to send by Mr. Jas Booker. Will
write another soon. Good bye Dear one. Yr
Richard

- - - - -

Letter from Mary Watkins to Lt. Richard Watkins

Linden July 17ᵗʰ 1862

My dear Husband –

I was disturbed very much yesterday by hearing through your letter
to Mama that you were sick. . . . I can't bear to think of you being
sick in camp or in one of those miserable Hospitals. I think of you
every minute . . . Mama and Cousin George are very hopeful about
this war and think it can't last much longer, but I am afraid it will be
years before we see the end of it.

Emmie is very much troubled about your being sick . . . I asked her just now what message she had to send you and she said, "Tell Papa to kiss me for he." . . . Emmie, Minnie, and I have very bad colds. . . . I reckon our colds will not last long though. . . .

Davy White is prizing your tobacco. We have a very good stand of tobacco this year but I don't know how many hills were planted. . . . Mama sends her love to you . . . Charley Redd is very anxious to get [Tom Haskins] as his substitute and put a substitute in Tom's Company for him. . . . If you have a chance I think you had better sell your place. I was very much opposed to it at first but think now it would be for the best. I don't believe after the war is over we will ever be able to pay for it. . . . Good bye dearest . . . Your own, Mary

– – – – –

Letter from Lt. Richard Watkins to Mary Watkins

Camp near Richmond
July 20th 1862

My Precious Mary

Your nice wee bit of a letter was handed me in Richmond yesterday by Cousin Barrett who says that you must continue to direct to the care of McKinney & Dupuy . . . So you see that I am well enough to be in Richmond . . . I will take the very best care of myself and will not in any event go into a Hospital. You said something about coming down [to Richmond] . . . but I almost dread the thought of you coming into such a place as Richmond is at present. The streets all the time full of sick soldiers and stragglers and provost guards and prisoners and ambulances and hearses. Oh tis a horrible place so filthy too. . . . Reminds me of Havana. A refined lady is seldom seen now on Main Street. Should you come I could meet you with a hack at the Depot and you would see very little of it. . . .

Do you really wish me to join Briery? However it will be time enough to talk of that after I get out of the army. . . . John Walton is at a private home near here extremely ill with typhoid fever. He can hardly live many days. Our surgeon got him a place . . . But with all their kind care he continues to sink under the fever. . . . Would astonish you to hear how vegetables and fruit sell here. Onions & beets sell at 12 ½ cents apiece. A few days ago I paid a quarter for two onions . . . They were not large either. Small indifferent peaches sell for a dollar a dozen. Tomatoes for the same. Cabbage 75 cents a head. Chickens small size a dollar apiece. Everything we buy is at these prices. Milk 50 cents a quart and butter one dollar a pound. Well Good bye precious one. Kiss Emmie & Minnie again & again for me and give heaps of love to all. . . .

Yr own

Richard

(ed: Mary in a July 25th letter noted, "made 200 shocks of wheat. Tobacco right fine. We have got distemper among our cattle, lost the best ox we had and a yearling. . . . We have only three calves (last years) left . . . no prospects of any this year. . . . Have not stacked wheat or oats yet. . . . Believe I will draw money from Cousin Barrett to pay for your horse.")

- - - - -

Letter from Lt. Richard Watkins to Mary Watkins

Richmond
July 26th 1862

My Precious Mary

I am getting better though my lungs feel quite sore yet, especially when I cough. . . . Sleep well and have a fine appetite. Got so tired of camp life that I came to Richmond yesterday and applied to a Hospital surgeon for the usual certificate for getting a furlough. It was Dr. Semple of Gwaltney Hospital a good physician considered so by all. He examined me carefully and said he did not think my lungs were afflicted but only the bronchial tubes. . . . Not satisfied

111

with that I called to Dr. William Carrington who nursed me in New York during my previous sickness . . . He agreed with Dr. Semple but that if I found myself at any time growing worse I must come to Richmond and he would pledge . . . That I should be sent home. . . . he is a brother in law of Andrew Venable. . . . Expect to remain in camp at least a week longer . . . Darling I want to see you very very much. Wish I could get a furlough but do not want to be sick in order to get one. . . . The discipline of our Army is entirely spasmodic. Very rigid for a time & then on the other extreme. . . . Have to write this very hurridly to get it off this morning. Give love to all . . . Good bye. Don't feel concerned about me. Your own
Richard

- - - - -

Letter from Mary Watkins to Lt. Richard Watkins

Linden July 29th 1862

My dear Husband

We are going to send a box down to McKinney & Dupuy for you tomorrow (Wednesday). I intended sending some hams and vegetables today . . . but Mama wanted to make a few additions to the box . . . If you can conveniently please send the butter pot back after you have used the butter out, they are getting rather scarce in this part of the country. . . . Mama has used nearly every box in the house and nearly all of her butter pots sending to the Hospitals. . . . I wanted to ride your horse yesterday but Mama would not let me. Cousin Purnall came up yesterday, says he is mighty sorry you could not get his horse . . . Pattie said Sunday, she had just received a letter from Nannie Watkins and Bro Nat was not at home. We had heard before that he was discharged. I hope you are getting well . . . Good bye
Your own
Mary

- - - - -

Letter from Pattie Watkins to Nannie Watkins

Mt. Pleasant
July 31ˢᵗ 1862

My Dear Sister

... Brother Dick has been quite sick & wasn't well when we heard from him. We feared he would have fever & he seemed afraid his lungs were affected again. He tried to get a furlough to come home but could not so many of the company were at home but the surgeon told him if he got any worse he would send him home.... There is a great deal of sickness throughout the country. Scarlet fever, roseola, measles & fever. Scarlet fever has been very fatal about Charlotte C. H. ... Cousin Pauline Purzear lost her baby not long ago which makes four children she has lost in the course of a year to diphtheria. ... The crops of corn in this neighborhood are fine the oats were very sorry & very little wheat. ... Brother Dick's wheat was very good. . . .

Your own Sister
Pattie 5

(ed: Roseola is a rose colored skin rash. Scarlet fever is an acute contagious disease marked by scarlet skin eruptions and high fever. Measles, as we all know, is an acute contagious virus also marked by red spotted skin eruptions. In the 1860's these were collectively know as the "eruptive diseases.")

- - - - -

Letter from Lt. Richard Watkins to Mary Watkins

Richmond Aug 1, 1862

My own dear Mary

I recd your nice box yesterday.... It would have made you glad to see how it was recd in our Camp. The boys got around it and soon the apples and pies disappeared, then the servants were put to cooking and we had a good dinner of vegetables and pickle. Capt. Berkeley happened to be in our sick camp . . . and enjoyed it as much as any. In the evening we had coffee and nice biscuit and bread & cold ham for supper. . . . Today I have been trying again to get a furlough for altho I am better . . . my cough is quite troublesome. Our Surgeon and Dr. Wm Carrington . . . have both given me recommendation for a furlough . . . may be several days [for the board to review and approve]. . . . You must not feel uneasy about me for I am taking every precaution . . .

No news from Richmond or the Army. Last night though about one o'clock heavy cannonading was heard on the River and it proved to be an attack on the gunboats by our batteries. . . .

. . . Have not time to write more now Darling so good bye – Will write again very soon. – Much love
Yr
Richard

- - - - -

Affidavit of Surgeon Wm. A. Carrington

Lt. Watkins Co K of the 3ʳᵈ Regiment of Va Cavalry having applied for a Certificate, on which to ground an Application for Leave of Absence, I do hereby certify, that I have carefully examined this Officer, and find that

He has Chronic Bronchitis with Debility & Emaciation – He has been off duty for 3 weeks – I attended him 3 years since in N. York when he had every symptom of <u>Phthisis</u> – an undoubted case (with vomicae Hemmorrhosso).

And that in consequence thereof, he is, in my opinion, unfit for duty. I further declare my belief that he will not be able to resume his duties in a less period than <u>30</u> days – as a temporary removal from the hardships of camp is necessary to enable him to overcome this predisposing disease to a [   ] to which he has a strong tendency.

Richmond August 1ˢᵗ 1862

Wm A Carrington
Surgeon
Genl Hos No 10   6

(ed: Phthisis would now be referred to as a disease of the lungs and could range from asthma to pulmonary tuberculosis. Vomicae means the expelling of putrid matter and this will often contain tissue from lung cavities that contain pus. "Hemmo" would refer to blood and " haemorrhos" refers to flowing with blood) 7

(ed: Richard got a medical furlough and went home to Prince Edward County. His furlough was good till the 21ˢᵗ. He departed home on the 19ᵗʰ for his trip back to Richmond.)

- - - - -

Letter from Mary Watkins to Lt. Richard Watkins

Linden Aug 20ᵗʰ 1862

My darling Husband

I feel so lonely today . . . came in the house and put away your clothes . . . I have concluded to begin that long letter I promised to write you. . . .

I received a note from Mother [Mrs. Watkins] yesterday telling me of the death of Cousin Sue Watkins Venable. She died at the birth of a child two months ago and her Mothers family never heard of it until Sunday. . . . Mr Baker had your machine mended at the shop and it is running very well again.

Aug 21st We had a very fine rain this morning enough to last some time, it is very sultry and cloudy now and I expect we will have more rain before night. Nannie and I busied ourselves . . . putting up tomatoes. . . .

Aug 23rd Received a letter from you today which has cheered me up . . . don't think I ever hated for you to leave home as much as I did this last time . . . Cousin Will Norton [has] just lost his second son with croup. . . . Minnie has just fallen down the stair again. She was sitting on the fourth step from the bottom . . . and she rocked over backwards . . . Emmie says frequently, "I wish my Papa would come back again." . . . They finally thrashed wheat at our house Thursday morning. . . . Good bye I must close

Your affectionate

Mary

- - - - -

Letter from Lt. Richard Watkins to Mary Watkins

Richmond
Aug 21st 62

My Precious Mary. – We reached Richmond today. All well – Quite a pleasant trip thus far except that I suffered more than ever from home-sickness. . . . the regiment is ninety miles from here and probably by this time a hundred, but that our camp is at Louisa Courthouse only 62 miles. All this journey we must make on horseback as so many troops are going out on the cars that there is no possibility of getting a horse on them. . . . I went to Minn's Gallery this evening . . . to have a likeness taken for you and sent it up by Mr Lockett of Farmville . . . But about our trip. First night just as I told you Henry Edmunds and I staid at Aunt Eggleston's . . . Aunt E gave us a late breakfast and we could get no further than Amelia Courthouse to dinner and staid last night with a Mr Goode nine miles this side of the Courthouse . . .

Darling I look back at the last fortnight spent with you as . . . the happiest . . . period of my life. Our children too are so sweet and interesting and love you so much I love them the more for that. . . . Wish I could Write you a longer letter but tis late at night . . . Give much love to all . . . Again good bye. Yr own Richard

- - - - -

Sharpsburg to Chambersburg
August 24 to October 22, 1862

With General McClellan out of the way, General Lee turns the Army of Northern Virginia north and goes after General Pope. He crushes Pope at the battle of Second Manassas on August 27th and on September 5th Lee has his men in Maryland. September 17th, the bloodiest day of the war, finds both armies in Sharpsburg, Maryland, facing each other across Antietam creek. By sunset 3,911 men are dead, 18,365 are wounded, and 2,136 are missing. Lee will withdraw back into Virginia. 1

In Kentucky, forces under General Bragg have been defeated at the battle of Perryville and they retreat back to Tennessee. President Lincoln, as commander in chief of the armies, decides to use the victory in Maryland as the opportunity to issue the Emancipation Proclamation. By edict he will declare the slaves free in all territories in open rebellion. Richard determines that, "Lincoln's proclamation will have no effect on the final result."

Mary writes that she is "lonely since you left." Minnie has fallen down the stairs backwards, Mary needs blankets for the negroes for winter, and scarlet fever is killing many children in the county. She sends Richard updates on the "tobacco, straw & spuds." There has been a draft of workers to build fortifications in Richmond and they have been tasked to provide one slave from Oldham. They were able to butcher 31 hogs and have a lot of hams curing in the smokehouse. Emmie "is needing" shoes for the winter but prices are "out of sight."

Richard's letters outline the declining operational condition of the both the cavalry and the entire army. On reaching Louisa Courthouse he finds many sick men and broken down horses from Co. K. In total 80 men from the 3rd Virginia Cavalry are here with broken down horses. He blames poor supply management and incompetent officers. On August 29th several men from Co. K are detailed to Prince Edward County for new horses. Richard deplores the poor condition and discipline of the army. Co. K, which has a normal compliment of 82 men, will have 12 men on the field at Sharpsburg.

After the withdrawal from Maryland, the 3rd Virginia is north of Winchester around Martinsburg. Richard has been living on "corn and apples." He does not like the mountains and plans to resign if the army will be staying in the mountains for the winter.

Letter from Lt. Richard Watkins to Mary Watkins

Louisa Courthouse
Aug 24th 62

My Darling

Evening before last we rode up to an old fashioned tavern kept by a Mrs. Goodall . . . Our camp here with some sick men and many disabled horses but the regiment still forty miles ahead . . . in Culpeper County. Will start again in pursuit tomorrow and hope to overtake them soon. Camp rumor says that [General] Pope is retreating and [General Stonewall] Jackson is pursuing. . . . I seem to be thousands of miles from home and it is a comforting thought that I am still within 24 hours ride of you. . . . The lands and crops in Louisa are very like those in Prince Edward and need rain quite as badly. . . .

. . . here in Camp are Leigh Redd with a sick horse and John Anderson who has been sick but is now well again. Jno Baker has had jaundice and is looking quite badly. No serious sickness in the regiment but eighty well men here with horses unfit for service. This indicates rather bad management on the part of our superior officers. . . . Good bye my precious one. . . .
Yr own
Richard

– – – – –

Letter from Lt. Richard Watkins to Mary Watkins

Camp at Brandy Station
Near Stevensburg
Aug 26th 1862

My own Dear Mary

I have overtaken the regiment at last. Rode 44 miles yesterday and about 8 o'clock at night came upon the regiment with their horses picketed . . . and the men all lying about on the ground without tents fast asleep. Waked up Capt. Berkeley and Lieut. Knight had a little conversation with them and Hal and I then spread our blankets near them and were soon asleep. . . . We are in a beautiful country in full view of the mountains. . . . The hills are covered with corn and hay. We crossed the Rapidan at Racoon ford 11 miles from this place which is a station on the Orange and Alexandria railroad. . . . Our regiment has been left in rear of the Army which is about 10 miles ahead and a portion of it at this time engaged with the enemy for while I am writing the canon is booming quite rapidly.

. . . Charley Redd's substitute is offering $500 more than Charley gave him for some man to take his place. He is looking very badly pale and emaciated and I fear cannot stand the service very long. . . . Please tell [Mr. Baker] to sow the winter oats as early as possible, the sooner the better. Write to me too how the tobacco is looking . . . Am anxious too to hear from my horse . . . Tell him to make haste and get well and fat that I greatly prefer him to his substitute. . . . Kiss often my dear little girls for me . . . Love to all Yr Richard

- - - - -

Letter from Pattie Watkins to Sgt. Nathaniel Watkins

Mt Pleasant
Aug 27th 1862

My own, Dear Brother

. . . we were all very much surprised to find that you had received the box so soon. We might have sent you some other kinds of vegetables if we had known how soon it would have reached you . . . Sister Maria made the Catsup & gave it to Brother Dick but he couldn't carry a box & Ma took it & sent it to you. Brother Dick staid about a fortnight. He looked right thin & coughed right badly when he came up. But said he fattened nearly a pound a day & was afraid to weigh before he went away. He got several new recruits from among the prisoners while here for the troop. Hal Edmunds was one. Henry Ewing, Frank Womack & Hal & one or two others went down with him horse back. His horse had given out so he had to get a new one. . . . Joe Daniel has joined the Charlotte troop but don't know whether he has started out or not. Poor fellow he hates so badly to leave his beautiful young wife . . .

We have had some very severe rains lately & Mr. Redd's tobacco has been right much injured but his corn crop is excellent. . . . we have very little fruit except apples. peaches are very scarce in the neighborhood & the watermelon vines have nearly all been killed by the drought. . . .
Your Ever Aff Sister
Pattie 2

(ed: The "prisoners" Pattie refers to are Confederate soldiers who were captured and have been paroled to their homes for a fixed period of time. They are honor bound not to rejoin the service during that fixed period. Their paroles have now expired and they can re-enter the service.)

- - - - -

Letter from Mary Watkins to Lt. Richard Watkins

Linden Aug 28th 1862

Well! Sir, It is time I was beginning another letter to you isn't it? . . . Mr Baker has just come in, says he is going to have the potatoes dug at our house today . . . I am going over presently . . . Aug 29th . . . Found a letter from you when I got back. Am glad to hear you have reached your regiment. Have not received your likeness yet. . . . It was nearly twelve o'clock before they got started on the potatoes . . . did not finish until after sundown and it was right dark. . . . I found Purnall and Beverly waiting to escort me home and they walked along behind the horse all the way. Met Isaac about half way coming for me. . . . The potatoes did not turn out quite as well as I expected . . . The tobacco has improved considerably since the rain . . . we put up thirteen stacks of straw, four more than we had last year. Mama will finish thrashing wheat today. I am going down to see your horse this evening. . . . Sam Davis . . . says he can never be made fat again there is something the matter with his lungs. I hope he is mistaken though.

. . . Cousin George is trying to get a substitute. Says he expects to pay $5000 for one. He is certainly in a delimma. His property is nearly all in Kentucky and will be confiscated if he joins the Southern army or gets a substitute. A good deal of his tobacco was burned . . . Good bye my paper is full
Your own Mary

- - - - -

Letter from Lt. Richard Watkins to Mary Watkins

Camp near Brandy Station
Aug 29th 29th 1862

My Darling Mary

. . . My last was written while the cannon was booming apparently eight or ten miles from us, at this time a heavy cannonading is going on apparently 25 or 30 miles from us . . . The Yankees tolerably quiet their minds no doubt occupied with Stonewall Jackson and his command. Hal Edmunds and I have been on picket once but the weather is so fine it is a poor initiation for Hal. I think he will make a fine soldier. . . . Lieut. Knight charges me with getting into bad habits while at home. . . . interrupted by an order from Col Thornton for the Prince Edward Troop to take a scout about the ford at Mountain Run, a creek running within five or six miles of our camp and emptying into the Rappahannock. . . . no Yankees to be found. . . . Lieut Bell of our Troop has just sent in his resignation on account of bad health, having been afflicted with rheumatism for several months. It has already been approved by the surgeon of the regiment and will be by Col Thornton . . . I will try to send this letter by him. Col. Thornton today detailed several of the Troop amongst them Leigh Redd to go home after fresh horses. I am glad that Leigh has a furlough, he deserves it having done good service the whole time. . . . when Leigh Redd returns please send my horse along with him and if Doug Mettauer [free black] will not come and no other servant can be had please fix up Purnall and send him. Tis absolutely necessary that I have a boy. I get so dirty currying my horse that I am not fit to appear with the other officers. And what is still worse I can't get anything to eat in this country without sending out a boy to buy it, and John Knight's boy has too much to do to wait on all of us. – I will try to take good care of Purnall but had rather hire a servant if I could get one. Hal Edmonds is messing with us and will continue to mess with me as long as we stay together in the Army. . . . Kiss Emmie and Minnie often for me & tell them that Papa loves them & wants to see them mightily. I love you, I love you, I love you, love you, love you, <u>love you</u> Yr Richard

(ed: Most of the officers in the 3rd Virginia Cavalry have a servant that is with them in camp and on the march. Richard desires to have one of the slaves at Oldham sent for this purpose. However, Richard will serve virtually the entire war without a servant at his disposal. The custom of officers having servants with them during the war is common throughout the Confederate armies and is the norm rather than the exception.)

- - - - -

Letter from Lt. Richard Watkins to Mary Watkins

On the road between
Manassas & Leesburg
Sep 2nd 1862

My own dear Mary

Here we go we know not where, perhaps into Maryland. Have obtained another signal victory at Bull Run. I have not time this morning to give the particulars. You will get them from the papers. Archer Haskins horse broke down yesterday and he is going to the rear this morning and I must send this to be mailed somewhere.

Your chances of getting letters from me are growing beautifully less but I intend to take every opportunity – Have not recd one from you yet. The order to mount our horses has been given so Good bye my own dear precious one. I am perfectly well. Kisses & love – Yr own Richard

Wish I had time to write more.

- - - - -

Letter from Lt. Richard Watkins to Mary Watkins

Dranesville
Sep 4th 1862

My Precious Mary

We reached this place today and are in the rear of the army the main body being as far ahead as Leesburg . . . Had a severe engagement near Fairfax Co H of which you have doubtless been apprised by the newspapers. Yesterday our company was on picket about 13 miles of Alexandria. About 1500 paroled prisoners passed us with a flag of truce on their way back to Yankeeland. I . . . wished them a long furlough and a happy time at home. . . . hundreds and hundreds of ambulances have been for several days passing, carrying to the enemy their wounded. . . .

My health is excellent and the health of the company is good. . . . Am glad to say that we seldom find any Union sentiment . . . in the vicinity of Alexandria and Washington City. . . . The people evince a most determined resolution to repay the Yankees for their depredations.

We are with an immense body of cavalry now. Would you not like to see a thousand men going at full speed on horseback together. We entered the little village of Fairfax Courthouse . . . just that way. . . .

. . . I should rather that you should not send Purnall now but would be very glad to have my horse and Doug Mettauer sent as I need a servant badly. Tis too far from home for Purnall, I know he would not feel satisfied. I am going to send this letter to Genl Lee [Gen. Fitzhugh Lee] our Brigadier – with a request that he send it to some post office along with his dispatches and hope you will get it continue to write and direct to Louisa CoHo. Good bye sweet one. I love you with my whole heart. . . .

Yr own Richard

(ed: The ambulances are transporting the Union wounded from the battlefield of Second Manassas to hospitals in Washington City.)

(ed: For the Maryland Campaign General Fitzhugh Lee's Cavalry Brigade will be composed of the 1ˢᵗ, 3ʳᵈ, 4ᵗʰ, 5ᵗʰ, and 9ᵗʰ Virginia Cavalry Regiments. The Cavalry Division is commanded by General J. E. B. Stuart. The other brigades are commanded by General Wade Hampton and General Beverly Robertson. Captain Pelham commands the artillery.) 3

- - - - -

Letter from Mary Watkins to Lt. Richard Watkins

Linden Sept. 5ᵗʰ 1862

Dear Mr Watkins

It has been nearly a week since I wrote you last . . . Minnie has bitten Emmie's toe and is telling me, "Toe Emmie Minnie bite mouth" and Emmie is crying about it, Minnie can make herself understood very well now but she will talk backwards. . . .

Isaac went to Farmville Tuesday and called at Mr Locketts for your daguerreotype. I did not think it a very good likeness at first but the more I look at it the more it looks like you. Mama says it looks very savage but she told me not to tell you she said so. I think it must be good though because I showed it to Emmie . . . when she woked up and she knew it directly. . . .

... By the way what in the world are we to do for blankets for the negroes this winter! I know some of them suffered for them last winter and I don't know what they will do this winter. The last few nights have been mighty cold ... Wish you had some of our peaches now they are such fine nice ones. I don't believe I ever saw finer. . . . I am going to stop to eat some. . . .

Sept 6th ... Haven't we had glourious news from Manassas? President Davis has appointed the 18th of this month as Thanksgiving day. . . .
Your loving
Mary

(ed: A daguerreotype is made using a photographic process where the image is made on a light sensitive silver-coated metallic plate. If you have daguerreotypes of ancestors you should take great care to avoid contacting the surface of the print with your fingers.) 4

- - - - -

Letter from Lt. Richard Watkins to Mary Watkins

New Market Maryland
Sep 7th 1862

Well Darlin here we are in Maryland only 36 miles from Baltimore and 18 or 20 from the Pennsylvania line. All well and getting on finely. Jackson ahead of us we know not where. The people receive us kindly many of them joyfully. Our squadron is here one mile out of town on picket and I am sitting down on a bag of oats this pleasant Sabbath afternoon with my arms on, writing to my precious one. . . . Recd your letter of the 21st & cannot thank you enough ... if our Army can meet with success a little longer I hope the great struggle will be over ... We crossed the Potomac at the Leesburg Ford on Thursday evening the 5th Va in front and ours next. We met with no opposition ... but came upon a squadron of Cavalry at Poolsville about 5 miles from the Ford. A squadron of our cavalry were dismounted as sharpshooters whilst a squadron of the 5th charged and we were soon in posession of 32 prisoners, one killed & one wounded. On our side only 1 slightly wounded and none killed. – New Market is in Frederick County. We have taken possession of the Baltimore & Ohio Railroad. . . . Direct your next to Leesburg Loudon County Virginia. John Redd is with us & well – Tell Mr Arvin if you see him that Mel is with us and well – Hal Edmunds, Archie Haskins & all well. . . . I must now close. Am very sorry that I cannot write more. . . . We will recd no boxes from home while about here . . . Good bye Darling . . . Love Love to all I love you Your own Richard

– – – – –

Letter from Mary Watkins to Lt. Richard Watkins

Linden Sept. 9th 1862

My dear Husband

This is the fourth letter I have written you since you left . . . They finished threashing our wheat the day after you left home I believe. There was thirteen right large stacks of straw. David White finished prizing the tobacco week before last, there are fourteen hogsheads and a little over. We have sent . . . for seed oats and have engaged some at last from Cousin Will Morton at $2.00 per bushel. I went over home one day and had the Irish potatoes dug . . . Believe I will send Purnall any how. I don't believe there is any danger of his leaving you, he loves home and his father and mother too well, expect the difficulty will be in getting him away from here. . . . I have just got some nice homespun dresses from the weaver for the children of which Emmie is very proud . . . Your daguerreotype is exactly like you I think and I thank you a thousand times for it. . . .

(Friday night) . . . I never heard of such dreadful fevers as are prevailing in Charlotte. A great many children have died of scarlet fever. Cousin Will Morton lost his second son and Fannie Spencer's three children are ill with it now. Jennie McPhail died week before last too. . . . I don't like it a bit your going way up into Maryland where I can hardly ever hear from you. . . . I wish I had a Gen Lee to forward my letters . . .

I expect we will lose all of our cattle with distemper, lost one cow with it since you left making three that have died . . . (Sunday evening) . . . Emmie says "tell Papa I am a good child now." It distresses her very much to tell her you will not love her if she is bad. Good bye darling.
Your own
Mary

(ed: Charlotte Court House is located in Charlotte County. Mary is hearing of fevers in the neighboring county to their west.)

- - - - -

Letter from Lt. Richard Watkins to Mary Watkins

New Market Maryland
Sep 11th 1862

My darling Mary

We are still here but expecting to go further towards Pennsylvania soon perhaps today . . . New Market is about as large as Farmville. We are on the right flank of the Army the main body . . . marching directly to Frederick a town of 10,000 inhabitants. We hear that yesterday they moved in the direction of the Pennsylvania line . . . one of our men (not a member of our company of course) having a broken down horse went to the house of a Union man and took one from him. He complained to . . . General Fitz Lee and he promptly placed the man under arrest and returned the horse to the owner and issued an order that if any trooper should be guilty of a like offense his horse should be taken from him & he made to march on foot carrying his saddle & baggage on his back and be made to keep up with the regiment. . . .

The health of our troop continues good . . . You may tell the friends of Henry Edmunds, Jno Redd, Archer & Tom Haskins, Henry & John Ewing & Mel Arvin that they are all with us and all well. . . . I hope that if this campaign proves successful on our part that it will lead to a speedy termination of the war. . . .

My bay horse is doing very well and I am very well satisfied with him. – Hal Edmunds is getting on finely . . . [*rest of the letter is missing*]

- - - - -

Letter from Pattie Watkins to Lt. Richard Watkins

Mt. Pleasant
Sep 14th /62

My own Dear Brother

. . . Nannie wrote me word that Mr. Daniel was selling Bro Nat's wheat at 3$ a bushel & his winter oats at 2$. He made quite a good crop of both, but no tobacco worth speaking of. John Daniel came down & staid a day or two staid most of the time with Nannie Dupuy. He looks very well & is very cheerful went to your house & looked around. Joe is speaking of joining the Charlotte troop. Jimmie Watkins got a substitute & since has been very sick with scarlet fever. Aunt Nancy lost 4 or 5 negroes with scarlet fever & had others very sick with it. Some of the cases run into diphtheria. Beverly Watkins has gotten a place as a surgeon in the Army & left Bro Nat & the other boys. Bro Nat has been acting as clerk in the Court Martial lately & hasn't been much with the Company, has had a great deal of writing to do.

All join me in much love to you.
Your ever loving Sister,
Pattie 5

- - - - -

Letter from Pattie Watkins to Nannie Watkins

Mt Pleasant
Sep 16th 1862

My Dear Sister.

. . . Poor Brother Dick he is so far off that we cannot even write to him except by private conveyance. He was on his way to Maryland when we last heard from him. We feel anxious about our Army there that we can't feel very glad to have them cross the Potomac. Mrs. Powell, the lady who is living here has just received the news of the death of her son her only one he was killed on the 24th of August . . . She had one killed at Manassas last year & the other near Warrenton this summer. He was only 22 years old . .

Mr Redd . . . he is gone today to try & get leather for the winter shoes. Ma says how do you come on with your spinning & your cards? Sister Maria has made 80 yds. Flannel for sale . . .

Kiss the little ones for me tell Charley I dreamed about him last night dreamed I was putting shoes on his feet. . . .
Your own Loving Sister
Pattie 6

- - - - -

Letter from Lt. Richard Watkins to Mary Watkins

Battlefield near Sharpsburg
Washington County Maryland
Sep: 18th 1862.

Thanksgiving Day Darling and with all my heart do I thank God for his many distinguishing mercies . . . We have just passed through an immense battle and driven the enemy back at every point. The fight may possibly be renewed today . . . A sad calamity though befel our regiment yesterday. The engagement had just commenced when a shell struck a pile of cordwood just by us & exploded a fragment of it fracturing Col Thornton's arm & injuring him we suppose internally to such an extent that he died last night. A fragment of the same shell seriously wounded Mr Hardy of Mecklinburg & killed his horse. I was only three or four yards from it at the time. A few days before in a skirmish with the enemy Col Thornton had his horse shot from under him. We mourn his loss deeply. . . . No other member of our regiment hurt yesterday though we were under fire nearly all day. . . . Mac Venable has a severe flesh wound and Pat Fitzgerald is wounded in the foot. We have had an active campaign here. Genl Jackson with his division & Genl A P Hills took Harpers Ferry with 10,000 or 12,000 prisoners, 60 pieces of artillery & 15,000 stand of arms only a few days ago & has rejoined the army here. Genl D H Hill with a portion of his command had a battle about the same time with a large body of enemy going to reinforce Harper's Ferry & succeeded in keeping them back. The battle Yesterday though was doubtless one of the greatest of the war I hope that we will never have another like it. . . . In yesterdays fight we lost Genl Branch & Genl Starke and a good number of other officers. In a skirmish at Boonesville we lost from our regiment one killed 7 or 8 wounded and 10 or 15 missing we do not know whether they are prisoners or not. Meredith alone is missing from our company. We hope he is not wounded and will yet come up. The bugle sounds and we must go. So good bye my precious precious Mary . . . Good bye Kisses & love to all Yr own Richard

- - - - -

Letter from Lt. Richard Watkins to Mary Watkins

Camp near Shepherdstown
Sep 22nd 1862

My Precious Mary

We are again in Virginia . . . When I last wrote we were on the battlefield of Sharpsburg one of the fiercest battles of the war. One which can never be forgotten by the people of Prince Edward. Col. Thornton, Wm Walton of Farmville and our Cousin John Booker were killed. Mac Venable, Dr. Walton and Pat Fitzgerald wounded. We drove the enemy back at every point, remained one day entirely quiet waiting for them to renew the attack and then withdrew our forces to Virginia. Our Generals strongly suspected that the enemy would renew the attack while we were crossing and if so our situation would have been perilous indeed. But they did not renew it and to our surprise after we were all safely over attempted to cross just after us when the rear guard of our army turned upon them and almost annihilated two or three regiments. . . . to our great surprise we hear that Genl Stuart with a portion of his command is again in Maryland away over beyond Hagerstown. The news comes to us through Genl Fitz Lee & I reckon is reliable. . . . Tis also reported that a portion of Jackson's command has recrossed and possibly all of us may be in Maryland again soon. . . . I know we were not defeated because I know where our forces were when the battle commenced and where when it closed and yet we left a portion of our wounded in the hands of the enemy. Our dead, so far as I know were buried. Wm Walton and John Booker were buried near each other and the spot marked. I did not hear that John was killed until after he was buried. . . . The feeling of hatred on both sides is becoming intensified and the battles more fierce and desperate. As soon as things get a little more quiet I mean to apply for a good long furlough and try to stay with you some. If the Army remains in the mountains I shall resign my commission for I shall be afraid to spend the winter in the mountains. . . .

. . . I hardly know what to suggest about blankets for the negroes. Could you not set the women to making quilts or comforts or would they be still more costly. Cousin Barrett might help you out of the dilemma by watching his opportunity. I reckon the negroes will have to suffer some along with the rest of us we cannot under present circumstances furnish them every thing that they really need and all that is left is to do our best. Will close for present and write again tomorrow if I have the time. Give love &c
Yrs Richard

- - - - -

Letter from Lt. Richard Watkins to Mary Watkins

Camp near Martinsburg

Sep: 23rd 1862

Mr Charles Crawley leaves today for home being over thirty five and not having re enlisted. One of the best men I ever knew and I am really sorry to part with him. . . . He came from Winchester yesterday (having been sent there a few days ago with a broken down horse.) and brought me . . . a letter from you (a good long dear letter) and a mighty good letter from Pattie . . . Also the news that Joe Cooper had reached Winchester with my other horse. . . .

Would you believe it Darling nearly the whole of our Company is at home and between here and Richmond. Tis shameful in the extreme. Even John Redd is going home after another horse. But I must not write more on this subject I might write imprudent remarks. The discipline of our army is entirely too slack and I am fearful that we will soon have a sad reverse unless it is made more rigid. – During the battle of Sharpsburg not more than twelve of our troop were present out of eighty-two. Is it not too bad. –

I am distressed at hearing of the death of Charles Hundley. Oh what will Fanny do . . .

I thank you for writing about Emmie & Minnie so much. I like to read about them. Tell Emmie that Papa loves his dear little girls. . . . Was glad to hear too so much about our farm. At any time that you think proper have the crops sold either the wheat or tobacco. Will get a furlough & come to see you as soon as possible.

Wish you could see how I have lived the past ten days and how well I am. Have not during that time had as much meat & bread as I could eat in one day. Have lived almost entirely on roasting ears and apples gathered on the roadsides as we go along and roasted whenever & wherever we stop. and yet strange to tell my health . . . is very good. Had it not been for the young corn and apples we could hardly have survived. We are now doing better – our wagons have overtaken us and we have had bread and beef. –

Well I must close for now . . . Give a great deal of love to all. Hal Edmunds always sends love. I must try to write to Pattie and thank her for her nice letter & presents. Oh I want to see you too bad. Again Goodbye Yr own Richard

(ed: The original upper end on the draft age was 35. Since Mr. Crawley is over 35 and his term of enlistment is up he is free to go home. This will soon change as the draft is expanded to both older and younger men to fill the needs of the Confederate service.)

- - - - -

Letter from Mary Watkins to Lt. Richard Watkins

Linden Sept. 24th 1862

My dear dear Husband

I received your letter today by Archer Haskins and assure you I felt relieved at the very sight of it. We heard Monday of Col. Thornton's death and I felt more anxious than ever to hear from you. . . . I dreamed Wednesday night that you were in a battle that day and it seems you were . . . there is some magnetic chain between us and I can almost always tell . . . when you are in danger. . . .

Sep 27th I have been sick in bed the last two days. had a very sore throat and pain in my head, neck and back. Took labelia all day Thursday and yesterday the Doctor scarrified my throat. Feel much better today though right weak and I almost faint if I stand . . .

Sep 29th Feel almost well this morning. . . . Am up and dressed and have just been begging Mama to cut off my hair. . . . Archer Haskins . . . will come again before he goes back to the Army and I will send you some money by him. . . .

Oct 4th I have been waiting to send this letter by Archer Haskins . . . and Archer must wait until he can have him a suit of winter clothes wove . . . I reckon . . . I will send it to Richmond as you directed. . . .

Good bye. All send love. Wish I could fill out this sheet but am in a great hurry.
Your own
Mary

(ed: Lobelia is any number of plants of the genus Lobelia which have terminal clusters of variously colored flowers. Mary is no doubt making some type of herbal tea from the lobelia.) 7

(ed: To be scarrified is to have a multiple bladed instrument, that is spring loaded, placed on some area of your body and triggered. In Mary's case, on her throat. The blades do multiple slices in your skin and the Doctor bleeds you. The process of bleeding a person to rid a person of "bad" blood is falling out of favor but is still practiced by many doctors.)

- - - - -

Letter from Pattie Watkins to Sgt. Nathaniel Watkins

Mt. Pleasant
Sep 26th 1862

My own Dear Brother,

. . . we have been anxious about Brother Dick but Mollie got a letter from him Monday written the 18th saying that he was well & that the whole company were safe except for Mr. Meredith who was missing but they hoped he would soon come up again. Col. Thornton was killed by a bursting of a shell also Dick was very near but escaped unhurt & Hal Edmunds was quite near where another burst & killed a horse in the same regiment. Col. T was the only one killed though there were others wounded. Mr. Venable received a very bad flesh wound & John Morton Booker was killed. We can get none of the particulars of J. Bookers death. . . . Our county has suffered very much from This war & now the Farmville Guards haven't been heard from at all they were in the 18th Regiment . . .
Your ever loving Sister
Pattie 8

- - - - -

Letter from Lt. Richard Watkins to Mary Watkins

Camp near Martinsburg
Sep 27th 1862

My own Dear Mary –

. . . This beautiful morning we are doing nothing sitting about in the forest talking cooking writing some twenty or thirty firing at a squirrel which has been so unfortunate as to find it's way into a hickory over us.

I have not seen Joe Cooper yet. He stopped at the wagons between Winchester & Martinsburg by the advice of Leigh Redd, his horses back being too sore for him to proceed farther. This was owing to my carelessness in not getting the saddle fixed before I left home. . . . Will go to wagons and see about him as soon as I can . . . I am greatly obliged to you and mother for sending him for if we remain in this country long he will be of great service to me.

Mel Arvin succeeded in killing the squirrel and he & Henry Edmunds are busily engaged in skinning it, anticipating doubtless a good stew. . . . Our horses and men are both poorly provided for in the Army at present. It must be owing greatly to carelessness & neglect & incompetence on the part of our quartermasters & commissaries. . . . the Army is in worse condition than I have ever known . . . so now at the height of our successes when our papers are calling loudly for us to invade the North I think that I see clearly that we are in the saddest plight imaginable for offensive operations. I am apprehensive that our very successes have tended to demoralize the army. We hear all too frequently of the bad conduct of our . . . stragglers whose name is Legion. . . .

Have been summoned to a meeting of the officers to take some suitable notice of the death of Col. Thornton. . . . He was highly respected and esteemed by all and his loss will be seriously felt. And now Good bye Darling. Be of good cheer write often. . . . Yr own Richard

- - - - -

Letter from Lt. Richard Watkins to Mary Watkins

Near Winchester
Oct 1 1862

My own dear Mary

Yesterday Tom Haskins and I got permission to visit Winchester. Left the Regiment at Charlestown about 12 o'clock . . . and six miles from Winchester we bought some corn for our horses and camped in a forest on the roadside. . . . Tom came to meet with his father and I have started in search of Joe Cooper. Joe is with the wagons in the rear . . .

Oct 1 – Am now here. We learn that Mr. Haskins has gone home. Am very sorry as I wanted to send this letter by him. Winchester in a dreadful plight just as Richmond was not long ago. full of sick & wounded & straggling soldiers. Nothing can be bought in the stores. Everything sold out. Nothing to eat at the hotels. Nothing – pshaw I will close this letter to get out of this place. Will call to see Mac Venable before I go who I hear is at the residence of Rev. A H H Boyd. Good bye my precious one. I love you more than ever. Yr own Richard

(ed: Mac Venable was brought to a hospital in Winchester following the Sharpsburg battle and, once his wounds were treated, he was transferred to a home in the community to recover. This freed up space in the hospital wards for more seriously wounded.)

- - - - -

Letter from Lt. Richard Watkins to Mary Watkins

Camp near Lee Town
Oct 4th 1862

My Precious Mary

Oh that I could see you this morning. I am almost crazy to get home again. Went to Winchester a few days ago by permission mainly to see Mac Venable who was seriously but not dangerously wounded at the battle of Sharpsburg. Found him ... doing well ... Our regiment is now about 8 miles NW of Charlestown near by a little place of three or four houses called Lee Town. . . . Recd your letter by Mr Sublett and thank you . . . I read it to Hal Edmunds . . . I would like for you to write me about Emmie & Minnie. It makes me love them more and realize now & more that they are my children. I like to hear of their running about . . .

The country around us is quite pretty . . . The forests are of oak and hickory and do not compare with the beautiful beech and maple which we saw in Indiana . . . The roads are fine nearby all of them macadamized and lime stone is so abundant that it is mainly used in building barns and fences . . . the cattle and stock of every kind are excellent. . . .

Our Army is mainly on the road between Winchester and Martinsburg the greater portion of McClellan's on the other side of the river but he has quite a large force at Harpers Ferry and their tents on Bolivar Heights can be seen from Charlestown where we are camped near. Charlestown you remember is the place where John Brown was tried and executed. Mr Sublett was present on the occasion and showed us where he stood and witnessed the execution. . . .

Oct 5 - ... This morning we were ordered to return to our Brigade at Martinsburg . . . but when on the way the order was countermanded. . . . John Flournoy who is sergeant for the Brigade Quartermaster . . . is about to go to Winchester . . . will draw this to a close & send it by him. . . . Our troops are enjoying fine health and the weather most beautiful.

Yr own

Richard

- - - - -

Letter from Mary Watkins to Lt. Richard Watkins

Linden Oct. 7th 1862

My dear Richard

I received a letter from you Sunday sent by Lucius Walton and another yesterday mailed in Winchester dated Oct. 1st. I am always so glad to get your letters and thank you very many times for writing so often. . . .

Oct 9th - . . . Mama, Nannie and I are sitting around the candle in the chamber. I have undressed, put on my wrapper and made myself comfortable . . . Isaac carried Emmie and me over in the little wagon [to the plantation] and he gathered apples whilst I had a fire made up in the cellar of the new house and melted over my lard and put it up in buckets ready to send to Richmond. I had the beds turned too. . . . We dined in real bachelor style on fried meat and eggs and corn bread with a chair for a table and apples for dessert. They have secured all the fodder . . . and cut four houses of tobacco. They had nearly finished fallowing the oats but the ground is so dry they can't sow now. One of our sheep got badly hurt the other day and I reckon will die. [Mr Baker says] one of the sheep horned it. Linny has a . . . baby and is doing very well. . . . Mr. and Mrs. Charles Redd and Branch are sick with Typhoid fever . . . not expected to live. Mr. Norwell is down with it too . . .

Oct 10th – Emmie has been crying . . . I told her I would have to write you about it. She says she is going to be a good child. . . . She is a great deal more of a baby than Minnie . . . if I get out of her sight

she cries . . . Good bye now I will write again soon. I sent a letter to Richmond for you last week . . .
Your own
Mary

- - - - -

Letter from Lt. Richard Watkins to Mary Watkins

Camp near Lee Town
Oct 8th 1862

My own dear Mary

. . . There seems to be at present a lull, a calm but my belief is that the storm will burst upon us again with greater fury than ever. There is great talk of peace, but nothing in the North that I can see to encourage such a belief . . . The present position . . . of our Troop forbids my carrying out for the present my cherished plan of spending the winter with you. If though Capt. Berkeley and John Knight return to the field well and healthy and our forces remain inactive and go quietly into winter quarters I will get a long furlough. . . .

I do not believe that they [Yankees] ever will or ever can subjugate or conquer the South. Lincoln's proclamation may make him more or less popular in the North but they can never intimidate the true men of the South. . . . His proclamation cannot in the least affect the final result which must inevitably be our recognition . . . as a distinct nationality. Pardon me darling for writing so much about the war. . . .

We are now getting letters regularly from Winchester. Think if you will direct to Co K 3rd Reg Cavalry 2nd Brigade and send to Winchester your letter will probably reach me . . . Good bye now for the present – always give love to every body & kisses to our dear little girls.

(ed: President Lincoln waited till his armies achieved the victory at Antietam [Sharpsburg] before he issued his Emancipation Proclamation. It was issued by President Lincoln, not as "President", but as "Commander in Chief" and upon "military necessity." He declared "That on the first day of January, 1863 all persons held as slaves within any State or designated part of a State the people whereof shall then be in rebellion against the United States, shall be then, . . . forever free." Slaves were not freed in Maryland, Missouri, Kentucky, most of Tennessee and portions of Virginia and Louisiana held by Union forces. No slaves were freed in any of the Northern states. All of those areas would have to wait for Congress to pass an amendment to the Constitution banning slavery following the war.) 9

(ed: Richard is the only Company K officer on duty. Capt. Berkeley is on furlough, Lt. Bell has been discharged for health reasons, and Lt. Knight home on sick leave.)

- - - - -

Letter from Pattie Watkins to Nannie Watkins

Mt Pleasant
Oct 9th 1862

My Dear Sister

. . . I hoped I would have been able to get to see you before now. . . . I hear of so much diphtheria & scarlet fever that I am afraid of carrying it either to your house or here. . . . I got a good long letter from Brother Dick a few days ago. He was in Martinsburg. Said he had been through a good deal of suffering since he left home last but had been mercifully spared through it all. He was under fire at Sharpsburg through the whole of the battle & one shell exploded near him & killed Col. Thornton one exploded near Hal Edmunds & killed a horse & wounded one of the [   ] troopers. . . . We have gotten through with the measles at last have had 43 cases & haven't lost any. . . . We have had one or two cases on hand ever since May.
. . .

Your Loving Sister
Pattie 10

(ed: *In an October 13th note to Richard, Pattie mentions that "Mr Redd selling six hogs heads of tobacco @ 18 & 19$ . . . Bro Nat selling his leaf @ 18$ but his was rather poor."*)

- - - - -

Letter from Lt. Richard Watkins to Mary Watkins

Camp near Lee Town Oct 15th 62

My Precious Mary

On last Thursday . . . Genl Stuart and I and a whole parcel of fellows about 1800 in all concluded that as times were getting dull on this side of the river we would ride over and see what the people were doing on the other side. Started about 10 o'clock in the morning in the direction of Winchester and then turning to the right we reached the Potomac about midnight . . . above Williamsport . . . At daybreak we crossed the river . . . taking 6 prisoners . . . passing rapidly through a portion of Maryland and entering Pennsylvania about midday . . . all the inhabitants astonished . . . suddenly turned pale, quaking trembling with fright. . . . The order was soon given to detail men to catch horses . . . Our large body continued to move rapidly to Mercersburg and over every field & in every direction men could be seen chasing horses. . . . Citizens on horses & in buggies were dismounted & turned loose afoot – it was really the greatest frolick that I ever witnessed. At Mercersburg we halted, fed our horses bountifully from the corn fields of the good old Dutchmen . . . At this place occurred the only thing which I sincerely regret about the trip. Some of the men broke open a store and rifled it of a great many goods . . . mainly such things as they needed badly such as shoes hats etc. . . . I doubt the propriety and the policy of even taking horses but this we were ordered to do by our Generals . . . From Mercersburg we continued our march to Chambersburg, a large and wealthy town which I reckon contains from fifteen to twenty thousand inhabitants ... Reached Chambersburg about sunset and the home guard threatened to oppose us. Genl Stuart sent in a flag of truce and informed them that if they made the least resistance he would shell the town. They at once gave him permission to enter. ... I burrowed under [a straw stack] and slept all night quite comfortably. ... The next morning ... took a most meandering rout from Chambersburg to Emmetsville, Md gathering several hundred horses as we went. When we touched the Maryland line near Emmetsville the order was given that nothing was to be seized under penalty of death. ... From Emmetsville we continued on going through Md & entirely around McClellans army first approaching near Hagerstown then through Woodville near Frederick, through Liberty ... New Market & then to Barnesville near the Potomac and thence to the river opposite Leesburg. We reached the river about 10 or 11 o'clock Sunday morning having marched 85 miles in 28 hours without dismounting a single time [since leaving Chambersburg] ... That night we encamped at Leesburg ... and we came on at our leisure to Camp. This morning I am perfectly well & entirely refreshed.

... I was sent out in charge of some videttes to watch [enemy] movements ... whilst there Genl Lee (Robt E), Genl Jackson & Genl Stuart rode by together going over to take a view of the enemy. Genl Jackson is entirely different in appearance from what I expected. He is about my size perhaps not quite so tall with dark hair & whiskers and entirely genteel in his appearance though plainly dressed. Nothing rough or uncouth about him ...

This morning I was delighted at the reception of another letter from you dated ... Oct 4th. ... My horse John Wesley broke down just as we crossed the Potomac ... but fortunately Magruder is in tolerable good order and I am riding him again. My little bay at home is worth two hundred and fifty or three hundred dollars according to his condition. ... Please write me about my tobacco and corn crop and write me about yourself ... Love to all & kisses for E & M.
Yr own
Richard

(ed: Emmetsville is actually Emmitsburg and is some 10 miles south of Gettysburg, Pa. and just across the border into Maryland.)

(ed: Richard does have interesting names for his horses. We met Henry earlier and now he is using John Wesley and Magruder, the latter no doubt being named for Genl. Magruder.)

(ed: In an October 18th note to Mary from Lee Town Richard wrote, "In the short time we were driven from our Camp yesterday they [Yankees] entered the dwelling of a Mr. Wiltshire a good respectable man being near here, took all of his clothes & his wifes & childrens clothing and almost everything that they had to eat and broke up his crockery and carried off his vegetables & strewed them along the road mere wanton cruelty.")

- - - - -

Letter from Mary Watkins to Lt. Richard Watkins

Linden Oct 22nd 1862

My dear Husband

It has really been a long time since I wrote you a letter ... Dr. Eggleston has been very ill for a week with diphtheria he has had a great many cases of it and caught it from some of his patients I reckon. . . . Now about the plantation. We cut five houses of tobacco, saved all the fodder ... will commence gathering corn tomorrow. Have not sowed any wheat or oats yet. Will commence sowing wheat as soon as the corn is gathered. The ground has been so dry . . . that they could not finish fallowing for oats before tobacco got ripe and the fodder ready to pull. Cousin Purnall rode over the plantation last week and advised Mr Baker not to sow them now before February. He says August is the right time to sow them and they will certainly get winter killed if sowed now. Mama sold some wheat a few days ago at three dollars ($3) it is a good deal higher now and we will send off some as soon as we get bags. . . . This county has been drafted for hands to work on the fortifications about Richmond and we will have to send one next week for sixty days. I have selected Patrick to send. Mr. Dick Thackston has been employed to go with the hands from this district at five dollars a head. . . .

Oct 24th . . . Mr Baker put up 31 hogs yesterday but most of them are very small. Mama had more than sixty up. We have a good deal of old bacon . . . which is one consolation. We have dug the late Irish potatoes and they turned out very well . . .

Mama is very much disturbed about Emmie going barefoot this winter but I am afraid she will have to do it. I sent to Farmville for a pair of shoes for her but they could not be bought for less than $7 ½ per pair . . . We had to pay $2 ½ a pound for leather and it is almost impossible to get . . . I had to pay $2 for a mean little tooth brush, the good ones are $4.00.

Oct 27th I was so sleepy Saturday night that I could not finish my letter and it rained so hard Sunday none of us went to church and I could not get it to Charley Flournoy but shall have to send it by mail. Good bye.
Your own
Mary

- - - - -

The Winter of Lost Horses
October 28, 1862 to March 30, 1863

Richard is promoted to Captain in late October when Captain Berkeley resigns his commission. He immediately starts ordering tents, blankets and winter clothing for the Prince Edward Troop in hopes of getting some key supplies before the onset of winter. He writes Mary and tells her he is "about as fit for the Captaincy of a Cavalry Company as I am for a Dance Master." On top of that, Richard is entering his hard luck winter. On October 31st, in a cavalry skirmish at Aldie, he is wounded by a saber blow to the head, falls off his horse to avoid capture, and his horse joins the Union cavalry and leaves the field with the enemy. After returning from wounded furlough, while on a scout near Hartwood Church in hot pursuit of the enemy, Magruder, his horse, becomes tangled in brush and snow and throws Richard "heel over head" into the snow and mud. Then Magruder joins the retreating Union cavalry and is last seen, with an empty saddle, leading the Union cavalry over the hill. Richard tells Mary that "the mud puddle was at least knee deep and for the remainder of the day my feet were almost freezing." It was indeed Richard's winter of lost horses. No doubt he received constant ribbing from his fellow officers and the men of Co. K.

Inflation and supply problems are beginning to impact the availability of key items. Mary is having trouble getting salt. When found, the salt is costing $25 a bushel. Shoes, and cloth for winter clothes for the negroes, are in short supply. Mary writes that they have butchered 13 hogs for 1380 pounds of meat. She also advises that as of December 16th the ice house is half full. The smallpox is in Lunenburg and Prince Edward counties. Thirty six cases of whooping cough are in the immediate area. Nat's wife Nannie has a serious case of typhoid fever and is bleeding from the nose. The county court supervises the selection of 13 slaves as Sister Maria Dupuy's dowry to her future husband.

The end of 1862 sees the Army of Northern Virginia winning the battle of Fredericksburg and the Army of Tennessee being defeated at the battle of Murfreesboro in Tennessee. West Virginia is admitted as a state to the Union. On January 1, 1863, the Emancipation Proclamation goes into effect. Confederate forces under General John Magruder recapture the port city of Galveston, Texas, and it will remain open for the balance of the war.

The fifth issue of Confederate currency is authorized on November 2, 1862, and $140,000,000 will be printed. 1 As we enter the year of 1863, Confederate currency is worth about 25 cents versus the United States dollar. 2

In the Mississippi River valley General Grant has launched his campaign to capture Vicksburg. His early attempts in the fall of 1862 and winter of 1863 fail at Chickasaw Bayou, Harper's Bluff, the Yazoo River and Steele's Bayou. However, Grant views a defeat as only a temporary setback and continues to move and work toward his goal. The Confederacy is beginning to learn that this general is unlike the other Union generals. The Union is learning that General Lee is unlike the other Confederate generals.

Richard has a wounded furlough at home after his injury at Aldie and also has a 30 day furlough that allows him to be home for most of March. Not only did Richard get to spend a lot of time with Mary, Emmie, and Minnie, but he also was able to be involved in the projects on their farm. Mary is pregnant and their third child will be arriving in the summer of 1863.

Letter from Captain Richard Watkins to Mary Watkins

Camp near Lee Town
Oct 28th 1862

My Precious Mary

. . . Capt. Berkeley left us a fortnight ago upon furlough and everything was going on very smoothly when to my surprise on the morning of the 23rd Col Owen met me and addressed me as Captain. . . . Capt Berkeley has resigned and that his resignation was accepted. . . . On dress parade the same evening an order came from Genl Stuart promoting me regularly to the Captaincy of the Company. I was then the only commissioned officer . . . I at once procured the Pay Rolls and drew all the money due the men present and paid them. Knowing that winter was approaching I set to work to get some additional tents and . . . to get blankets & clothing for the Company. . . . Archer Haskins has been unanimously elected Jr 2nd Lieutenant and then promoted to 2nd Lieutenant the resignation of Jas Bell having been accepted. Jno Knight is thus our 1st Lieut. . . . I want mightily to be at Sister Maria's wedding [to Capt. Abner Anderson of Danville, Va.]. . . .If [Mr. Anderson] doesn't love her and make her a good husband he ought to be whipped.

Darling what sort of a Captain do you think I will make . . . I am about as fit for the Captaincy of a Cavalry Company as I am for a Dancing Master. . . . my mistake was in allowing myself to be elected Lieutenant . . . now like the bear who thrust his head into a bee hive, having eaten to my satisfaction, I stand with my head so swollen that I am unable to extricate it . . .

The weather is becoming quite cold, but my health is most excellent. . . . Our troop is in fine health & spirits and I believe are best contented when they have most to do. Hal Edmunds still sleeps with me and yesterday our Quartermaster furnished me with a good comfortable tent. . . . the Yankees . . . have been very quiet of late. . . . Our fare

is beef and bread . . . Tell Emmie that Papa wants to see her and Minnie too bad. That Papa loves her dearly . . . Good bye now . . .
Yr own
Richard

- - - - -

Letter from Captain R. Watkins to Major Genl. J. E. B. Stuart

Camp near Upperville
Nov 1. 1862

I most respectfully ask leave of absence from Camp for twenty five days to visit my home in the County of Prince Edward for the following reasons: I am wounded by a severe blow from a carbine or saber on the head, and in the charge lost my horse saddle bridle & my blankets – overcoat.

I have the honor to be Yr Obt. Servt.

R. H. Watkins, Capt
Co K 3 Reg Va Cavalry
To: Major Genl. J. E. B. Stuart

Approval Endorsement

Granted with the hope that his Co will soon again have the services of such a gallant leader –

J. E. B. Stuart
Major Genl – Commd 3

(ed: On October 31ˢᵗ, during a skirmish near Aldie, Captain Watkins was struck in the head during a cavalry charge and wounded. In the process, adding insult to injury, his horse left the field with the Union cavalry. Richard will return to Prince Edward County for the rest of November to recuperate.)

- - - - -

Reimbursement Request from Captain R. H. Watkins to C.S.A. Government

The Confederate States of America
1862
Oct 31

To R H Watkins, Capt. Co K 3rd Reg Va Cavalry
To one horse & equipment unavoidably lost this day in a skirmish with the enemy near Aldie, Loudoun County, Virginia

Horse	$225.00
Equip	25.00
	$250.00

I certify that on the 31st October 1862 in a hand to hand fight with the cavalry of the enemy near Aldie in the County of Loudoun State of Virginia I received on the head a sabre blow so stunning on discovering which I fell from him in the ranks of the enemy and so unavoidably lost him. The enemy rapidly retreated and carrying my horse & equipment along with them in their column. The said horse & equipments were valued as above by a boards of officers regularly appointed for the purpose. Given under my hand this 22 January 1863

R. H. Watkins, Capt Co K
3rd Regt Virginia Cavalry

- - - - -

Hdgtr 3rd Va Cavalry
Jany 23d 1863

I hereby certify that the above mentioned horse was valued by a regularly authorized Board of Officers, on the   Aug 1862 – at the sum of two hundred & twenty five (225) dollars – as is shown by a record of the regiment.

H. B. McClellan
Adjt 3rd Va Cavalry

- - - - -

HdQrs 3rd Va Cavalry
King William Cavalry
Jany 23rd 1863

I hereby certify to the truth of the facts as set forth by Capt Watkins, Co K, of this Regt having been an eye witness of the affair.

W. R. Carter Col
Comdg 3 Va Cavalry

- - - - -

In all cases where horses are lost in an engagement with the enemy, as in this in my opinion they should be paid for as a matter of rights & Justice but under the law I am not allowed to pay for any horse unless killed in an engagement with the enemy; furthermore I have been directed by Major Nelson, Brigade QM, Lees Brigade not to pay for any horse killed unless the said horse appears upon the Original Muster Roll, all other cases are referenced to a Auditor for settlement.

Jno A Palmer, Capt
& AQM 3 Va Cavalry

April 4 1863
Hqtrs Lees Cav Brig 4

- - - - -

Letter from Pattie Watkins to Sgt. Nathaniel Watkins

Mt Pleasant
Nov 13, 1862

My Dear Brother

. . . Brother Dick was here Monday his wound is very slight & is healing very fast. It is on the back part of his head & bled very freely & they feared at first that the skull might be injured, but he seems perfectly well. . . . He says he wants to join your company [King & Queen Heavy Artillery] very badly but there is no chance now since he is made Capt.

He says during the raid into Penn they went 28 hours without stopping even to water their horses. Some of them are back here . . . after new horses.
Pattie 5

- - - - -

Letter from Fannie Edmunds Hundley to Capt. Richard Watkins

Nov 18th 1862

Dear Uncle Dick

I feel it my duty to write to you and ask your advice . . . I am sorry to have to trouble you with any of my matters especially in these times of trouble. . . . I received your very kind and comforting letter while I was at Papa's & I thank you for it. . . . I asked Papa's advice about several things but he said he knew so little about Law he did not give me any satisfaction. Now my dear Uncle I hope you will not feel any hesitancy in coming up here . . . while you are at home to make some arrangements about the property . . . or if you cannot do that come up and appoint someone that can attend to it. Papa does not seem willing to have anything to do with the estate . . . I think myself it will be best to sell all the perishable property belonging to the estate and pay Mr. Hundleys [Fannie's husband] individual debts . . . I also wanted to know if the law allowed me a bed & bed clothing and any of my chamber furniture also if the negroes are not sold can I still keep one of them another year for a nurse without paying hire as you know they were all Deeded. If I have to pay hire I do not wish to keep one of them. . . . I want to go down to Papa's to live before Xmas and I would like to take such things down with me if it is proper for one to have them. I greatly prefer seeing you personally but for fear you could not come up I concluded I had better write to you while you were at home.

You can imagine at what a loss I feel not to have any person I can get advice from . . . I feel very lonely at times but my dear little children are a great comfort to me. . . . I was sorry to hear of your wound but was glad it was so slight hope you will soon be well. It is late so I must close by send[ing] much love to Aunt Mary and a kiss to the dear little children. Write to me . . .
from your affct
Niece Fannie Hundley 6

(ed: In Virginia, in 1862, the estate would normally pass to the oldest son. However, the oldest son in this case is seven. Unless the will stipulates property and monetary awards for the wife, she has no standing but is allowed to live at the home with the oldest son until she marries again. In this case Fannie moved to her father's home with Edwin and his two younger siblings Henry and Nannie. Perhaps it took the sale of all the property, both real and personal, to settle the debts of the estate. We do not have a response from Richard in the collection. Only a search of Prince Edward deeds, wills, and estate settlements could possibly provide the answer.)

- - - - -

Letter from Pattie Watkins to Nannie Watkins

Mt Pleasant
Nov 21, 1862

My Dear Sister

. . . I have just finished a cap for Bro Dick I had knit him one but he hadn't had it more than six weeks before the Yankees hit him on the head & took it away from him. I suppose you have heard before now

that he is home slightly wounded, but the wound is so slight that we are glad he got it so as to be able to come home. It is almost healed now. For a moment he was stunned a little so that he lost command of his horse & when he recovered himself his horse had gotten so far in among the enemy that he had to fall off to prevent them taking him prisoner & in that way he lost his horse, overcoat, & all of his blankets. He says he cut three of them terribly before he was cut. He made a very narrow escape but a merciful Providence spared him to us. . . . He gives a very amusing account of Stewarts [Stuarts] raid into Penn. Thinks Stewart is one of the greatest generals of all. . . . Ma wants to know what your prospects are for salt & whetha you got your negroes cloth done & their shoes. Mr Redd is selling his tobacco very fast now he got $26 for the last no of heads he sent off . . . Mr Anderson who used to be overseer for Mr Redd is living at Brother Dicks . . .
Pattie 7

(ed: On the first of November, before Richard returned on wounded leave, Mary sold the bay horse for $200. Mr. Baker will concentrate on overseeing Mrs. Watkins fields and slaves and a Mr. Anderson has been hired to run Richard and Mary's plantation.)

(ed: Richard and Mary are able to attend the wedding of Maria Dupuy and Captain Abner Anderson in Danville. Abner is the editor of the **Danville Register** *and connected with the* **Richmond Whig***. Future references will usually be Brother Abner and Sister Maria.)*

- - - - -

Special Orders No.   Headquarters, Cavalry Div.,
                                      Army of Northern Virginia
                                      December _____ 1862

The following named soldiers being dismounted are hereby detailed to go to their homes in Prince Edward County, Va. to remount themselves. They will return to their commands in (20) twenty days or else be treated as deserters.

Private _____ _____ Company K, 3rd Virginia Cavalry

Appd. By orders of	By command of
Gen. R. E. Lee	Major Gen. J. E. B. Stuart
R. H. Chilton, A.A.G.	R. Channing Price, A.A.G.
December, 1862 8	

(ed: The problem of broken down horses has become a continuous situation in the Confederate cavalry. There were from 100 to 200 men in the 3rd Virginia that needed new mounts after the Maryland Campaign. A formal program was needed and the above furlough format was instituted to detail soldiers home to replace their mounts. Inadequate feed, and over marching poorly fed animals, would constantly reduce the abilities of the Confederate cavalry throughout the war.)

- - - - -

Letter from Captain Richard Watkins to Mary Watkins

Camp near Mt Pleasant
Spotsylvania Dec 13th 62

My Precious Mary

I reached camp last night, have slept out one night and eaten my beef and bread and feel very well indeed . . . Charley Redd did leave one day ahead of us though we all reached camp yesterday. John Knight started but had a chill at Cumberland CoHo and returned. The Regiment is 20 or 30 miles from here on duty and they are expected back tonight. . . . fighting is going on about Fredericksburg again today, almost as rapid & heavy cannonading as I ever heard. Camp rumor says Genl Lee suffered a portion of the yankee army to cross [the Rappahannock] yesterday in order to get a fair chance at them. Our regiment is on the extreme left of the army and possibly as far from the fighting as we are here. . . . I am wanting a furlough again as bad as ever. Will always look back upon my last as one of the happiest periods of my life!! . . . Tell Emmie and Minnie that Papa

wants to see them again muchly . . . Good bye my precious, precious one. Yr own
Richard

(ed: Mary is four months pregnant with their third child. I am confident Richard found out when home on leave unless Mary told him in a prior letter and that letter is not in the collection. There has been no mention of the pregnancy in any of their correspondence.)

(ed: CoHo and CoH are Richard's shorthand for Courthouse.)

- - - - -

Letter from Mary Watkins to Captain Richard Watkins

Linden Dec 16th 1862

My dear Husband

It has been a week since you left home and I have not written you a line yet. Shameful, isn't it? . . . I missed you so much for two or three days . . . Oh How I wish this war would end and let you come home again. . . . Nannie Watkins has been sick for a fortnight with continued fever, the Doctor did not think it a very bad case . . . they had several cases of small pox in that neighborhood and had just vaccinated Charlie and Minnie. Mama intended having her hogs killed this morning . . . Mr. Anderson killed 13 of our hogs Thursday and Lavallette and I went over Friday and dried up a part of the lard and made sausages. . . . The thirteen hogs weighed 1380 lbs. . . .

Dec 17th [Mr Anderson] nearly half filled the ice house too the day after you left got all of the ice off of the pond. Mama filled hers the day you left and I hope we can give you a plenty of cool milk and ice cream too next summer if you will promise to come home.

. . . Cousin Purnall and the commissioners met here yesterday to divide the negroes. Sister Maria drew John Nelson, Simon, Aunt Sally, Catharine and four children, Fanny & child, Betty, Dotia, and

Martha John, thirteen in all. . . . Brother Abner is going down to Richmond today . . . Emmie fell down with a little flat iron in her hand and smashed one of her fingers very badly. The nail and end of the finger are right black, they are so bruised. . . . Minnie sleeps with me every night and she is a real nice little bed fellow, keeps me as warm as a toast . . . Have plenty of money at present but should like to pay Cousin Robert Smith for the salt and several other little debts in the neighborhood. I believe our salt amounts to about $25 per bushel. . . .

Dec 24th I have just time this morning to close my letter. Mammy Jinny send howdye to you. All send love.
Your own
Mary

(ed: It would appear that the thirteen slaves are the dowry provided with Maria when she married Abner Anderson. One can postulate that a similar dowry was provided with Mary when she married Richard and those slaves provided a significant portion of the "personal property" shown on the 1860 census for Richard and Mary Watkins. [see Appendix 2])

- - - - -

Letter from Captain Richard Watkins to Mary Watkins

Camp 10 miles from Fredericksburg
Dec 20th 1862

My precious Mary

. . . The enemy were successfully repulsed and have retreated across the River. The battle lasted the whole day. Our troops fought from behind earthworks & stone walls and our loss was comparatively small. The loss of the enemy was very great. . . . Our regiment was on pickett on the extreme left of the line and was not engaged in the fight . . . while the fight was going on our pickets were in a most quiet manner conversing with the enemy pickets across the

Rappahannock . . . Henry Ewing [and some of our men] actually gone over and taken breakfast with a portion of the 6th New York cavalry.

The weather is quite cold but our health is excellent and that of the troop good. . . . Henry Edmunds, Archer Haskins, John Ewing, Lucius Walton are sitting listening to Ned Price who was just arrived and is telling them about home. . . . Please ask Mr Geo Redd to buy me a second rate saddle and send Mr Young or Younger on Magruder as soon as possible. Please also get Mr Anderson or Mr Baker to ride down to Farmville and have my boots cut out and made as soon as possible, those that I now have will not last me long . . .

Give much love to Ma and all . . .
Richard

- - - - -

Letter from Mary Watkins to Captain Richard Watkins

Linden Dec 31st 1862

My dear Husband –

Christmas has come and gone and a very quiet time we have had too. . . . Lavallette, Nannie and Willie went to a molasses stew at Uncle Joe's the only frolic I have heard of in this neighborhood. We have not even had a caller this Christmas. Mr A [Brother Abner] carried some of the servants back with him and will come down in a few days for the others. I paid Cousin Robert Smith for the salt yesterday. It was a good deal higher than I expected $101 for four bushels. It can be bought in Richmond for $18 . . . I believe there is a great deal of small pox about home now. Lunenburg is full of it and there was a good many cases in Prince George too. . . . Mr Haskins is going to start to your camp next Thursday and has offered to take charge of your servant and horse [Magruder]. I only hope that the boots and saddle will be ready by that time. . . . I received a letter from you a few days ago and when I opened it I thought you had sent me blank paper . . . I reckon you poured water in you ink and made it too pale. . . .

Jan 3rd A happy new year to you my dear . . . I hope the war will be over before next January. . . . He [Mr Anderson] succeeded in buying a saddle from a Brother Mason for $5.50 . . . Flowers promises to have your boots at the Depot Tuesday evening . . . He has fourteen lambs but two of them got smothered by putting the sheep up nights . . . Magruder begins to look like he did when he first went into service . . . His back entirely well and he is in very good order.

Brother Abner seems to be a real businessman. Has hired out . . . John Nelson and Jim Watson at $20 per month . . . Mama exchanged Jim for Simon this year . . . he has hired out Robert too . . . at $30 a month or more if he proves to be an accomplished blacksmith. Catharine & her children and Bettie he has hired in Danville somewhere, Aunt Sally & Fannie Mama says she can't spare very well this year. They are her main spinners so he lets her keep them for their victuals and clothes. . . .

Jan 5th . . . Purnall Dickinson . . . is going back last of the week and I don't know but I shall send your horse and servant by him. I heard yesterday that Mr Haskins had concluded to go by public conveyance. Will send this letter off today . . . Good bye. All send love.
Your loving
Mary

(ed: Richard wrote a four page letter from "Camp near Guinea Station – Richmd & Fredksbg RR Dec 28th 62" and Mary can't read it. The letter is in the correspondence collection and two of the four pages are totally impossible. The 146 years since Mary tried to read the other two pages have made it no easier for anyone else. We will just do without Richard's year end stories.)

- - - - -

Letter from Captain Richard Watkins to Mary Watkins

Camp near Guinea Station
Jany 4th 1863

My Darling Mary

... You have no doubt seen in the papers an account of our last raid. Our brigade went within eight or ten miles of Washington City burnt bridges tore up rail roads &c &c. At one point Genl Stuart took a message from the telegraph and discovered the whole plan which the enemy had for entrapping him. I told you in my last letter that I started with them but was taken sick and returned the third day ... Hope we are going into winter quarters some where for I am tired of moving about so much. .... I recd a letter from Mr Tom Anderson a few days ago. Thank him for me, ... I will answer his letter as soon as possible. .... Has Patrick returned from Drewry's Bluff? I recd a letter from Bro Wm telling me that he has sold the mill to Bro Geo Redd for twenty four hundred dollars. It is the cheapest sale of <u>anything</u> that I have heard since the war commenced. .... at present prices of real estate [the mill was worth] at least five thousand dollars. It is worth more than that to Bro Geo Redd.

I hope Sister Maria is still with you. .... How did she like her lot of negroes and what is she about to do with them? I received a letter from old Mr Hundley telling me that he had advertised Charles Hundleys negroes for sale at Charlotte Court (tomorrow) ... I hope too that if our present crop of tobacco will bring as good prices as the last we will soon be out of debt. .... Oh I am so glad that you are my wife. I love you too dearly. Now don't you read my love letters to everybody. Oh I long to be with you this very evening. .... Kiss Emmie & Minnie every day for me & write to me every day to.
Yr own
Richard 9

- - - - -

Letter from Mary Watkins to Captain Richard Watkins

Linden Jan 6th 1863

My dear Husband

I sent off a letter to you yesterday . . . I have not received a letter from you since Christmas . . . Your horse, saddle, bridle and boots are ready and waiting. I am afraid too you are suffering for boots. . . . Purnall Dickinson is going to leave the last of this week and I can send by him . . . Mr Anderson . . . let me know that he is going to kill hogs tomorrow morning and I suppose I will have to dip with lard again Thursday and Friday . . . Maria had the ground prepared to sow her peas yesterday . . . Good night sir. . . . Hope you are well again by this time.
Your own
Mary

- - - - -

Letter from Mary Watkins to Captain Richard Watkins

Jan 13th 1863

Purnall Dickinson is here and starts back to the army tomorrow so I will write and send the letter by him. . . . we persuaded him to stay until Wednesday hoping that we might find a servant to send with your horse. . . . Mr. Anderson . . . thinks it would be a very bad place to send Purnall [slave] . . . Mr A . . . sent a bucket of the fresh meat and a bucket of very good sausages Saturday evening. . . . The last hogs weighed 1088 lbs. Mr Anderson has just measured up the new corn and finds that he has 125 barrels to begin the year with after fattening the hogs. . . .

Dr Dabney called here this morning on his way to Danville and is going to leave his horse and buggy. . . . Nannie Watkins is very low with typhoid fever, has bleeding at the nose, a great deal of very bad symptoms. . . . Brother Nat has been with her a fortnight. Mama has

a good many sick negroes here. Dr. Eggleston was here yesterday ...
Patience he thinks will go off in consumption like the other women
we have lost here. .... Mr Baker heard from his brother who was
taken prisoner at Fort Donelson he has taken the oath of allegiance
to the United States Government and married a Union lady. ...
Write me soon whether to send Purnall or not ... Minnies mouth
is still very sore her limbs and back are covered with sores too. ....
Good bye
Your own
Mary

*(ed: Dr. Robert L. Dabney is an eminent theologian serving on the Union
Theological Seminary staff at Hampden-Sydney College. He also served
the CSA on the personal staff of General T. J. "Stonewall" Jackson.)*

*(ed: "Typhoid fever is an acute, highly infectious disease caused by the
typhoid bacillus, Salmonella typhosa, transmitted by contaminated food
or water and characterized by red rashes, high fever, bronchitis and
intestinal hemorrhaging.") 10*

*(ed: Patience [a slave] has tuberculosis which was called consumption in
the 1860's.)*

– – – – –

Letter from Mary Watkins to Captain Richard Watkins

Linden Jan 26th 1863

My dear Husband

It is a beautiful quiet day ... Brother Nat was at Mr Redds last
Monday, he staid only one night and I did not see him at all. He said
he lifted Nannie into a chair the day before he left home and the Dr.
thought she was free from disease now and would soon be well. Jan
28th ... Edna and I have just been setting some rat traps ... Willie
met one today on the steps and it didn't even turn back, just looked
at her a minute and kept on up the stairs. Do you remember the rat

you caught by the tail last summer? I can't help laughing whenever I think of it. I believe they are even bolder and more impudent now . . . Archer Haskins and Taylor Johns staid here last night and we had a real pleasant evening in the parlor. . . . All send love. – Your own Mary

(ed: Mary would note in a February 5th letter, "Snowing hard again this morning . . . I have been trying ever since breakfast to get a chance to write some but the children are so mischievous it is almost impossible . . . Minnie . . . comes back to tell me for the tenth time this morning "that the Yankees took a great big knife and cut Papa right on his head." . . . ")

- - - - -

Letter from Captain Richard Watkins to Mary Watkins

Camp in King William
Febry 5th 63

My own dear Mary –

Archer Haskins reached here yesterday and brought with him that long good letter for which I waited . . . We have been ordered to move back to Culpeper Courthouse next week. . . . have had another heavy fall of snow . . . I will try to write to Ma soon, though I cannot promise to come up to Nat in that particular . . . I ought to write to Ma frequently and will try to turn over a new leaf . . . Good bye Yr own Richard

P.S. I forgot to tell Mr Anderson in my letter to him to keep my colt Button separate from the mules & horses and not to let him go with the mules at all.

(ed: Nat writes their mother regularly and she seldom gets mail from Richard. Richard tries to justify it with Mary by saying that the cavalry is much busier than the artillery and especially heavy artillery staying in one spot at Drewry's Bluff.)

(ed: Richard is sending his backup horse, a mare, back to Farmville via Cousin Barrett in Richmond. There is no need for two horses while in winter quarters near Culpeper. He will keep Magruder and tells Mary to look for the mare, Lizzie Leigh, at the Depot.)

- - - - -

Letter from Captain Richard Watkins to Mary Watkins

Camp in King William
Febry 9th 1863

My own dear Mary

Hal Edmunds will probably go home today after a fresh horse. We march in the opposite direction to Culpeper Courthouse. The day is beautiful just suited to such a march . . . Saturday I went down to Ayletts on the Mattapony [Mattaponi River] to see the smugglers but their goods had all been sent to Richmond . . . Have no time to write more. . . . Understand that John Knight will return soon when he comes will try to get a furlough. Goodbye precious one. Yr Richard
Much love to all.

(ed: Mary writes in a February 12 letter that Richard's spare horse, "Lizzie Leigh," has returned and been picked up at the Depot. She also notes that Mrs. Watkins overseer, Mr. Baker, is being examined by the Board of Physicians for fitness to be drafted into the army and lose his exemption.)

- - - - -

Letter from Pattie Watkins to Nannie Watkins

Mt. Pleasant
Feb 12 1863

My Dear Sister

. . . Ma got a letter last night from Hal Edmunds saying that he & Brother Dick were both well & in fine spirits they are now in King William Co. & are very snugly fixed in winter quarters but he was afraid they would have to go up to Culpepper C Ho to relieve Hampton's Legion. He said they had a chimny to their tent & could get anything almost they wanted to eat by paying right high for it, They had even had a bowl of eggnog. Brother Dick wrote sometime ago to Mr Redd that he wished they had some tobacco to strip this bad weather while they were roasting the "taters" & stewing his oysters. . . .

. . . Brother Nat said he told you to send for a bale of cotton for me when you sent for yours please send for no 16 or 18 if you haven't sent already. All join me in love to you all.
Your Ever Aff Sister
Pattie 11

- - - - -

Letter from Captain Richard Watkins to Mary Watkins

Camp near Culpeper Coho
Feby 19th 1863

My darling Mary

Here we are snowed up. Snow from six to eight inches deep yesterday. not quite so deep this morning, the roads without bottoms, our horses standing in mortar. Ourselves in soak, surrounded by melting snow. . . . Quite a gay time Miss Purnall. Wish you could . . . take a squint at your old man as he pens these lines. see him sitting down on a little pile of wet straw surrounded by damp blankets & wet saddles . . . with a pair of saddle bags in his lap for his writing desk. . . . Last night I dreamed that I applied for a furlough & wrote to old Genl Rob E Lee that I had not been blessed with a furlough or indulgence since last February but that old Genl sent it back with a note that he had not had one since the war commenced. Ha Ha Ha! Twas all but a dream. . . .

No news in camp. All quiet. A few days ago a Halifax trooper in cleaning a loaded cylinder in his pistol shot himself through the hand and this morning I noticed that one of his fingers had mortified. . . . Billy Womack and Tom Flournoy reached our camp last night. . . . Hope Hal Edmunds called to see you and will bring me a letter. Hope still more that Genl Lee will grant my furlough . . .

Good bye . . . kiss Emmie & Minnie all over their cheeks & mouths & foreheads for me . . . All honor to Mr Flowers my boots are prime . . . my pants thick & warm, my blankets soft & heavy – my night cap warm & fitting closely about my ears – socks & shirts in plenty & good as new – my breakfast & dinners of hot biscuits buttered, broiled beans & coffee with good sugar, who wouldn't want to be a Confederate soldier & contend for his rights & his home & his country. . . . HURRAH FOR JEFF DAVIS & SOUTH RIGHTS

Good bye Darling
Yr own
Richard

(ed: If a finger or body part mortifies it means that it has become gangrenous or necrosed. Necrosis is the pathologic death of living tissue.) 12

- - - - -

Letter from Mary Watkins to Captain Richard Watkins

Linden Feb 23rd 1863

My dear Mr Watkins

I must thank you for the nice present you sent us of shoes, spools, cotton, buttons, pins &c. The shoes are very nice and fit me exactly . . . I have not received a letter from you for more than a week . . . Willie Dupuy spent today here. He has left college and is trying to take the measles before going in the army. . . . What do you think? A letter came here Saturday from Camp Chase, Ohio directed to Miss Maria

Dupuy. It was from Cousin Willie [William Hart] Dupuy. He was taken prisoner at Arkansas Post was Lieutenant and Adjutant in Crawfords Battalion [Arkansas Infantry], Gen Hindmans Division. Cousin Ann is greatly distressed . . . It is the first time she has heard from him in a year.

Minnie talks a great deal about Papa . . . Lavallette and Nannie send much love to you. My ink is so bad I can hardly write at all. Good bye.
Yours
Mary

(ed: Lt. Willie Dupuy is the son of James Dupuy who is a brother of Col. Asa Dupuy of Linden. In the 1850's James moved to Tennessee and then later to Missouri. On January 11, 1863 Confederate forces at Arkansas Post and Fort Hindman surrendered to Union forces. Camp Chase is a prison camp in Columbus, Ohio.)

- - - - -

Letter from Captain Richard Watkins to Mary Watkins

Camp near Culpeper CoHo
Febry 27th 1863

In my last letter Darling I told you of our tramp through the snow . . . the big snow came the heaviest that I have see since the winter of 1856-57 and all so snug in our little tent . . . we congratulated ourselves and concluded that on the second day after the snow we would go out & lay in a supply of rabbits & opossums. On the evening before . . . an order came detailing me to go on the picket . . . [orders changed] to a scout with the 2nd & 1st Regiments . . . we moved down in the direction of Fredericksburg near the junction of the Rapidan & Rappahannock then crossed the latter and marched directly toward the Yankee camp. . . . Early the next morning . . . we came upon a large body of Yankee cavalry going also on a scout. They threw themselves into a line of battle in a large open field. The 2nd Regt charged a regt on the road the 1st Regt charged another regt on the left . . . we were held in reserve . . . Our 3rd Regt was drawn up under cover of a narrow strip of woods, our sharpshooters retreating rapidly through us . . . the Yankees were almost upon us . . . Genl [Fitzhugh] Lee in a excited manner rode up to Col Carter & ordered him to charge . . . now was our turn . . . we dashed off and to our agreeable surprise the Yankees though outnumbering us two to one instantly wheeled about and scampered off with all their might . . . But Darling your unfortunate husband while pressing on at full speed in the charge & almost upon the Yankees found himself suddenly precipitated heels over head in a enormous mud puddle. His war horse had fallen by having his feet entangled in some brush . . . and what is worse than all the horse [Magruder] jumped up before the rider, out ran every other horse in the charge and when last seen was leading the Yankee column with his beautiful mane still waving in the breeze.

I now ride a very pretty dark iron gray Yankee mare with a beautiful Yankee saddle, with a splendid Yankee bridle & halter with two new large heavy dark gray blankets. This given me in place of Magruder by Col Carter with consent of Genl Lee and Genl Lee also sent me word that if I would make out my account for horse & equipage lost at Aldie it should be paid me. This ends the chapter so far as the fight. . . . We returned at our leisure with one hundred and forty three prisoners, besides several killed & wounded. Our loss was 1 man in 2nd Regt killed & 4 wounded none in the 3rd Regt hurt at all.

After the fight we marched about 8 miles . . . rekindled our fires unsaddled our horses took off our boots toasted our feet and were soon again sound asleep: soon the rain began to pour but we only drew our heads under the blankets and slept on. Next morning returned to camp . . . our horses almost swimming at the Rappahannock and the rain pouring the whole way in torrents. I was not hurt at all by my fall . . . but I must confess my ardor was considerably cooled by the mud puddle which was at least knee deep and for the remainder of the day my feet were almost freezing . . .

Good bye Darling this is all for the present . . .
Love to all
Yr
Richard

(ed: Richard received a furlough from February 28 through March 28 and immediately departed for Farmville.)

- - - - -

Letter from Pattie Watkins to Nannie Watkins

Mt. Pleasant
Mar 21, 1863

My Dear Sister

. . . Mr Redd . . . has had a great deal of sickness in his family this winter. We all dread the whooping cough very much some of the negro children are very sick with it the white ones are coughing very badly . . .

Brother Dick is home now. He had twenty day furlough. He was in a charge a few days before he came home & lost another horse though he got a very good one in exchange. They were on a scout, it was during the last snow, & were ordered to charge on the Yankees, which they met in a large force. He was commanding a squadron (2 companies) . . . his horse ran up in some brush . . . and fell throwing Dick over his head into a very large mud hole. He gathered himself & looked for his horse. He had run on a head & gone to the Yankees. . . . Gen. Fitz Lee gave him a beautiful iron gray Yankee horse with an elegant army saddle & two yankee blankets new that were almost as good as his own. . . . He was wringing wet . . . as they were twenty or thirty miles from camp & his feet were almost frozen.
Pattie 13

(ed: Richard has now had a second horse desert to the Yankees but got a beautiful "iron gray" Yankee horse in trade. The ribbing from his

fellow officers should be pretty regular with two horses "going up" in five months.)

- - - - -

Letter from Pattie Watkins to Sgt. Nathaniel Watkins

Mt Pleasant
Mar 25 1863

My Dear Brother

. . . while he [Dick] was home the Yankees crossed at Kellys Ford & his company were again engaged. I suppose you have seen Gen Stuarts official report . . . Saturday we heard that Hal Edmunds was killed but Sunday Brother Dick sent us a letter . . . saying that is was thought at first that he was mortally wounded but as he was better it was hoped that the wound would not prove fatal. . . .
Your own Loving Sister
Pattie 14

- - - - -

Letter from Sue Watkins Redd to Sgt. Nathaniel Watkins

March 28th 1863

My dear Brother

I have been wanting to write you for a long time but first one thing & then another had to be done and letter writing has always been put off . . . However I believe Pattie keeps you well posted in Pr Edward news. We are just through with one of the worst spells of weather we have had during this remarkably bad, wet winter; today is a real March day, almost the first fair windy day this month. Crops and gardens very backward. Mr. Redd has not commenced sowing oats yet, and I have done very little in my garden, have a fine pea patch 3 or 4 inches tall and a good many onions, <u>thats</u> <u>all</u>. Lambs, chickens &c all froze in the long snow storm . . . I was very glad to

hear you had gotten another furlough . . . We saw very little of Dick while he was at home, was truly glad he was not in that battle. . . . We are in the midst of the whooping cough, about 20 negroes with it, and all 5 of our children . . . 36 in all have it. . . . Mr. Redd and all join in much love to you.
Your aff Sister
S. Watkins Redd 15

(ed: "Whooping cough is an infectious disease involving inflammation of the mucous membranes of the nose and throat and is characterized by spasms of coughing interspersed with deep, noisy inspiration" [raspy attemps to breathe air in].) 16

- - - - -

Letter from Captain Richard Watkins to Mary Watkins

Gordonsville
Sunday evening 29 March

My own Dear Mary

I reached here about noon today. Met Mr Haskins & Charley Redd at the Depot . . . Had heard in Richmond that Hal Edmunds was better and that strong hopes were entertained of his recovery, and cannot therefore describe to you my bitter disappointment on learning from Mr Haskins that he has sunken rapidly and could live only a few days . . . I hardly think it probable that he will live 24 hours longer . . . on [Friday] evening seemed to be attacked with pneumonia. His breathing is now very rapid pulse quick (exceedingly so). Has frequent coughing and constant rattle in his windpipe. Yet his voice is strong and clear . . . Poor Bob Cunningham lies quietly in another room apparently improving though not yet past the most critical period. Just now Hal turned and asked who I was writing to. I told him to you. He told me as he has always . . . "Give my love to her." I expect to remain with him until a change takes place in his condition. . . .

Monday evening 30th Hal I am happy to say very much better this morning – Breathing better coughing but little and the rattle in his windpipe entirely ceased. He rested well under the influence of morphine. . . . He has too a little appetite and has eaten a boiled egg and cracker with some relish. . . . His situation is as comfortable as it can be in a Confederate Hospital – Bob Cunningham also better. His sister is with him.

Isaac has not yet arrived [with my horse] but I am expecting him hourly. Will go to the Regiment if he comes today. Oh what a beautiful spring morning and how glad I would be if I could take a long walk or ride with you today. . . .
Yr own
Richard

- - - - -

Letter from Mary Watkins to Captain Richard Watkins

Linden
March 30th/63

My dear dear Husband

You don't know how much I miss you. I have felt lost ever since you left. . . . I expect this war will end some of these days and then if we live we will be all the happier for having had some trials. . . . Minnie coughing nearly all night and I certainly count on the whooping cough . . . though it may be a common cold. Emmie does not cough any yet. Have not heard from Henry Edmunds since you left and feel very anxious to get a letter from you. . . . Poor fellow! I think a great deal about him and do hope he may get well. I sent your pistol down to Hester Walton Sunday morning by Purnall. He was just about starting when Purnall got there but said he would take it. . . . I must make haste and close this scrawl. Good bye, and write soon to
Your own
Mary

- - - - -

Chancellorsville
April 3 to May 13, 1863

Spring activity in 1863 opens with Union naval attacks on both Fort Sumter and the Charleston defenses. General Grierson leads a cavalry raid from LaGrange, Tennessee, through Mississippi to Baton Rouge, Louisiana, leaving bridge and railroad destruction in his wake. General Grant crosses the Mississippi River south of Vicksburg and captures Port Gibson on May 1st, wins a battle at Raymond on May 12th, and moves toward Jackson on May 13th. Clement Vallandigham, the leader of the Copperheads, is arrested in Dayton, Ohio, on May 5th and President Lincoln banishes him to the Confederacy rather than imprison him in the North.

In Virginia General Longstreet and the 1st Corps of Lee's Army is besieging Suffolk. General Hooker, the new commander of the Army of the Potomac, crosses the Rappahannock on April 28th and the campaign that will culminate in Confederate victory at Chancellorsville is under way.

Richard writes of visiting the Co K wounded again in Gordonsville. As actions begin around Kelly's Ford, the 3rd Virginia is dispatched as reinforcements. He gets the good news that Minnie is doing better with the whooping cough and he tells Mary he would like to be with her to help her with the children as she enters the end of her pregnancy. A letter arrives from his brother Nat containing the news of the typhus epidemic in Granville County and the death of their young son Charley. Richard pens a couple of notes about the actions at Chancellorsville and Fredericksburg in defeating Hooker.

On April 24th the Confederate Congress passes a 10% tithe on farm produce. This will be collected by commissioners in each county and forwarded into the supply system.

The sixth issue of Confederate currency is authorized on March 23, 1863, and the series will be dated April 6, 1863. The government has been unable to slow the demand to increase the printing of bills. This act authorizes the printing of no more than $50,000,000 monthly in $5 to $100 denominations. A total of $15,000,000 can be printed in the 50 cent, $1 and $2 denominations. A total of some $525,856,000 of issue number six will be printed between April 6 and February 17, 1864. 1

Mary's letters advise Richard that the beets, spuds, peas and other vegetables have been planted. There is considerable family sickness including Mrs. Watkins spitting up blood and the children, at least Minnie, getting the whooping cough. She writes Richard that people are refusing to take Confederate money in payment of debts. On a lighter note, Emmie and Minnie are torturing two little kittens with their attention. In mid May the government commissioners stop at Oldham and impress almost 300 pounds of bacon.

During the night of May 13th Mary delivers a baby girl named Mary Purnell. Amid all the death in Virginia and North Carolina, from both whooping cough and the virulent strain of typhus, a brand new bouncing baby sister arrives for Emmie and Minnie.

Letter from Captain Richard Watkins to Mary Watkins

Gordonsville
(Friday) Apl 3rd 1863

My Darling Mary

. . . I thank you . . . for sending my pistol so promptly by Hester Walton. After writing you last Monday I put Lizzie Leigh [horse] on the cars and we went to camp. Found the boys all well their horses though looking very badly for want of proper feeding. On Wednesday heard that Hals Pa had left him and that he was worse applied at once for leave of absense for 36 hours . . . I came down again . . . His condition is still extremely critical but I think there is a chance of his recovery. Mac Venable & Leigh Redd are nursing him . . . must go back to the regiment today & will in a day or two try to write you a long letter. I love you my own dear one . . .
Yr own
Richard

- - - - -

Letter from Mary Watkins to Captain Richard Watkins

Linden. Apr 5th 1863

My dear, precious Husband

It is Sunday night and I am sitting by a cozy little fire . . . Thinking about someone who is away in the army . . . and imagining him sitting on the floor of his tent before a good warm fire with his head reposing comfortably on his saddle or roll of blankets taking an evening nap. . . . I wish I had a pair of wings and could fly down close by you without anybodys seeing me I comb your hair whilst you are asleep. I do want to see you so bad, I mean to borrow some tonight and go to see you in my dreams any how. . . .

Tuesday April 7th . . . I walked over home and back again Friday morning . . . Mr Anderson was planting potatoes, had sowed beets, snaps and some other vegetables . . . I inquired about the pigs that Bro Edwin gave you and was mortified to learn that the largest shoat and two pigs has broken out . . . and could not be found anywhere . . .

April 8th . . . Cousin Johnny [John James Dupuy] came yesterday . . . He is now Adjt [adjutant] for the 4th Tenn Reg . . . He says I haven't changed at all in the last five years. Cousin Ann got a letter from Cousin Asa's wife [Julia] who is in Memphis. The saddest letter I ever read. One by one her children have all [3] been taken from her and lastly her husband [killed at Shiloh] and now she says she has not one earthly object to cling to. She is in the enemys lines too separated from all of her own and her husbands relations. . . . Cousin Johnny says he heard in Richmond that Rich Venable was killed in Texas. . . . Cousin John says he is surprised to find so many of his college mates and young men of his acquaintance here had put in for substitutes. There is a great deal more of it in this army [Virginia] than that of the West and South he says. . . . I must send this letter to the Office now or I would finish the sheet. Good bye and write to me soon . . . Emmie and Minnie continue well and I hope may avoid the whooping cough. Mr Redd has lost two cases with it . . .
Your own
Mary

- - - - -

Letter from Captain Richard Watkins to Mary Watkins

Camp near Culpepper Courthouse
April 7th 1863

My Precious Mary

I want to see you so bad . . . I almost feel like running away from the army or getting out of it any way that I can, and going home to stay with you. . . . I believe my last visit home has unfitted me all together for camp life. There is nothing here to interest me. I think of you and of our dear little ones all the time. . . .

We are still in our old camp with the same comfortable tent and chimney and plenty to eat and tolerably good fare for our horses. Everything quiet. Recd a letter from Leigh Redd (who is staying with the wounded at Gordonsville) yesterday saying that Hal Edmunds and Robt Cunningham are both improving and we begin to entertain hope of recovery. . . . the bugle sounds and I must go to drill the squadron . . . Quite exhilarating this cool weather and vastly more pleasant than fighting.

. . . Please tell Mr Anderson to prize my tobacco & let it go as quick as possible to Messr McKinney Dupuy & Archer – when Willie Dupuy comes please send by him my bay horse and the blue flannel shirt I wore when at home. . . . Tell Ma I will write to her as soon as possible. . . . Tell Mr Anderson to be careful when they plow my young orchard that they do not plow too near the trees. Good bye my precious, precious one . . .
Yrs
Richard

- - - - -

Letter from Mary Watkins to Captain Richard Watkins

Linden Apr 11th 1863

My dear Husband

. . . Mother was very unwell . . . had been spitting up blood and felt very weak and low spirited. . . . I believe she gets worse whenever Pattie is away from her. The children are in the height of the whooping cough . . .

Apr. 16th John Redd has just sent me word that he intends to start back to the company tomorrow and will take a letter for me . . . Willie Dupuy intends starting next Monday week with Willie

Booker . . . Cousin Johnny [Dupuy] left this morning . . . He is going to Petersburg first to see if he can hear anything from Cousin Willie who he thinks was sent with the other prisoners [from Camp Chase, Ohio] to be exchanged last week, and then he is to start for Vicksburg. . . . I got a bushel of flax seed from Mama last week and [Mr Anderson] promised to have "as fine a parcel of flax as I ever saw" for me next year. . . . It is so hard to get any spinning done on account of the cards and it seems to me before I get the negroes winter clothes they will be calling for summer ones. Have just got 60 yards of osnaburg [heavy coarse cotton cloth] from the weavers and will have to have sixty more before summer . . . What will we do next winter when blankets and thick clothes & shoes will be needed . . . People all around are refusing to take Confederate money now and I am afraid you will find some difficulty in paying off your debts if you had the money.

. . . Cousin Will refused some Confederate money which Mr Edmunds wanted to pay him. I think both of them should be sent to the Army and kept there until they can find some use for their Confederate notes. It makes me mad to think of these men who are staying at home getting rich refusing to take Confederate money. Well I have spent my wrath . . . it is time to stop. . . . Mama and the girls send love. Write soon to
Your own
Mary

(ed: Cotton cards and wool cards were needed to process the raw cotton. The cards were used to straighten the fiber to prepare it for spinning. Cotton cards, wool cards, and the wire to repair them were regular items brought into Charleston and Wilmington on the blockade runners.) 2

(ed: Inflation continues to devalue the Confederate dollar. In mid-April of 1863 it is worth about 20 cents to the U. S. dollar. Less than two years ago it was worth 95 cents.) 3

- - - - -

Letter from Captain Richard Watkins to Mary Watkins

Camp near Sperryville Rapphannock
Apl 18th 1863

My Dear Dear Mary

When I last wrote we were in Culpepper. Immediately thereafter I was sent in charge of our picket on the Hazel River a branch of the Rappahannock. Spent four days very pleasantly most of the time fishing, sleeping at night in an old deserted house. . . . Whilst there our brigade moved over to Salem in Fauquier some 26 miles distant. . . . On Wednesday our relief came and we started for the regiment. Had gone about 15 miles when we heard heavy artillery firing behind us and soon met our brigade returning. A large force of the enemy's cavalry were again attempting to cross at Kellys Ford. Had been met by Wm H F Lee's brigade and ours was returning to reinforce. . . . night came on. We lay down in the woods without our tents a hard rain commenced and poured on us all night. I drew my head under my blankets and slept well. . . . In a day or two move again . . . probably back to Salem in Fauquier County.

As has always been the case just when the hardships of the service come in their worst form . . . a sweet cheering letter from you . . . takes my thoughts entirely off . . . I would not take anything in the world for your last letter. No husband ever recd a better one. I can read it for days & days.

Have not heard a word from Henry Edmunds & Cunningham, since the 10th. They were then better and strong hopes were entertained of their recovery . . . The weather is becoming mild now and the mountain scenery is quite pretty . . . Hope [Mr. Anderson] is getting on quietly with his business and that I will soon get from him a "letter of information." . . . I did not succeed in getting clothes in Richmond. Very little cloth was allowed Genl. Stuarts Division and all of it has been distributed. . . . send my thin brown pants with a thin lining in them. If Willy Dupuy has not started please send them instead of my blue shirt. . . . Mr Flowers boots are beginning to rip right badly and I must go this morning to Sperryville to get them mended and therefore cannot write more at present. Will write again soon. Give love as usual to all. Oh I would give everything in the world to be with you.

Goodbye

Yr own Richard

- - - - -

Letter from Mary Watkins to Captain Richard Watkins

Linden Apr 22nd/63

My Darling Husband

. . . Willie Dupuy was here this morning and told me he did not expect to go to the army until Tom Haskins went back and he thought I had better send your horse by Willie Booker who starts out next Monday . . . Will send your brown pants as soon as I can . . . I was surprised yesterday by a bundle containing two neat, pretty calicoes. I need not tell you . . . how much I thank you . . . you are too thoughtful and kind to me . . . you displayed excellent taste in your selection of dresses, they suit me exactly and when you come home next time you can expect to see me dressed up in one of them.

Guess who we had to dine with us Saturday? <u>Twenty</u> <u>one</u> <u>soldiers</u> belonging to the 1st S. C. Reg part of Hampton's Legion. The whole Reg. camped within a mile and a half of here . . . Sixteen dined here Sunday, . . . and two staid all night. One of them had pneumonia and excited Mama's sympathy . . . she was fixing up pepper and sugar stews for him . . . Mama said some of them were real intelligent nice gentlemen and all of them well behaved . . . I was very sick . . . drank some sour buttermilk which was the cause of my sickness . . . I took my usual quota of salt water, soda water, brandy water, warm water, sage tea, lobe lia &c but was not relieved until Sunday when I took some oil. Minnie is getting along well with the whooping cough and Emmie has not taken it yet.

Minnie is about the most headstrong, obstinate child that I ever saw .
. . I have to whip her nearly every day. She and Emmie have two little
kittens which Minnie tortures half to death. She . . . pours water on
them and squeezes them and kisses and rocks them by turns. . . . Mr.
James Daniel has lost his youngest child [typhus fever] and several
negroes with it and his three other daughters were down with it.
Lucy they thought would not recover. Mary Graham (the one who
died) was taken sick Saturday and died Sunday and a good many
cases died in three hours. . . . Dr Wilson said . . . he did not know
what to do for it. It [the disease] was brought from Weldon [North
Carolina] by the hands which were sent to work on the fortifications
there; 90 out of 100 who went from neighborhood have died with
it. I reckon Bro Nat feels very anxious about his little family. Heard
yesterday that Hal E. and Mr Cunningham were both considered
out of danger now. . . . I want to see you too bad. Good bye
Your own
Mary

*(ed: In an April 26 letter Mary noted, "O! how I wish this war was over
and you and I could live at home together again. It makes me right sick
to think of there being more battles this summer and all the horrors of
another siege around Richmond. I really think it is time for the Yankees
to give up and conclude that Richmond cannot be taken nor the South
subjugated if they ever intend doing so.")*

- - - - -

Letter from Captain Richard Watkins to Mary Watkins

Camp near Culpepper CoHo
April 27th 1863

Another of your precious letters Darling has found its way into my
letter bag. I am so glad to see you write so cheerfully and to hear that
you are well & that little Minnie is getting on so smoothly with the
whooping cough. I feel very sorry though that I cannot be there with
you just at this time [8 months pregnant] to aid you in controling

& taking care of her & Emmie. It amused us all to hear how many soldiers mother was feeding . . . I am glad that you are pleased with your dresses . . . You need feel no concern about my clothes I have quite enough for the present . . .

Please tell Mr Tom Anderson that I would like to hear from him soon. Want to hear particularly about my tobacco crop. Has it been prized? Have my winter oats disappeared. Has any corn been planted &c &c. Tell him to send the tob to McKinney Dupuy & Archer as soon as the whole crop has been prized. Must close now darling – Give love to all. Good bye. Write often.
Yr Richard

(ed: This is the only letter without a salutation in all of his letters to Mary.)

- - - - -

Letter from Mary Watkins to Captain Richard Watkins

May 1ˢᵗ 1863

My dear Husband

I am only going to write you a few lines to tell you that I am entirely well. I know you feel anxious about me all the time now and I will write with any chance I get. . . . Brother Nat's little Charley died last week of dyptheria and Minnie [Charley's little sister] was thought to be dying when we last heard from there. Charley was taken sick Friday and died Saturday. He had convulsions until just before he died when he became quiet and commenced saying a little prayer – very fast . . . The Dr. at first called it typhus fever but says now it was dyptheria. . . . Emmie is the only one left of the three little ones who were baptized together three years ago and she seemed then far more delicate and most likely to die of the three. How distressing it must be for Bro Nat to be away from home when his family are so afflicted. I really should not blame him if he got a substitute. . . . Tom Haskins was here this morning and will take your pants to you. I will

send this letter over soon tomorrow morning and get him to carry it too. . . . Good bye
Your own
Mary

(ed: Nathaniel and Nannie Watkins live in Granville County, N. C. and have had two children. Charles Read Watkins was born in 1860 and Mildred Henry (Minnie) Watkins was born in 1862. Earlier letters spoke of the typhus killing 90 out of 100 workers sent to Weldon. Charley either died of typhus or virulent diphtheria.)

(ed: Typhus can be several forms of an infectious disease caused by the microorganisms of the genus Rickettsia. Both the flea borne and louse borne types lead to endemic typhus. Both are characterized by severe headache, sustained high fever, delirium and red rashes.) 4

(ed: Diphtheria is an acute contagious disease caused by the infection with the bacillus Cornebacterium diphtheriae. It is characterized by the formation of false membranes in the throat and other air passages causing difficult breathing, high fever, and weakness.) 5

- - - - -

Letter from Captain Richard Watkins to Mary Watkins

Spottsylvania CoHo
May 4th 1863

My own dear Mary

Another great battle has been fought, another horrible scene of carnage and bloodshed. Thus far we are successfull and victory seems to be on our side, but the fighting may possibly be resumed tomorrow and therefore the result is not positively certain. When the enemy advanced and forced us back from Culpeper CoHo I was quite sick with dysentery and with the Col's cousin went to the rear. . . . When the battle commenced I made an effort to get back to the Regiment but as Cousin Tom Walker said was so "scattered"

that I did not succeed till today. Am now well again. The fighting was all day yesterday and a good part of the day before and now is too dark for me to write more & the fighting has again commenced at Fredericksburg 8 miles below here. . . . a squadron [of cavalry] including my company is here guarding a train of wagons at present. May 5th Genl. Stonewall Jackson lost an arm and Genl Stuart took command of his corps – of the Pr Edward men I heard of none killed but Gus Bass – Chas Hutcheson of Charlotte was shot thro the hand. We hear no firing this morning all seems to be quiet . . . the slaughter on both sides has been terrific . . . Good bye my precious one. Will write again in a day or two.
Yr own
Richard

- - - - -

Letter from Captain Richard Watkins to Mary Watkins

Camp near Spottsylvania CoHo
May 7th 1863

My Precious Mary

God has blessed us with another victory. The enemy has been driven back at all points and have re-crossed the Rappahannock. . . . We have taken a large number of prisoners, variously estimated from 10 to 12,000. Our regiment was engaged in picket duty on the flank of the army and did no fighting except a little skirmishing with sharpshooters . . . Of Prince Edward men I hear that Lieut Gus Bass of the Central Guards was killed . . . among the wounded are Thom and Sam Hines (one shot in the foot the other in the hand) and Drury Lacy shot thro the arm. We are now located 7 or 8 miles from the battlefield and can hear very little news. . . . When this battle commenced I hardly thought it possible for us to maintain our position Hooker had advanced so rapidly and taken so good a position but soon Genl Jackson came along with his forces attacked the enemy in front, left a parcel of his force fighting, took the remains & moved rapidly up in their rear & drove them from their entrenchments . . . a courier came full speed from Fredericksburg stating that a large force crossed & already had possession of Mayre's Hill! Then I began to think we would be certainly defeated but the battle went on – we had regained the Heights and driven them out of Fredericksburg. . . . This has been going on for nearly a week . . . I do not think I ever spent a week of such painful suspense. Concerned about you and about the great battle. . . . May God ever bless & protect you . . . and our dear little children and all who are near and dear to us.

Yr own

Richard

(ed: The battle of Chancellorsville is a very expensive victory for General Lee and his Army of Northern Virginia. General Stonewall Jackson dies a few days after having his arm amputated. Some 12,800 Confederates were killed and wounded. Union losses were some 17,300. The casualty rate for Lee was 22% while the Union percentage was only 13%. Taken over the long course of the war, the South with finite resources and manpower, cannot replace their losses.) 6

- - - - -

Letter from Sgt. Nathaniel Watkins to Captain Richard Watkins

Chaffin's Bluff Batteries
May 6th 1863

Dear Brother

About two weeks since I received a letter from Nannie writing of the death of our dear little Charley after an illness of twenty seven hours – the sickness of little Minnie – the death of Mary (Nannie's youngest sister), and the sickness of all of Mr. Daniel's daughters – the death of several of his little negroes & the sickness of others. The disease very violent & unmanageable, unknown to the physicians, prevailing & very fatal all through the country . . . thought to have been brought from Weldon by the negroes who had been engaged on the fortifications. I immediately applied for and got a ten day

furlough ... On getting home I found that the disease had abated very much – scarcely any new cases & much more manageable. The Drs. think it a form of typhus fever – more malignant than usual. Strong & healthy negroe men were taken & dead in six or eight hours.... Our dear little boy was a little over four years of age – was baptized with your Emmie & Sis Lou's Lilie. – we loved him too much. A little while after they found he was sick, he sunk into a stupor & remained so until God took him. ... Nannie was almost crushed at first ... God give & has taken away, blessed be His holy name. – Let me hear from you ...
Your brother
NVW 7

- - - - -

Letter from Mary Watkins to Captain Richard Watkins

Linden May 8th 1863

My own dear Husband

...I am so glad Hal Edmunds got home before the battles commenced again. Hope he will improve rapidly now. I continue well though I get right low spirited sometimes ... Minnie ... I have not heard her whoop but once yet. ... Edna has been whooping some time and there are nearly thirty other cases of it ... I want to stop my ears and run away from it ... strange Emmie has not taken it. ... received a letter from Bro Nat a few days ago saying little Minnie was better . .. He said that disease was more like a plague ... Hardly a family in the neighborhood escaped it and it proved fatal in a few hours. Little Charley ate a hearty breakfast one morning and went out to play but came in about ten o'clock complaining of his head and back and the next day about the same time was a corpse. ... I don't know when I may be able to write again, but you must write me as often as you can. Believe me as ever
Your own
Mary

Sunday May 10th . . . Emmie and I have just been walking in the garden and Emmie is completely carried away with the beautiful flowers. I never saw a child so fond of flowers. Whenever I go out to walk she begs me to bring her wildflowers and sit and talks to them by the hour. . . . Emmie has worn out three prs of shoes this winter and is getting through her fourth pair right rapidly. . . . Mr Tom Anderson called . . . the day after he wrote you, his leaf tobacco came in order and he had taken it all down and bulked it nicely and would prize it as soon as he could. He had finished making his potatoe hills and would finish hilling up tobacco and be ready to go weeding corn Monday. The commissioners were at our house Thursday and impressed 250 or 300 lbs of bacon. . . .

Cousin Willie Dupuy has been exchanged at last after four months of imprisonment [Camp Chase, Ohio] and reached Petersburg last week. He wrote . . . that he was horribly treated, subjected to every kind of insult, had all of his clothes stolen and they even stripped the shirt off his back . . .

Well Good bye. I have written quite a long letter and must send it to the Depot.
Your loving
Mary

- - - - -

Letter from Mary Watkins and Mrs. E. H. Dupuy to Captain Richard Watkins

Linden May 13th 1863

My dear Husband

. . . Sent off for the Doctor and have had him waiting all day upon a false alarm. . . . Cousin Willie Hall [Dupuy] has been here two days but left this morning on his way to Vicksburg . . . He is looking rather badly . . . I reckon he is glad to get out of prison, He says he was never better treated in his life than at Fort Delaware. It was some of the Federal prisoners [guards] at Camp Chase who stripped them of their clothes and abused them pretending that was the way they had been treated in Richmond. . . .

May 14ᵗʰ – No false alarm at all my dear son, for about midnight Mary gave birth to a fine _____ Oh you are hoping it is a son but our Heavenly Father knows what is best, it is a daughter . . . The Mother bore the trial well, & is quite comfortable this morning . . . You never saw happier children than Emmie & Minnie were this morning upon being introduced to their little sister. . . . Mary sends love and says don't be uneasy about her.

Your mother

E. H. Dupuy

(ed: Mary named the girl after herself. So the third Watkins daughter is Mary Purnell.)

- - - - -

Gettysburg
May 14 to August 7, 1863

Mary writes Richard, "I was sorry it was a girl … Capt. Watkins would be pleased with a boy." Mary P. is fat and plump and Emmie and Minnie are growing fast. Tempering that good news is the spreading whooping cough. Mrs. Dupuy has lost three negroe children at Linden and one more is expected to die. Mary and Richard have lost three negroe children at Oldham and the rest seem to be improving. Mary reports that, "the corn and wheat both survived the rains, oats may be a half crop and one sow has died from eating mushrooms in the woods." Mary cannot believe that General Pemberton would surrender Vicksburg on the 4th of July. She thinks "Pemberton was so hungry he didn't remember it was July 4th when he surrendered." The Watkins may need to start searching for a new overseer for next year as Mr. Anderson has indicated he will be leaving. Minnie is running around the house screaming a great ovation about the moon being broken. It is just another normal day with three little girls.

There are no letters from Richard in the month of June reporting on the happenings with Co. K at either Brandy Station or Aldie. In a wonderful letter dated July 5th, Richard gives a marvelous recap of General J. E. B. Stuart's raid into Pennsylvania. The 3rd Virginia was involved in heavy rear guard actions almost daily during the retreat back to Virginia. On July 18th Richard writes that he is "again on Virginia soil." He also notes that the, "Army is certainly in much worse condition than when we left." He does not feel the invasion was the thing that should have been done. Richard also does not realize that Stuart totally failed Lee by riding off on his raid and not providing cover, intelligence, scouting, and reconnaissance as the Army of Northern Virginia moved northward. General Lee was blind without his cavalry. Richard is also upset that his tobacco was sold for only $26 per hundred when he was offered $40 per hundred on his last furlough home.

Moving quickly, in mid-May, General Grant captures Jackson, Mississippi, on May 14th and then turns westward and on May 16th and 17th wins victories at Champions Hill and Big Black Creek, forcing General Pemberton into his defensive works around Vicksburg. He attacks Pemberton on the 19th and 22nd of May; both assaults fail, and Grant establishes siege lines around Vicksburg. Vicksburg will surrender on July 4th and Port Hudson, Louisiana, on July 8th. The Mississippi River belongs to the Union.

Gold is discovered in Virginia City, Montana, in late May. On July 13th and 14th draft riots in New York City leave many buildings burned and more than 300 dead. Federal troops are sent from Gettysburg to secure the city.

Letter from Captain Richard Watkins to Sgt. Nathaniel Watkins

Camp near Orange CorHo
May 14th 1863

Dear Bro Nat

The announcement of the death of dear little Charley affected me deeply. I had heard of the fatal character of the disease prevailing in the neighborhood but was wholly unprepared for such an event. But oh how grateful we ought to feel that his death corresponded so beautifully with his life . . . He is now beyond the reach of suffering & sorrow his parents and his little sister must struggle on with the ills of life a few more days with the . . . hand of a merciful God laid heavily upon . . . themselves when they too will be lead by the same Gentle Shepherd to the bright & happy world . . .

With regard to the business part of your letter I of course cannot carry out my plans after the hints which you have given me, but am not the less tired of the Cavalry service, completely worn out by constantly moving & marching & watching. My health however continues good, very good. The health of our whole command has been excellent for many months past altho we have passed through many and great hardships. The death of Genl. Jackson has cast a deep gloom over the army. His life will ever be regarded as one of the most brilliant on record, as well by other nations, as our own . . .

Our Regiment is at present enjoying a brief resting spell in a beautiful forest of oak & hickory we are lounging about, surrounded with green pastures in which hundreds of horses are grazing. Gen. Stuart is collecting a very large force of cavalry just here of course we know not the object. Hampton's Brigade, Wm. H. Lee's Brigade, Fitz Lee's Brigade, The 3rd Arkansas Mounted Rifle men are all here and we hear that Genl. Jenkins cavalry is not far off. It may be that he intends punishing Stoneman for his late raid or retaliating by going over into Maryland or Pennsylvania. Our brigade has been doing so much of late that we need rest more than plunder but if a raid is made we will doubtless be required to go along. We find it difficult to get newspapers and hear very little news. I hear it said this morning that Lincoln has called out 500,000 additional troops and thus this horrible war goes on. Well, if I am not killed I hope to see the old fellow through some of those days.

Am a member of a Board to examine & condemn horses unfit for service and as that Board will soon meet must bring my letter to a close. Give my kindest regard to all of my acquaintances in your Company. I will always be delighted to hear from you and can get a letter at any time addressed to Co. K 3rd Regt Va Cavalry 2nd Brigade – Richmond Va.
Farewell Yr Bro
Richard 1

– – – – –

Letter from Mary Watkins to Captain Richard Watkins

Linden June 1st 1863

My dear Husband

. . . I wanted to write to you a week ago but thought I would wait till I was a little stronger and then I was taken right sick again and could not write. My breast threatened to rise I had right high fevers and felt very badly for several days . . . Well! it is just like all other babies I reckon, not pretty at all with real white hair and eye lashes, dark blue eyes, right large mouth and nose can't tell whether the latter will be straight or not yet, and small ears. . . . I am afraid she is taking whooping cough . . . Emmie gets along better than I expected with whooping cough . . . We have some very bad cases of it here and I can hear the whooping most all night. . . . Minnie keeps well and is as full of mischief as she can hold. She is very fond of the babe, and if Emmie calls it babe she says directly, "He is named Mary Purnall. Papa says so." Then strokes her head and says, "poor little creeter." . . . I was so sorry it was a girl I didn't know what to do. I knew Capt. Watkins would be pleased with a boy. . . . I hope you will come home

again soon want to see you so bad. Give my love to Cousin John
Knight and Willie Dupuy....
Your own
Mary

- - - - -

Letter from Mary Watkins to Captain Richard Watkins

Linden June 6th 1863

My dear Husband

... Mama is right unwell this morning, is in bed now. Lavallette
is most always sick and Nannie and everybody else here have the
whooping cough. The Doctor has just come to see one of the little
negroes who is very ill with it. Mama has lost two negro children
with it and there are two others that she thinks will die. Oh it is
dreadful.... it makes me right nervous to see the little negroes cough
out in the yard. They ... whoop and strangle and look as if they would
die before they can get their breath.... Our negroes are beginning to
whoop and I dread it mightily for those little babes over there. Old
Uncle Frank sent me some snake oil root to put around my baby's
neck, said he had put it around all the childrens necks over there and
he knew it would not go so hard on them.... June 11th – Mama lost
another little negro with it last night ... The babe is right fretful this
morning and I must stop and take her. Good bye Write often to
Your own
Mary

- - - - -

Letter from Pattie Watkins to Captain Richard Watkins

Mt. Pleasant
June 8th 1863

My Dear Brother

... Little Mary ... is a fat, plump little thing & they say is generally very good. Emmie & Minnie grow very fast Minnie is over the whooping cough & Emmie hasn't it very badly. They were out doors almost all day & were very good children ...

... Next Sunday Mr. Wharey will preach a sermon in reference to Gen Jackson's death.

The crops are suffering very much for rain every thing is parching up & it is so cool & clear that it looks right gloomy. Mr. Redd's wheat crop is very poor. ...

All join me in love to you.

Your own Loving Sister
Pattie 2

- - - - -

Letter from Private H. W. Edmunds to Captain Richard Watkins

Home June 16th 1863

My Very dear Uncle

Your most welcome letter was received some time ago but you must not wonder that it has been neglected for I must confess that I have been thinking rather more of getting married than about writing to Uncle Dick ... I will be married June 30th & would be much gratified if Capt. Watkins & Lady wd honor me with their presence.

... I have been improving every day since I got home with the exception of two or three days that I stood still & that was caused by putting a [   ] too deep in the wound which causes a little bleeding from lungs. The wound has healed except a very small hole kept open by a [   ] it does still discharge and now the lower part of my left lung is very much injured if not ultimately destroyed & does not work at all yet. Cannot use the shoulder joint of my left arm but very little yet . . .

Remember me to all the member of your company & to other friends in the Regmt. Tell Dr. Leigh that I will act by his prescription.

My respect to Archer Haskins & Leigh Redd tell them that I would like to have their assistance on 30th & you will do what you can to get them a leave of absence. Hoping to see you soon I remain your true & humble Svt. V Affectionable respects

H. W. Edmunds

PS Please let me know if there is any prospect of my being paid for the two horses that that I lost / with the last horse I lost saddle bridle & baggage. Do what you can to secure the money for me will you. Tell Lieut that I have been paid $50.00 by his wife.

Truly Yrs   H W Edmunds 3

(ed: H. W. was badly wounded in the battle of Kelly's Ford (March 17, 1863) and three months later is still having seepage from his chest wound. I am unable to identify the type of drainage apparatus they placed in his chest that caused the bleeding he mentions. The Army of Northern Virginia is heading toward Maryland and Pennsylvania on what will be known as the Gettysburg Campaign. There will be no furloughs for anyone to attend a wedding.)

- - - - -

Letter from Sue Watkins Redd to Sgt. Nathaniel Watkins

June 26, 1863

My dear Brother –

I received your letter to Pattie yesterday and as she is at Bro Edwin's I will reply to it, though Tom is waiting to go to the Depot, and I have time to write only a few lines . . . We had quite a severe hail storm about a week since . . . the hail injured the wheat & corn very much & ruined our watermelon vines . . . I feel very uneasy about Dick, they are having a hard time of it, the last news we had was through Willie Booker written last Thursday evening they had just had a fight, in which Willie lost everything he had, and were then drawn up in line of battle for another fight. Hope we will hear from him today.

Love to you & all of our friends from all here
Your aff Sister
S W Redd 4

- - - - -

Letter from Captain Richard Watkins to Mary Watkins

9 miles north of Chambersburg, Penn
July 5th 1863

My Dear Dear Mary

I know you feel concerned about me not having heard from me for such a length of time. But you will not think hard of me or believe me at all remiss when are more acquainted with the facts. About a fortnight ago Genl Stuart commenced his 2nd raid into Pennsylvania. We left Loudoun County went back almost to Warrenton . . . then came into Fairfax approached within 6 miles of Alexandria, U turned almost to Drainesville, crossed the Potomac at midnight burned 5 canal boats at break of day next morning. Then went in the direction of Washington City to Rockville . . . took a train of almost 180 wagons & almost 1200 mules with a good number of prisoners then went in the direction of Baltimore till we approached within 15 or 20 miles of that city turned off to the Pennsylvania line west to Hanover, Penn: where we had a sharp cavalry fight and took several prisoners, went from there to Westminster and then to Carlisle, found a large force of infantry at Carlisle, called upon them to surrender the town which was refused & the town shelled by

Genl Stuart & the public buildings burned. We then came across in the direction of Gettysburg and joined our forces, the raid occupying 10 days during which time we marched the whole of each day & the whole of six nights & the half of one or two others our only time for sleep being whilst our horses were grazing or feeding in the day. Upon joining our forces at Gettysburg found that Genl Longstreet had in the meantime marched across through Chambersburg joined Gen Ewell and had engaged Gen Hookers Army. A most furious & bloody battle was fought on the 1st 2nd & 3rd of this month which like the Battle of Sharpsburg seems to be claimed as a victory by both sides. Whilst this was going on On the 3rd we (the Cavalry) engaged the cavalry of the enemy on our left wing & had a very severe engagement. finally repulsing them but finding that they are supported by infantry could gain no advantage. . . . My company has dwindled to about 10 or 15 the horses of the rest having completely broken down. Have lost as yet no members of my company & only two wounded . . . they are Jenkins & Chas Anderson. Wm Dupuy & Willie Booker, the Haskins & Henry Ewing . . . are with me yet. They are all well. . . . Last night we marched the entire night in a hard rain. . . . Have unsaddled our horses only for two nights of the fortnight. . . . My health strange to say continues good though . . . much exhausted from fatigue. I feel that my preservation is owing entirely to the goodness and mercy of God. . . . From present appearances I think that our Army is falling back and will probably recross the Potomac . . . I still think it is a very bad policy for us to attempt an invasion of the North but our great men are wiser than I & much more courageous. . . . Much very much love to all. May God take care of you my own Dear one. Good bye Yr Richard

(ed: The official account of the Rockville wagon train ambushcade credits Genl. Stuart with the capture of 125 wagons, 900 mules and 400 teamsters.) 5

(ed: While the cavalry has been off on their own, Lee has been deprived of valuable intelligence, and Stuart and his cavalrymen are unaware that General Hooker has been replaced by General George G. Meade.)

- - - - -

Letter from Captain Richard Watkins to Mary Watkins

Camp near Funk Town
Maryland July 9th 1863

My own Dear Mary

I have only time to write you that I am alive and entirely well. So with every member of my Company except Charley Anderson & Jenkins who are wounded but not seriously. We have had much the most arduous time which we have ever had during the past fortnight an account of which I gave you in a short letter written on the 5th. - We are still fighting nearly every day & night. . . . We have been thro Pennsylvania but have returned to Maryland. Our army defeated at Gettysburg or if not defeated it was a drawn battle. Our loss immensely heavy I reckon. Though I have not the particulars . . . Good bye my Precious one. May God . . . protect you and all those who are dear to us. Give love to all
Yr own Richard

Write often to me. Can't get your letters now but will get them as soon as I return to Va

(ed: Gettysburg is the bloodiest battle ever fought on the American continent. A total of some 50,000 men killed, wounded and missing. Confederate losses were 3,903 killed, 18,735 wounded, and 5,425 missing. The totals in Gen. Meade's Union army were 3,155 killed, 14,529 wounded, and 5,365 missing. The Confederate army lost 30% of their force. One in every three Confederates who came to Gettysburg was either killed or wounded.) 6

- - - - -

Letter from Captain Richard Watkins to Mary Watkins

Washington County, Maryland
July 11th 1863

My own Dear Mary

God still preserves my life and health and that of every member of my company. We have been fighting or rather skirmishing every day for many days past and are now expecting another great battle here. Our work has been hard indeed . . . every morning at day break advance two or three miles and meet up with the enemy, fight at intervals all day first with carbines & rifles then artillery occasionally with pistols & sabers, at 8 o'clock P.M. retire two or three miles to a wheat field or clover lot, then cut grass or wheat with our pocket knives to feed our horses on & get to sleep about 11 or 12 o'clock with peremptory orders to be in our saddles again at daybreak. We are now enjoying a few moments of leisure our regiment being sent back to graze our horses for a time. I have slept in wet blankets for several nights . . . whenever I dismount & lie down on the wet ground . . . am asleep in from 3 to 5 minutes. By this means I keep up and am always as fresh as men who are much stronger & more active than myself. Have to send this by a free negro to Richmond & he says he cannot wait for me to write more. . . . Much very much love to all. Will write you again as soon as possible. Good bye
Yr own
Richard

- - - - -

Letter from Mary Watkins to Captain Richard Watkins

Linden July 13th 1863

My dear Husband

It seems so long since I received a letter from you . . . I suppose you are on the march most of the time . . . Mr. Dance dined here yesterday . . . he has just lost another son. Fletcher who died July 6th just a year lacking one day from the time that Henry died. He was taken with a hemorrhage six weeks ago and never recovered . . . Mr. Bob Williams was killed while sitting at the supper table with his wife and little children around him. Some one shot him through the window . . . They have no clue as to the murderer but suppose it was a deserter he had arrested . . .

Mr Anderson came over to see me Saturday morning, his corn and wheat had not been very much injured by the rains . . . thought he would make half a crop of oats . . . one sow had died from eating mushrooms in the woods. . . . Fancy and her colt look in fine order, the colt grows very fast and bids fair to be a large horse. I haven't time to write more. We are all well. Tell Willie Dupuy they are well at his Pas. . . . Hal Edmunds was to have been married last Wednesday but was very sick and the wedding had to be postponed. Good bye
Your own
Mary

I could not believe for several days that Vicksburg had surrendered on the 4th of July too, it was too bad. I think Pemberton might have done it a day sooner or later, but I suppose the poor fellow was so hungry he didn't remember what day of the month it was. We have had a series of disasters lately and I am afraid the war is right far from an end yet.

- - - - -

Letter from Captain Richard Watkins to Mary Watkins

Camp near Charlestown, Va
July 18th 1863

I am happy to announce to you Darling that I am again upon Virginia soil . . . Was greeted upon my return with two dear letters from yourself . . . how glad I was to get them, having heard not a word from you for a month or more. . . .

As strange as it may appear all of my troop are alive and well excepting three who are supposed to have been taken prisoner and one Jenkins who is right badly but not mortally wounded. The missing are Frank Penick, Nat Thackston, & Geo Hart they were in the rear with the wagons, their horses having broken down. An attack was made by some Yankee cavalry . . . and these three have not since been seen. . . . The Mecklinburg Company being a company of sharpshooters has lost heavily 2 killed 9 or 10 wounded and 5 or 6 prisoners. No other company has lost as heavily . . . we see no papers . . . I reckon you know more of the particulars of the Gettysburg fight than I do. . . . Our army is certainly in much worse condition than when we left Va. Our loss was immensely heavy. Nearly every acquaintance of mine in the infantry seems either to have been killed or wounded . . . most of them belonged to Genl Picketts Division . . . In addition to the return of our army from Pennsylvania I hear of the fall of Vicksburg. I cannot regard that in such a serious light as most persons . . . The commerce of the enemy will not be safe yet on the Mississippi whilst our communications with Texas and Arkansas through Vicksburg was more nominal than real. At least I have always so regarded it. . . .

Rec a letter from McKinney, Dupuy & Archer *[see Appendix 5]* with an account of my tobacco sales net proceeds $2,156.27, only seven hogsheads at an average of $26 per hundred. . . . I was offered $40 pr hundred when at home . . . McKinney & Dupuy since taking on their new partner have so much business that they cannot attend to a small crop like mine. I know that it could have been sold for more . . . Kiss our little girls often for me . . . Good bye Yr own Richard

(ed: Richard doesn't belabor the McKinney & Dupuy problem in this letter. Since the Dupuys, are Mary's relatives, they probably have to sell through this wholesaler to keep family peace. After years of good service, Richard lets Mary know he is not pleased and that they lost a significant amount of money.)

- - - - -

Letter from Captain Richard Watkins to Mary Watkins

Camp near Charlestown, Va
July 21st 1863

My own Dear Mary

Since my last written 3 or 4 days ago we have enjoyed perfect rest and quiet, lying under the shade of the large oaks and walnuts which abound in this fertile limestone country.... It will require a very large force to garrison [Vicksburg] and other towns on the River which of course will be taken from the field and will add greatly to the taxes already laid on the Northern people.... There is no good reason for despair ... We have still in the field more than 300,000 soldiers well armed, well disciplined and under able & experienced officers our cause is just and right & a great and merciful God oversees all....

We have orders to prepare three days rations the army will again be in motion tomorrow. Rumor says that we go toward Richmond, that the enemy is advancing on the south side of the James River. Others have it that we return to Pennsylvania ... Thank you for the letters . .. The murder of Mr Williams was truly a sad affair.... Leigh Redd was detailed before we moved into Pennsylvania to nurse the sick and wounded at Upperville. He has not yet returned to us ... Leigh attempted to ford the Shenandoah and went in over his head but managed to get back again to the shore and could not be induced to try again but went round to Front Royal, so he will not overtake us for several days yet.... Tis growing late and I must close ... Will write more in the morning if I have time ... I am quite thin and not altogether as strong as heretofore yet I feel perfectly well. Good night my precious one. Give ever so much love to all ... Tell Mr Anderson he must manage the farm as he thinks best. If he thinks the clover ought to be grazed [by the pigs] let it go. Do as he thinks best. Good bye. Kiss Emmie Minnie & Mary P for Papa. Yr own Richard

- - - - -

Letter from Mary Watkins to Captain Richard Watkins

Linden July 21st 1863

My dear dear Husband

You can imagine how glad I was at receiving your letters last Friday, I had not heard from you in three weeks . . . Well baby is asleep again and I will resume my letter. Minnie is sitting on the floor by me . . . she says Mama must tell Papa Minnie loves him "heep o times." Emmie goes from the breakfast table out doors and I can hardly get her in again before night. She is very much sunburned but looks more healthy than Minnie . . . I rode Lizzie Leigh over home yesterday and staid several hours . . . I rode with Mr Anderson out in the plantation to see the crops. We have a splendid crop of corn now and if we could only have a little dry weather I should be sure of a fine crop. The hail and hot weather has injured the wheat . . . Mr A is having it hauled up to the grainery ready for threshing . . . He hadn't finished cutting oats and I didn't see any of the tobacco. . . . Sister Sue told me Sunday that Mr Anderson thought it was time for you to let him know whether you wanted him another year. He asks a very high salary but Mr. Redd and Bro. William advise that you employ him again. . . . I reckon we have the best [corn] crop in the neighborhood now but if it continues to rain as it is doing now, ours will go like the rest.

So we were defeated at Gettysburg . . . .

(ed: An incomplete letter. The additional page or pages is missing.)

- - - - -

Letter from Mary Watkins to Captain Richard Watkins

Linden July 27ᵗʰ 1863

My Dear Husband

I got home today to a late dinner and found a good long letter awaiting me . . . Lucy's [slave] youngest child died whilst I was over there [at the farm] the oldest died last night and Liny's Friday morning. Nellie's child is right sick now though I hope he is out of danger. Dr Owen came to see Susan [Lucy's oldest] several times, said she had scrofillo, though he thought the whooping cough shortened her life some. . . . they coughed so hard their brains became affected and they had spasms . . . Mr Anderson was very attentive to them and did all he could. . . . Mr A will not agree to live there by himself another year . . . What do you think of my going over there to live? They say it is almost impossible to get an overseer now and I understand Mr. Andersons only objection is living there by himself. . . .

I heard her [Minnie] the other evening out doors making a great ovation over the moon and asked her what was the matter, she said, "somebody had broke the moon right in two" She had never seen the moon before except when it was full and did not know what to make of half of it being gone.

. . . I believe us Southern people can make everything at home now, unless it is cotton cards, if we could only get them we wouldn't ask the Yankees any odds except to let us alone and go home and attend to their own concerns. Lavallette made a pretty straw fan and sent Cousin Sarah Skinner to let her see what we could do and Mama sent her samples of all our homespun dresses and told Willie to tell her that we could make our own hats, bonnets, dresses, shoes, bedcords, fans and everything else we needed. I am getting sleepy now and must go to bed. Good night my dear husband. I want to see you so bad.
Your loving
Mary

(ed: In the margins of the letter Mary wrote, "Mama sent for Mr Anderson this morning and tried to employ him to overlook her business and yours too and live here as he objected to living alone but he said his health was bad and he should not do business for any one next year.")

(ed: Scrofillas or scrofillo [Mary's spelling] is tuberculosis of the lymph glands.) 7

- - - - -

Letter from Captain Richard Watkins to Mary Watkins

Camp near Fredericksburg
Aug 5th 1863

My Darling Mary

Immediately after writing my last we recd marching orders. Marched the whole of the night and a part of the next day and encamped here in a clear field, without a single shade tree near us and have been broiling in the hot sun for three or four days (the hottest weather that I have ever felt). All are well however, the Yankees reported again at Falmouth and a strong possibility of another great battle soon. Perhaps you have seen an account of a late Cavalry fight in Culpeper. . . . no part of our Brigade was engaged. . . . have heard that Hampton's loss was considerable. . . . Tis sad news you write from our home, the death of three little children in so short a time. I did not know the whooping cough was ever so fatal. And Mr Tom Anderson has not the manliness to live on our farm <u>alone</u>. Well I am not willing that you shall humor the old man so much as to subject yourself to such inconvenience for him. . . . We may be called upon for the next year or two to experience trials even greater than those which we have already passed through. . . . If we can get no overseer let our negroes take care of themselves. . . The bugle calls to 'saddle boys' and I must close for the present.

Merely moved camp about three quarters of a mile to a cooler place and better pasture. We are now almost in sight of Fredksbg. A few evenings ago Col. Carter and I rode down to town to examine the old battlefield . . . The town has not suffered to the extent to which I had supposed. Only a few buildings burnt the rest perforated by a few shells, but . . . a few bricklayers & plasterers might very soon repair the whole town. . . . Only a few citizens remain and they hold themselves in readiness to move . . . We went to Mayre's hill where the fighting had been very hot, at the foot of the hill is the stone fence which our men held so obstinately and where Meagher's Irish Brigade was destroyed. A Mr. Watson who lives nearby pointed out to us the trenches and ice house in which they were buried two ditches containing about 340 each and a large ice-house filled, supposed to contain about 500. Mr Watsons house is completely riddled by grape & canister & minnie balls ... I enquired of Mr Watson if any citizens were killed in Fredericksburg and especially if any women & children. His reply was not one. ...

Recd a letter from Hal Edmunds a few days ago written in a most cheerful spirit ... Hope to hear of his entire recovery ere long and of his happy marriage.... Robert Cunningham has been more successful, is almost entirely well and married. How is it with Fayette Scott.... Darling I am thinking seriously of resigning my commission (this is secret) and becoming a private in the ranks again. Am getting very tired of the responsibilities and duties of my office. There is such a lack of discipline in our Regiment, our Colonel is so inefficient that I cannot manage my company at all to my liking and cannot provide for them ... without constantly complaining to the Col & about the Col. – Altogether my situation as an officer is much more disagreeable than it was as a private. ... What do you think of it? Write me in your next. Now don't tell <u>anybody</u>.... Wish I could see our dear children. ... Good bye make haste and write me another letter precious, a long letter. Give heaps of love to Mother and all. Please ask Mr. Redd to look me up another overseer ... I will come to see you just as soon as I can.
Yr own
Richard

(ed: Falmouth is on the north bank of the Rappahannock just across from Fredericksburg.)

- - - - -

Letter from Mary Watkins to Captain Richard Watkins

Linden Aug 7th 1863

My Darling Husband

... I wish so often that you could come home and get some peaches and vegetables and fatten up a little. I am so impatient for this war to end though I see no prospect of peace ... Do you reckon the war will last our lifetime?

I have taken a right bad cold this warm weather and have been so hoarse I could hardly speak. . . . Emmie and Minnie are both well and just as sunburnt as they can be. I am afraid you would not know Emmie she is so black. Minnie stays out just as much but her skin does not burn half as badly as Emmies. . . . Cousin John Knight spent the day with us Thursday. he said he promised you that he would come to see me and the children before he went back. . . . You wrote something about your wheat. Mr. George Redd I believe wants fifty bushels for seed. It is a right poor crop I am afraid, was late and took the rust. Mr Anderson says he will stay until the crops are secured and will try to get you another overseer. . . . Mama seems at a loss to know what to do about keeping Mr. Baker next year he asks $500 wages. Uncle Joe has engaged his for another year for $250. . . .

Aug. 8th . . . Oh I want to see you so bad. I have so much to talk to you about that I can't write. I am so glad that you write so often I ought to be ashamed of myself for not writing oftener, will try to do better hereafter.
Your own
Mary

- - - - -

The Rapidan Line & Bristoe Station
August 18 to December 14, 1863

Things quiet down and the armies rest after the battles at Gettysburg and Vicksburg. The Army of Tennessee is in northwestern Georgia and the Army of Northern Virginia is in camps near the Rapidan and Rappahannock Rivers. The Confederates rest and recover while waiting for the Union to make a move.

Mary writes in August that they are drying fruit, pickling, and making cider and vinegar. Minnie is learning to ride a horse and she is fearless on top of Lizzie Lee. Mary asks Richard to try to find some coats and blankets for their negroes for the winter. Mrs. Dupuy is making molasses and Mary plans to grow more sorghum next year. Cotton cards are costing $27. The fall harvest, recapped in November and December letters, is yielding 29 ½ stacks of fodder, 1300 head of cabbage, over 400 barrels of corn. The winter wheat is sowed, and they slaughtered 12 hogs for 980 pounds of meat. Their overseer, Mr. Anderson, departs in December and Tom (a slave) is placed in charge of operations. Mary goes over to Oldham twice a week to meet with Tom. He feels he can manage during the winter but wants an overseer in the spring.

After a short furlough, for medical reasons, Richard is back with Co. K in the Fredericksburg area and then in Orange County. He is able to procure some coats and blankets that folks have recovered from the battlefields and forwards these to Mary. Once in Orange the cavalry is constantly skirmishing with the Union cavalry. October finds the 3rd Virginia in the vicinity of Warrenton and Bristoe Station. While near Buckland they have a brisk fight with the Union cavalry and Richard reports that we "gave them a severe drubbing." Co. K camps near Orange Courthouse, and also in Madison County, during the month of November. Richard comments that half of the company needs new mounts. The Confederate government wants each man to keep two horses at the front to avoid the details going back to Prince Edward for horses. That policy, of course, would lead to each soldier having two horses that are starving. On December 7th Richard writes that John Wesley (his bay horse) has broken down and he will be sending him home to be fattened up. Richard has bought another horse.

A Confederate victory at Chickamauga, in Georgia, is followed by a defeat in the battles around Chattanooga, Tennessee. As the year draws to a close virtually all of Tennessee is under Union control, the westerns states of Arkansas, Louisiana, Texas and Missouri have been cut off from the rest of the Confederacy, and the economy of the Confederacy is teetering.

Letter from Captain Richard Watkins to Mary Watkins

Hanover Academy
20 miles from Richmond
Aug 18th 1863

Darling

Where do you reckon I am? At Hanover Academy Hospital, and a patient. Not very sick just too unwell to do duty. . . . I was taken with a violent cold about the same time that you were. Was obliged to report sick for two or three days when I improved so much that I again took charge of the company. The cold returned upon me accompanied with severe headaches and some fever. . . . the cold still hangs on . . . applied to Surgeon Leigh to be sent to Farmville Hospital as others had been heretofore. He said that it has lately been forbidden and that the order of Genl Lee now were that the cavalry sick should all be sent this place and the infantry to Staunton that I could not even be sent to Richmond. Accordingly I came here and am happy to inform you that it is decidedly the most comfortable & apparently best regulated Confederate Hospital that I have ever seen. Everything neat & clean & well arranged & the meals very nicely prepared indeed with the best bread and the freshest coolest water I ever saw in a Hospital. The Academy is a large frame building two stories surrounded by many little cabins . . . Some distance from the main building are two single story oblong buildings which were formerly used as debating Halls for the students. These two constitute the officers Ward and from the appearance of the patients you would not judge that there was a sick man among them. All looking as well and cheerful & well content as any men I ever saw. I do not believe there is a sick man among them at all.

I reached here yesterday evening, reported to the Surgeon (Dr Kinney) and immediately asked a transfer to Farmville. He said he would try to get me one and would today . . . forward it [the application] to the Medical Director in Richmond and that I would hear from it in two or three days . . . Will write you again in a day

215

or two. John Knight returned just as I left. Said you were looking as well as ever in your life & had one of the finest best babies in the world. All this I believed before. Give love to all.

Yr own

Richard

P.S. I am not confined to my bed at all, am very much in the same condition that I was last August when I went home from Richmond.

(ed: Richard was transferred to Farmville and released to Linden which is some 15 miles south from town. He recuperated at home and checked in with the hospital. Richard gets to meet his new daughter Mary P. and spend 2 weeks with his wife and 3 girls.)

- - - - -

Letter from Mary Watkins to Captain Richard Watkins

Linden Sept 12th 1863

My dear precious Husband

I cannot resist the temptation of writing . . . to tell you how much I miss you and how very much I want to see you again. . . . your last visit . . . made a very bright spot in my life and I look back upon the last two weeks (except the parting with you) as the happiest I ever spent. . . .

Sept 17th . . . Little Mary has had a dreadful cold with some fever too but she is getting well now. . . . Mama is busy as she can drying fruit and pickling and making cider and vinegar. She got $100 for that little keg of pickled peaches that she sent down last week. The last two barrels of peaches brought only $20 apiece . . .

Minnie is learning a new accomplishment . . . She mounts Lizzie Lee and walks off with her as fearlessly as I could. Emmie looks on almost ready to cry and says Mama please make Minnie get down she will fall. but Minnie just laughs and says get up behind me sister. I don't believe the child knows what fear is and I am afraid she will get killed some of these days. I saw her yesterday go up behind Lizzie Lee and stroke her legs and she will stand up in the saddle just as quick as any way. . . . Please try and get some more blankets if you have an opportunity. They are badly needed [by the negroes this winter]. Did you leave any money in Farmville or any where to pay your taxes?

Your loving

Mary

(ed: Inflation is growing rapidly. The Confederate dollar is now worth about 10 cents to the U. S. dollar. Said another way, it takes $10 Confederate to equal $1 U. S.) 1

- - - - -

Letter from Captain Richard Watkins to Mary Watkins

Camp near Fredericksburg
Sep. 13 1863. –

My Darling Mary

I reached camp on Wednesday and found all well and every thing perfectly quiet. Met our Col & Dr Leigh and James Baker at Hamilton Crossing going home on furloughs looking very cheerful and happy. How I did wish I could turn back and go with them, but a long time must elapse before I can have that good fortune. . . . William Berkeley I am glad to say has attracted the attention of Genl Fitz Lee. On Friday he was invited to dine with him and yesterday the Genl took him with him to Richmond to remain five days I hope that he will promote him in some way, not so much on Williams account as for the sake of the old Capt. – who certainly did good service while here. Reckon you have already learned by the papers that Genl Fitz Lee has been promoted to . . . Major Genl and Col. Wickham to that of Brigadier. He now commands our Brigade. His appointment gives general satisfaction. His profanity is the only objection to him. We hope that the dignity of his position . . . will induce him to amend his habits in that respect. How sad it is . . . that some of our officers set such examples before the men.

. . . Was glad to find on my return that a Christian association has been formed and it consisting of 40 or 50 members and that there are already several applicants for the Chaplains officer. Amongst them is Rev. Mr. Christian formerly Presiding Elder in the Methodist Church in Pr Edward. Rev. Mr. Conrad (Methodist) . . . seems very anxious to be our Chaplain even asked the Col to take him a month on trial.

. . . We have been ordered this evening to cook up three days rations. Probably a move or a scout intended of course we know nothing until the time comes. Darling I long for the time to come when I can be with you again Oh tis such a severe trial to be separated from you so much and from our dear little children. . . . Good night my precious one. If I have time in the morning will write a little more, if not will send this off by Mr Ewing. . . .

Monday Morning Sep 14th – This morning rode to Fredericksburg and for the sum of eighty dollars purchased six good coats and three blankets for our negroes. If Nelly will wash them thoroughly I reckon you will find them worth the money at any rate you will have less sewing & cutting & weaving to do. If another opportunity presents itself soon will try to get some more blankets. These are clothes picked up by poor people from the battle fields and I buy them the more willingly because the people need the money. At the same time they are well worth what I have paid.

Have nothing to write more at present. Good bye again my precious precious one. Write to me very soon and tell me what you think of the clothes & blankets. The usual quantities of love to all –
Your own
Richard

- - - - -

Letter from Captain Richard Watkins to Mary Watkins

Camp near Fredericksburg
Orange County
Sep 19th 1863

My Darling Mary

A few days after my last was written we were ordered to this place which is about 30 miles above Fredericksburg on the Rapidan River. The enemy now occupies the whole of Culpeper County. The Rapidan is the line and a battle has for several days seemed imminent. We are doing nothing. . . . Our army in good spirits. Since our arrival have had regular prayer meetings. . . . Rev. Mr Conrad is becoming very popular and will in all probability be our next Chaplin. . . . Col. Berkeley is still with us and doing well – He went five days ago to Richmond with Genl Fitz Lee and expected to have a gay time but on stepping from the cars met a friend who told him of the death of Alice (Mrs. Robt. Berkeley) without stopping he passed right on to the Danville cars & went home . . . Poor Bob did not get home in time to see her at all. . . . Have a great mind this morning to mount old John Wesley and ride right straight home . . . What say you about it?

Hope you have recd the clothes and blankets sent by Mr Ewing for the negroes, Since then have bought four more excellent blankets which I will send . . . Hope Mr Anderson and the negroes are getting on smoothly at home . . . God grant that we may soon be living together again in peace & quiet. Give love to all . . . Write to me dear one.
Yr own
Richard

(ed: Mary wrote on Sept. 23, "Mr Anderson has just put up hogs and such hogs I hope not to see again soon. . . . Mama lost 2 hogs last night, they were killed . . . Mr Baker has just come to Mama with the feet . . . You don't know how glad I am for the blankets and overcoats . . . so glad you are having prayer meetings every day . . . Emmie and Minnie send love to Papa.")

- - - - -

Letter from Captain Richard Watkins to Mary Watkins

Camp near Vidiersville
Orange County
Sep 24th 1863

My Precious Mary

. . . we have been on the march the object of which was to reinforce Genl Stuart who with the rest of the cavalry at Madison Court House was endeavoring to prevent Genl Pleasonton making a raid upon Charlottesville. We reached him in time and Genl Pleasonton at once retired rapidly across Robinson River into Culpeper again. Our 1st & 2nd Regiments came up with his rear guard consisting of two Michigan Regts and charged him just before crossed killing and wounding several and taking 15 prisoners . . . Am sincerely glad that you were pleased with blankets & coats . . . You said something about the taxes. Mr William Walton will deposit to my credit in the Farmville Bank $450 & George Crump $800 (money which they owe me) sometime this month or early next month. If this not be deposited when the taxes are due . . . draw upon McKinney Dupuy & Archer for the amount . . . Am glad to find that you think about these things . . . Has Mr Geo Redd succeeded in getting me an overseer? If we fail in this must try to get Mr Tom Anderson to give the plantation some little attention . . . [or] take your plan for it & trust in Providence. . . . Were it not for you and our dear little ones would care very little for life. - . . .

Good night my precious Mary . . . Love & kisses –
Yr own
Richard

(ed: General Alfred Pleasonton is the cavalry commander for the Army of the Potomac.)

- - - - -

Letter from Captain Richard Watkins to Mary Watkins

Camp near Vidiersville
Orange County
Sep 28th 1863

My Precious Mary

. . . I send today four additional blankets by Lt. Meredith which he will leave with Dr Wood in Farmville unless he finds an opportunity of sending them directly to Meherrin. . . . They will reach Farmville or Meherrin tomorrow. I send herewith a check on the Farmers Bank of Farmville for Five Hundred Dollars. . . . The five hundred is already there to my credit. . . .

Have heard nothing from my wheat. Was it sent to market? . . . If the wheat has been sold you can get this money also by writing a few lines to Cousin Barrett. . . .

Today we have had a very close inspection of horses, equipment and arms by an old foreigner who Genl Stuart sent here whose name I did not learn. . . .

Mr. Conrad has been appointed Chaplain of the 12th Regt & will probably leave us this week. . . . Whilst writing this have recd orders to move camp a few miles for better grazing so good bye. With all my heart I love you. Am hoping for another letter from you soon. Love & kisses to all.
Yr own
Richard

- - - - -

Letter from Mary Watkins to Captain Richard Watkins

Linden, Oct 2nd 1863

My dear Husband

... I received a letter from you today enclosing a check and telling me that you had sent some blankets. . . . Am happy to say the blankets arrived before your letter. . . . Mama and Uncle Joe have just sent hands down to Richmond to work on the fortifications. They overlooked us this time . . . Sister Sue told me Sunday if I would send my wool over to her house Monday evening she would have it sent with hers to a carding machine up in Charlotte Tuesday. So I got up early Monday morning took Minnie, baby and Edna [servant] and went over home to spend the day and have the wool picked over. . . . Emmie was very anxious to go but when she saw I could not carry both she said "Mama let Minnie go I will stay home and be a good child." Wasn't that sweet . . . ? I packed the bags, sewed them up, and labeled them [6 servants picked & sorted the wool] and . . . stayed till 8 OC and got it all ready to send to Mr Redd's before day the next morning. . . . we didn't have but fifty lbs. after the Government wool was taken out. I had no idea it took so much work to get it ready to be carded. . . . Mr Redd got James Foster to carry it down to Amelia yesterday though and I hope it will be nicely done there. . . .

Mama has just got her sorghum mill done and is going right in making molasses tomorrow. . . . I expect her corn is entirely too ripe. . . . Little Mary is calling me and I must go to her now. Good bye Your Mary

(ed: In an October 7 letter Mary noted that, " wheat so indifferent in quality the millers in Richmond would not buy it." Cousin Barrett sold it for $5.50 a bushel. Mama was only able to get $5.00 at Govt. price. Cousin Barrett also sent some cotton cards @ $27 each and some #15 cotton @ $30 a bale and #6 cotton @ $14 a bale. Cousin Mary Marshall and her daughter, who are refugees, want to rent the Watkins house, garden, & a few acres for $20. Mary thinks the house needs an occupant & tells Richard she thinks that this is a very good idea.)

(ed: In September, 1863 the Commissioners for Virginia in Farmville, Mr. E. W. Hubard & Mr. Robert Gibboney, had the below listed fixed prices they were paying for goods sold to the Government: Flour - $25

per barrel; Bacon - $1 per pound; Salt - $5 per bushel; Soap — 40 cents per pound; Coffee - $3 per pound; Beef cattle - $16 per hundred weight; Wool socks - $1.25 pair; Mules - $300; Molasses $8 per gallon. Many of these items sold for more on the open market and were worth more in barter.) 2

- - - - -

Letter from Pattie Watkins to Captain Richard Watkins

Mt Pleasant
Oct 7th/63

My Dear Brother

Ma and I went down to see Mary & the children yesterday . . . Mary is looking very well indeed . . . she was making an apron for Emmie. Emmie has grown very fast . . . she & Minnie both have a small remnant of the whooping cough. . . . Minnie is as fat as a little pig, eating sorghum molasses. And little Mary Purnall is the sweetest, whitest, best little baby you ever saw . . .

When we heard from Brother Nat last he was on his way to Charleston with Wise's Brigade. He wrote in very good spirits & seemed very willing to go. They will be in Heavy Artillery. . . .

Mr Redd has finished cutting tobacco & said yesterday he had gotten out about 16 bu of peas & expected to be able to get as many more. . . .
All join me in love to you.
Your own Loving Sister
Pattie 3

- - - - -

Letter from Mary Watkins to Captain Richard Watkins

Linden Oct 12th 1863

Mr Watkins
        Dear Sir

... Sister Sue wrote me this morning that all our wool had been returned without being carded, they had so many orders on hand that they could not touch ours. .... it will throw us back mightily about our winter cloth. Don't know what I should have done if you had not sent those overcoats. I reckon it will be after Christmas before I get the wool carded and spun then the weaving will have to be done. I intended also having a piece of flannel wove and had just got a nice bale of cotton for that purpose. ...

Aunt Jane wishes me to mention to you again her proposition of renting our house, yard and garden. .... It seems a pity for the house to stand unoccupied whilst there are so many homeless families ...

Mother got a letter from Bro Nat last week. His company have been turned into <u>Infantry</u> and are encamped three miles from Charleston. [South Carolina] The company is very unhealthy, I think he said forty of them were sick there. He was having chills every other day. I am so glad you did not join that company.

Oct. 15th – Emmie sends her love to Papa and Minnie says, "remember me very affectionately to Papa." Your loving
Mary

(ed: The 4th Battalion Virginia Heavy Artillery (Wharton's Battery) has been transferred from Drewry's Bluff to the defenses around Charleston, S. C. Nat is in Company K which is the King and Queen Heavy Artillery.)

- - - - -

Letter from Captain Richard Watkins to Mary Watkins

(Thursday morning)
Near Manassas
Oct 15th 1863

My Precious Mary

We crossed the Rapidan Sunday morning early and fought the enemy cavalry & artillery the whole day driving them steadily before us through Culpeper – Monday night crossed the Rappahannock .. . Tuesday night our infantry under Gen Ewell over took the infantry of the enemy below Catlett's Station. Yesterday hard fighting all day but driving the enemy. The fight is to be renewed this morning near Bristoe Station and the pickets are now firing. We are on the extreme left of Gen A. P. Hills Corp. All of my company well in the fight of Sunday. Drury Armistead recd a flesh wound in the arm my company recd no other damage. Both our Col & Lt Col had horses shot under them & Col Carter was taken prisoner but we rescued him – No time to write more. Cousin Barrett has $800 dollars of my money in hand for the sale of wheat. This you can get by writing to him. I hope too that Crump has deposited $800 more for me in Farmville . . . Again Good bye I love you . . . and long to be with you.
Yr own
Richard

– – – – –

Letter from Captain Richard Watkins to Mary Watkins

Culpeper Oct 21 1863

My Precious Mary

Our Army is again on the South of the Rappahannock Contrary to my expectations . . . Our infantry advanced as far as Bristow Station on the Orange & Alexandria Railroad. Genl Meade withdrew into his fortifications at Manassas. . . . We then tore up and destroyed the whole railroad back to the Rappahannock and recrossed it. In the meantime a portion of A. P. Hills Corps became engaged at Bristow Station, a North Carolina Brigade stampeded and we lost four pieces of artillery and a few prisoners. We (the Cavalry) had a hard time of it without rations nearly the whole time. . . . where scarcely anything could be obtained for our horses. At the same time our work was hard but it was well done. Whenever we fought the Yankee cavalry we drove them in confusion from the field. Day before yesterday we had a terrible fight near Warrenton against both cavalry and infantry and gave them a severe drubbing taking a good many prisoners from each. Genl Fitz Lee has rather distinguished himself and is rapidly gaining the confidence of his Division. . . . He is certainly one of the most reckless daring men I ever saw . . . He is always in the thickest of the fight and above all the noise and confusion his full rich voice can be heard cheering on the men. But . . . like all others, he has his weakness. He drinks to excess and rumor says the habit is growing . . . that persisted this habit will soon ruin him. In our last fight Willie Dupuy received a wound on the head which our surgeon pronounced a slight one. I was very near him. He fell and I had him taken up immediately and carried to the surgeon in the rear. . . . his scalp alone suffered. He was sent back to Culpeper CoHo and I heard last night that he was on his way home. . . . I was truly sorry that . . . I could not carry him myself from the field . . . Fayette Scott & Wm Booker went with him. The rest of the boys are all well . . .

. . . Will send some more blankets by the first opportunity. Good bye precious. I love you more & more every day.
Yr own
Richard

(ed: The correct spelling is Bristoe Station as in his October 21 letter. General A. P. Hill made an impetuous attack on a well prepared Union position and lost some 1400 killed and wounded and an additional 450 captured. The Union losses totaled about 300 and only 50 of those were killed. Sometimes this battle is called "Third Manassas.") 4

(ed: Pvt. Willie Dupuy was wounded in the battle of Buckland, or Buckland Mills, which is the "terrible fight near Warrenton" that Richard notes above. This fight is known to most Confederates as the "Buckland Races.") 5

- - - - -

Letter from Mary Watkins to Captain Richard Watkins

Linden Oct 23rd 1863

My Precious Husband

... I walked over home and while I was resting sent Lewis to the Depot. Mr. Anderson was just starting to Lunenburg and I did not have him to talk with and I got right lonesome waiting for Lewis to bring the mail. I went in the front porch and sat there a long time by myself and thought about you ... I like to have had a good cry before I thought what I was about. ... I am getting to be a good walker, went over home last week and walked all over the cornfield with Mr Anderson and then back home ... I think the fattening hogs are improving, they are very young most of them but I reckon we can make out meat enough. ... I think I shall have some sorghum planted next year for molasses. Some [neighbors] made 150 gallons of molasses from one acre of sorghum and I think it would be better for the negroes not to have as much meat. ... Mr A is gathering corn and sowing wheat.

Poor Mr Pollard died last Sunday of inflammation of the stomach ... He will be right much missed ... He has done nearly all the shoemaking since the war commenced. Poor Mrs Pollard is left with nine children (oldest just sixteen) and is expecting another. Isn't she to be pitied? Mama ... is afraid her mind will become unbalanced. ...

Oct 26th We heard last night that Willie Dupuy was shot but have not yet learned how badly. Oh dear how I wish this cruel war was over. ... Was disappointed that Tom Haskins did not bring me a letter ... Must wash the baby now. Good bye
Your own
Mary

- - - - -

Letter from Captain Richard Watkins to Mary Watkins

Culpeper Oct 25th 63

My Darling

Henry & Josh Ewing are going after fresh horses and I write to let you know that I am still in the enjoyment of excellent health . . . the boys are well. Have not heard from Willy Dupuy since he was sent to Gordonsville. . . . a cold northeaster blowing with constant rain – I lost my little tent in a charge last Sunday week and have the full benefit of the refreshing showers. . . .

Nothing new to communicate. The army is quiet and the Quartermasters are distributing new clothes . . . John Knight, _ _ _ _ _ and I sleep together (three in a bed) and such pulling for blankets you have seldom seen . . . I send two additional blankets by Henry Ewing . . . if more yet are needed please write to me and I will try to procure them.

. . . reflection comes up that I am nearer a furlough, that we will soon go into winter quarters and then I can apply . . . with some prospect of success . . .

In the morning we arise at day break, attend roll call, turn our horses out to graze, make up a good many little smoking fires & stand around them, some cooking some washing their faces others laughing cracking jokes, some abusing quartermasters . . . and others hollering & singing & whistling &c &c. Thus our time glides on in a beautiful forest with fields still green around us.

A great many horses played out on our last campaign and nearly one half of my company will have to get fresh ones. Some are talking about going into infantry the price of horses is so high. And I fear that unless our horses are better fed many will be compelled to change their branch of service. Old John Wesley still keeps up though considerably reduced. . . .

Make haste and write to me & kiss again & again our dear children for me. Where is Nat. Give heaps of love to all & especially to Ma when you see her. Good bye my dear dear one.
Yr own
Richard

- - - - -

Letter from Captain Richard Watkins to Mary Watkins

Culpeper Oct. 25th 63

. . . I do not think the suggestion to rent out our house & yard & garden a good one unless at the same time we rent out the whole plantation. If Aunt Jane . . . rents the house . . . where will she get her firewood. Are we to supply that? and if so to haul it? Or will she keep servants & horses. If the latter then she will need a stable & forage house and an additional negroe cabin – [would] our hands without an overseer be likely to have the time, or to give satisifaction . . . Tis always a bad plan to have two sets of negroes on the same plantation especially controlled by different persons . . . One thing might be considered however. If Mrs M be a refugee and her husband in the army, then I for one am willing to make almost any sacrifice to aid her. And if you & mother still think the plan is feasible after the suggestions I have made do not hesitate to carry it out and let her have it for a moderate fee.

No news here except that a small fraction of our Army have been fighting the Yankees about some railroad iron this morning . . . I long to see you . . . Kiss often & often our children for me . . . Love to all . . .
Yr own
Richard

- - - - -

Letter from Mary Watkins to Captain Richard Watkins

Linden Nov 3ʳᵈ 1863

My darling Husband

I received a letter from you today dated Oct 21ˢᵗ . . . I have received two others of later date in the mean time though. . . . This is such a warm, still night. I am always inclined to be low spirited in such weather . . . I have been quite busy making up some winter clothes for the children . . . Have just finished two pairs of flannel drawers for you too. Mary Brown keeps sick and I can't have any spinning done and don't know when I can have my flannel so Mama let me have enough for your drawers. Emmie and Mary are asleep and Minnie is lying on the floor at my feet playing with a handkerchief . . . The negroes are shucking corn out in the horse lot and singing some beautiful old tunes . . . "The Old Ship of Zion" and "When I can read my title clear." It sounds so sweet coming on the still night air. . . .
from Your loving
Mary

- - - - -

Letter from Mary Watkins to Captain Richard Watkins

Linden Nov 5ᵗʰ 1863

My dear Husband

. . . Mr Anderson took me the usual rounds to the grainery, cornhouse, hog pen, smoke house, dairy and garden. He was filling the corn house from the grainery where he has been drying it out. They had gathered 240 barrels . . . and not more than half done. Finished sowing wheat this morning. We have had fine weather for sowing wheat and drying out corn. Mr A has . . . twenty nine and a half stacks of fodder. The hogs are really improving right fast. . . . Mr. Anderson has all of that back square of the garden that we used to have in potatoes full of cabbages ... he told me he had thirteen hundred heads of cabbage in that square ... think we might sell some ...

... Little Mary has had a cold and been very fretful night and day but is getting over it and is much better now.

I am going to send you two pair of flannel drawers by Henry Ewing. I reckon they will be very comfortable this winter. Aunt Jane is going to send a flannel shirt to Cousin Willie of the Nottoway Troop by him too. . . .
Your own
Mary

- - - - -

Letter from Captain Richard Watkins to Mary Watkins

Camp near Orange Courthouse
Nov: 11th 1863

My own Dear Mary

... Archer Haskins horse was wounded and broke down on our late Manassas Campaign and he has been trying ever since to get a detail to go home after a fresh one but Genl Stuart throws every obstacle possible in the way. When his application first went up Genl S. sent it back with the inquiry "how many horses has the Lt" He answered the question and this morning it returned with the endorsement that it will not be approved unless the Lt will obligate himself to procure two horses. The number which the law authorizes him to keep in the field. Archer is in a great bother. He does not want to keep two horses starving at a time and yet the poor fellow wants to go home terribly. . . .

What did you decide on about renting the farm house? As to the blankets, we are now so far from Fredericksburg that it is hardly possible for me to get any more nor can I get the overcoats I fear. . . .
Breakfast comes now and then Court Martial again so good bye for

the present . . . Kiss our dear children for me and tell them that Papa loves to hear that they are good children. . . . Poor Mary Pollard . . . cannot we contribute something to the support of her family - . . . I love you dearly
Yr own
Richard

(ed: As you have noticed, in many letters, the men of the 3rd Virginia are constantly being detailed back home for new mounts. Cavalrymen in the Confederate service own their own horses and equipment. The government is not providing enough feed to keep the horses serviceable and yet the government would like the men to each keep 2 horses available. Archer is correct that he would then have 2 horses starving. On top of this the cost of horses keeps rising and Confederate currency keeps dropping in value. More and more Confederate cavalry units are becoming dismounted units. Dismounted cavalry is a nuanced name for infantry.)

- - - - -

Letter from Mary Watkins to Captain Richard Watkins

Linden Nov 21st 1863

My dear Husband

. . . Edna was taken with diphtheria [a week after Mary's Nov. 15 letter] and I had nearly all of the nursing . . . She did not have a very severe attack though and was out again in four or five days. Emmie and Minnie have been sick ever since she got well. I thought for a day or two that they would have pneumonia. . . . The baby is beginning to take it too. . . . It seems to be an epidemic, all the children on the land [slaves] and at our house have been sick with it. . . .

Mama went to Farmville last week and I sent your boots by her to be half soled. I sent some leather and tried to get Booker Jackson to make you another pair . . . they had taken all of his hands and he didn't do any shoe making now. He agreed to mend your boots though. I drew $500 from the bank and paid our State and county taxes which amounted to $384. I think George Crump has never deposited any money . . . I paid $91 for a side of sole leather and $3.50 a yard from some unbleached domestic. Mama staid all night with Cousin Cornelia Knight . . . she was dressed in homespun from head to foot. . . .

(Nov 24th) . . . The children are all better, nearly well now and slept very well last night. Mr. Tom Anderson leaves us today he came over Sunday to tell us good bye. I was right much amused at a parting lecture that he gave the negroes, he made them all get in a line before him and commenced by telling them that their Master was off in the army enduring all kinds of privations and hardships . . . That next year they would be without an overseer and they must let Tom tell them what to do and to do it without fuss. . . . Then he made them all promise to do their best and they would do well he knew.

. . . Capt. Marshall Cousin Mary's husband has been very badly wounded lately near Pasqaqoula [Pascagoula, Mississippi] and I reckon she will go south as soon as he can be moved to where she can reach him.

. . . Will write again soon
Your loving
Mary

(ed: Inflation is gaining momentum. Today the Confederate dollar is worth 5 ½ cents versus the U. S. dollar. Said another way it takes $18 Confederate to equal $1 U. S.) 6

- - - - -

Letter from Mary Watkins to Captain Richard Watkins

Linden Nov 30th 1863

Good Morning Mr. Watkins

Will you believe it Sir! I am up by day this morning writing by a lightwood blaze. . . . Emmie and Minnie are both dressed and little Mary is setting in the corner . . . Mama got up one night to give [Mary] some calomel but I persuaded her to wait until morning and by that time she was better.

I am going over home directly after breakfast to give out meal and corn. I go over twice a week. . . . Tom thinks he can do very well this winter but wants an overseer next spring. Cousin Robert Smith says he and Mr. George Redd are going to measure the corn in the grainery. They think Mr Anderson over stated his crop of corn. . . .

Dec 1ˢᵗ I slept so cold last night that I was glad when day came . . . I felt very glad that I had carried the blankets over home yesterday and given them out to the negroes. I did not have one to give Lucy's little children but I am going to send them that old bed quilt that you sent home while you were on the Peninsula. . . .

. . . Write as often as you can to
Your loving
Mary

- - - - -

Letter from Captain Richard Watkins to Mary Watkins

Orange CoHo
Dec 1 1863

My own Dear Mary

. . . Genl Meade's army has crossed the Rapidan. . . . a great fight is impending when our Regiment was ordered from camp I recd an order from the Col to go back with the wagon trains to the rear and take command of the dismounted men & of those with unserviceable horses. (Company Q as it is called) and to examine the horses carefully and see that no man went to the rear without proper authority. On Sunday I recd an order from Genl Stuart to take all of the dismounted men . . .

belonging to Genl Fitz Lees Division organize them into a force and bring them to this place and protect this place and the Government property (mainly commissary and Quartermaster stores.) Am now occupying that unenviable position with about 300 men under my command. . . . We are about 12 miles from the main army. . . . if the Yankees make a raid will do the best I can. . . . weather very cold. . . .

When the armies get quiet again I mean to apply for a furlough . . . write again in a few days. . . .
Good bye
Yr
Richard

- - - - -

Letter from Mary Watkins to Captain Richard Watkins

Linden, Dec 5th 1863

My dear Husband

Did you know it had been two weeks tomorrow . . . since I received a letter from you. I have no doubt you have written unless you are paying me back in my very own coin, which I don't think you would do intentionally. . . .

Mama had her pork killed this week and has just got through with tying up lard, smoking sausage meat &c. &c. I expect to have a hog killing next week if it turns cold enough . . . Mr. Redd thought I had better have all my meat brought over here . . . be safer . . . Mr. Baker made a very short crop of corn this year and Mama took thirty three bushels of ours in payment for the seed wheat and oats that she let us have. Mr. Redd sold the remainder in the grainery at $51 per barrel. I don't reckon there will be more than fifty or sixty barrels though after the Government corn is taken out. . . . They have come for Mr Redd's papers and I want to send this along with them. Good bye from your loving
Mary

- - - - -

Letter from Captain Richard Watkins to Mary Watkins

Camp Troymann
Madison County Dec 7th 63

Darling:

Your last letter bearing the good news that all are well again has been recd ... I wish you would send me one every day but that I know is asking too much more specially as the plantation now is claiming so much more of your attention. ...

... Meade's Army ... withdrew again into Culpeper. ... I was ordered by Genl. Stuart to take command of the dismounted men ... Genl Chilton Adjutant for Genl R. E. Lee finding that I was there ordered me to act as Commander of the Post, to take charge of all soldiers coming on the cars and send them to Genl. Lee ... to take charge of all Federal Prisoners and send them to Richmond, to arrest deserters & those improperly going to the rear, to institute a Provost Guard & preserve order in the Town &c. &c. Quite enough for one man was it not? Yet I undertook it all and succeeded far better than I expected. Fortunately for me my administration did not last more than four days. ... As soon as Meade's army returned ... I was relieved.

... On returning to our Camp & feeling satisfied that the active duties of the year are over & not wishing to be in Command another year I resigned my commission unconditionally and asked again to be enrolled as a private. ... This resignation I forwarded to Genl Stuart and have not yet heard whether he has accepted it. ... Most persons say Genl Stuart will not accept it but I think otherwise ... Our Squadron is today on pickett and I have stolen away ... to write you this wee bit ... Jno Knight is on the sick list with a cold ... he is very sorry you have such a headstrong husband ... I don't think that he has altogether the same aversion to HeadQuarters men and red tape that I have ...

Have you heard anything lately from Nat. Is he still at Charleston?

... Wish I could spend Xmas with you but there is not much chance. ... I will try to get an overseer when I come home again. My bay horse (John Wesley) is entirely broken down, will send him home by the first opportunity. Have bought a very handsome horse lately and it seems a pity to keep him here to starve. Tell Tom I want him to fatten John Wesley as soon as possible. Give him as much as he can eat. . . . Tell Emmie that Papa is coming home just as soon as he can and will try to bring her candy. . . . Am sorry that I have not succeeded in getting the overcoats or additional blankets. . . . Good bye again now my precious one . . .
Yr own
Richard

- - - - -

Letter from Captain Richard Watkins to Mary Watkins

Camp Troymann
Madison County
Dec 11th 1863

Darling –

I have just returned from pickett – Have been on six days and now tis almost dark, but Jno Redd has recd a detail to go home after a fresh horse and my letter must be written at once . . . I was riding along today with fingers almost frozen when Ned Price rode up and handed me the gloves [from Mrs. Dupuy] . . . Tomorrow our Brigade moves back to Albemarle to go into winterquarters until the 15th January when we will again come to the front on the pickett line. . . . I will try to get a furlough as soon as possible . . . We are all well . . . Recd a letter from Bro Wm yesterday, was surprised and sorry to hear that Henry has almost reached the age of 18 & will soon have to join the Army. Bro wanted to know whether he should join my company but I cannot advise him to do so. The Cavalry service is too hard for Henry and entirely too expensive. Will answer in a day or two & will write you again . . .

Rec yesterday a letter from Gus Anderson (A. F. Anderson) stating that he wanted to settle a debt of $1400 dollars & interest which he owes me. If he applies to you . . . do not by any means . . . let him . . . settle it in any way. He has treated me badly and I will not receive Confederate money from him but am willing to receive it from any body else! – In the beginning of the War I applied to him for the money when I really needed it, and although he had it . . . he refused to pay & invested in 8 per cent Government bonds whilst he was paying me only 6 per cent. Now when Confederate money is cheap he wishes to settle. Do not take a dollar of it. . . . It is growing dark and we have no candles! I am getting almost crazy to see you & must come soon. John Redd will take my bay horse home. Tell Tom to take the very best care of him I prize him very highly. Love Love Love to Everybody
Yr own
Richard

- - - - -

Letter from Mary Watkins to Captain Richard Watkins

Linden Dec 14th 1863

My dear Husband

I have a great mind to get mad with you for resigning your office as Captain, indeed I sat down with the intention of abusing you soundly and calling you a grand rascal. and a great many other ugly names . . . but if you would be better satisfied a private I ought certainly not to complain . . .

Mr. Redd and Cousin Robert Smith found upon measuring the corn in the grainery that there was 114 barrels for sale after Mama had taken out 33 and the Government corn had been taken. . . . it [sold] at $51 per barrel $5814 would almost get you out of debt if people would take Confederate money wouldn't it? If we were only out of debt I should feel right satisfied.

We killed 12 hogs last Tuesday . . . had them brought over here. Then Lucy, Liny and I turned in and soon had all the fat dried up and sausages made. I sent Sister Marie a pot of sausages. Our twelve hogs averaged 90 lbs. and the twelve in the pen are very much smaller.

. . . John Redd reached home last night and sent over your letter and horse this morning. I am real glad you are going into winter quarters and have the prospect of a little rest at last. Wish you could come home and spend Christmas with us.

Minnie is talking to me so fast and combing my hair at such a rate I hardly know what I am about. She came in just now and said "Mama I don't believe your hair has been combed this morning . . . let me brush it nice." So I let her comb it to keep her out of other mischief . . . The baby is crying and I must go to her. She can sit alone very well now. Good bye
Your loving
Mary

(ed: The government takes a 10% tithe of the crops to help feed the armies. Mary probably had some 163 barrels of corn. The government took 16, Mrs. Dupuy took 33 and that left 114 for Mary to sell. It is also possible some grain was hidden to provide for planting in 1864 and avoid not only the tithe but also the impressing agents that would come along to either buy or impress additional grain. The local county boards will soon be adding a 10% crop tithe of their own to help feed indigent soldier's families.)

- - - - -

Pursuit of Averell
December 20, 1863 to March 6, 1864

The armies are in winter camps. The 3rd Virginia is camped in Madison County north of Charlottesville. Orders come to cook three days rations and they are off in pursuit of Union cavalry, under General Averell, which is on a raid toward Salem, Virginia and the Tennessee railroad. It is a hopeless chase when the enemy has a 30 mile lead. The weather is miserable with rain, snow, sleet and freezing temperatures. Richard writes three marvelous letters detailing the travails of the pursuit. They chase Averell back down the Shenandoah Valley and then raid into counties in West Virginia and get "400-500 mules and horses & as many cattle." That is about all that is accomplished. The 3rd Virginia departed Charlottesville with 227 men and 23 officers and returned about 30 days later with 40 men and four officers. All of the loss is due to horses breaking down and sickness.

Mary opens her Christmas letter with several lines from *The Night before Christmas* and tells Richard stories of Emmie and Minnie getting apples, "ground peas" and candy in their stockings. Emmie gets soot all over herself looking up the chimney for Santa. Mary also notes that the negroe men bring their corn, grown in their personal gardens, and Mary pays them for 18 barrels of corn and gives them their winter coats.

Inflation continues to worsen. The demand for currency continues to grow. On February 17th Congress authorizes the seventh issue of currency. It is to be printed in unlimited quantities and some one billion dollars are eventually printed. All earlier notes are to be retired after being funded into bonds. Specific dates are set for certain value notes to be redeemed. Unbonded notes are to be taxed at 33% upon exchange. This converse effort to reduce circulation and improve the value of CSA notes is unsuccessful. Large quantities of earlier notes remain in use and the money has little value. 1

On February 17th, near the harbor entrance to Charleston, South Carolina, the Confederate submarine *Hunley* sinks the U.S.S. *Housatonic* with a torpedo. Confederate forces in Florida claim victory at the battle of Olustee. Some minor sparring is taking place near Tunnel Hill, Georgia between the two opposing armies.

After the pursuit of Averell things are quiet and the Prince Edward Troop relaxes in winter quarters. Richard receives a furlough on January 15th and does not depart Prince Edward to return to the 3rd Virginia Cavalry until March 3rd, 1864.

Letter from Captain Richard Watkins to Mary Watkins

On the roadside near Fincastle
Bottetourt County Dec 20th 1863

My Precious Mary

When I last wrote we were in Madison joyful in the anticipation of going into winter quarters at Charlottesville. . . . the orders came to draw three days rations of hard bread & bacon and be ready to march at once. In an hour thereafter we were in our saddles marching towards the Blue Ridge. Reached Browns Gap at nightfall and crossed the mountains in the night. It was extremely cold a sharp wind blowing in our faces. Entered the Valley about 10 o'clock and camped the night. Next day moved to the Valley Turnpike midway between Harrisonburg and Staunton & on toward Staunton Wednesday . . . A cold freezing rain poured upon us wetting out blankets & clothes thoroughly, next morning marched through Staunton in the direction of Lexington a most terrific rain pouring upon us all day & freezing, the trees fences grass & everything covered with ice, when night came went into camp with orders to march again at midnight, stood shivering around our smoking fires the rain pouring in torrents . . . the rain ceased about daybreak . . . We passed through Lexington today Friday in the direction of Covington but yesterday turned toward Buchanan passed through that & camped again. This extremely cold morning we commenced our march at 3 o'clock A M and now about 9 o'clock have stopped on the Sweet Spring Road to feed our horses having just passed through Fincastle. The object of it all is to intercept Averill [Averell] who has made a raid upon Salem (Roanoke). He is reported to be about 30 miles ahead of us and whether we shall be able to overtake him is extremely doubtful as our men & horses are nearly exhausted. . . . Lee Redd Wm Booker, the Ewings & Archer Haskins are with us & all well. Tom Haskins horse was unserviceable & he remained at Charlottesville. My ink is freezing as I write . . . Had applied for a furlough the morning we left Charlottesville and hope to get it upon my return. . . . May he [God] bless & protect you and all who we love . . .

Write to me
Yr own
Richard

- - - - -

Letter from Mary Watkins to Captain Richard Watkins

Linden. Dec 24th 1863

> "Tis the night before Christmas and all
> through the house not a creature was
> stirring, not even a mouse" <u>except</u> <u>one</u>.

My darling Husband

It seems a very long time since I heard from you ... [thought] perhaps you would drop in from [winter quarters]. Willie Dupuy dispelled that illusion this morning with the information that the 3rd Regt was in pursuit of Averill ... Emmie and Minnie hung up their stockings before going to bed and I have just filled them with apples, ground peas [home grown peanuts] some candy . . . and some cakes Mrs Baker sent them. Our negro men have been over to get pay for their corn and get their overcoats. They made eighteen barrels of corn this year. [from the servant gardens]

Dec 25th Little Mary waked up last night and would not go back to sleep again until I went to bed with her so I could not finish my letter. She and Minnie both sleep with me. Minnie sleeps at the foot to keep my foots warm she says and she is a regular little stove. . . . You never saw children more delighted than Emmie and Minnie were at finding their stockings full Christmas morning . . . Emmie was rather expecting a china doll but I told her the Yankees would not let Santa Claus get such things nowadays. . . . I asked [Minnie] how she got so black [with soot] she said she had been looking up the chimney to see if Santa Claus was up there now. . . .

. . . I can't help thinking about you shivering in a cold rain and can hardly enjoy a good fire when I think that you are perhaps suffering with cold.

We are all well here. Little Mary has one tooth . . . I want to send this letter to the Depot now. Good bye for the present. Hope too see you at home soon as you get here . . . begin to think about your going back.
Your own
Mary

P.S. Please get me some stamps when you come through Richmond

(ed: It was also noted that the Meherrin Depot burned. Mr. George Redd lost a good deal of tobacco which was at the Depot awaiting shipment. Mrs. Owen of Nottoway lost some bed steads, table linen, silver spoons, & most of her & childrens clothes. She has come from Nottoway and is moving into the Womack place.)

(ed: Reverend Clement Moore had composed "The Night Before Christmas" for his children in 1822. It was officially published in Manhatten, N.Y. in 1844 and caught on rapidly throughout the United States as is evidenced by Mary quoting from it 19 years later.) 2

- - - - -

Letter from Captain Richard Watkins to Mary Watkins

Camp near New Market
Shenandoah County Dec. 30th 1863

My Precious Mary

Here I am again, no telling where I will be tomorrow. 'Push along keep moving' seems to be the plan of our General. . . . he has suffered us to rest here two days, night here, which have been the only rest days I have had for a month. Tomorrow we start again, down the Valley, in the direction of Winchester . . . then . . . over into Hardy or

Hampshire . . . Can sit down by a log fire in the woods and eat nearly a half pound of raw bacon (the fattest that can be found) and two or three hard crackers, then make up a shelter of fence rails, with oil cloth over them, rake up a pile of leaves, roll myself in my blankets . . . and sleep as soundly as if . . . on the best mattress. Many of the Regiment have been badly frost bitten on the late chase after Averill but fortunately I escaped, owing mainly to the fact that I walked a great deal. Whenever pinched by the cold would jump down and walk or run until the circulation was completely restored then mount and ride again. Often wished that you could see us crossing the mountains. At times there was so much ice on the roads that the whole command would have to dismount and walk . . . the most hazardous parts of the march consisted in crossing the rivers . . . near Covington a member of the 2nd Regiment was drowned and but for the vigilance of Genl Wickham I reckon more would have been . . . but he stood on the bank to order and direct . . . until the whole column passed. . . . we went almost to White Sulphur and then to the Hot, Warm, Jordon's Springs &c. . . . Am satisfied that I can get a furlough. Am too eager for the time to come. . . . I have been favorably impressed [with] the counties of Augusta, Rockingham and Shenandoah. The people too are very loyal and kind and the boys tell me of fine dinners that they eat. I have eaten only one meal in a house since we left Charlottesville. . . . They occasionally bring in with them some nice light bread and apple butter & always give me a share. No Captain was ever treated more kindly by his company. . . . You really astonished me with the news about the corn, what a pity now that the currency is so depreciated. How much more comfortable would I feel if the whole of that amount could be immediately applied to my debts . . . Perhaps some of my creditors can be persuaded to take part of it when I am home. The warm gloves that mother knit me have been invaluable on this trip. Thank her all the time for them. Papa sends many kisses to Emmie, Minnie and Mary.

Please ask Bro Geo Redd to pay Mr Tom Anderson his wages as soon as possible. Mr A. selected Frank D. Redd to determine what he should be paid for the extra time and I am perfectly satisfied with

him. Tis growing late so good bye for the present – Give love to all –
I long to see you & all at home . . . The boys all well – at least the few
who are here. – My Company I believe is the largest in the regiment
and it numbers only 17 – some companies are reduced to three or four
– The rest all broken down & gone back to Charlottesville. Cousin
Wm Dupuy broke down & went back about three days ago. –
Yr own
Richard

*(ed: On December 27, 1863 brokers were offering $50 Confederate for $1
gold. So from an approximate value of 33 cents in July the Confederate
dollar has fallen to 2 cents.)* 3

*(ed: Richard's comment about fatback and crackers echoes the basics of the
standard diet for the Confederate soldier. Fatback, sometimes eaten raw,
and cornbread or hardtack/crackers was the daily ration. When possible
the fatback was fried and then the cornbread was made in the grease or
the hardtack was soaked/cooked in the grease and the cooked hardtack was
then called a 'muck.' The soldier was expected to forage for any additions
to this diet. Over time the soldier's health broke down, no differently than
the health of their horses failed, from poor diet.)*

- - - - -

Letter from Mary Watkins to Captain Richard Watkins

Linden Jan. 1st 1864

My dear Husband

I had a sneaking notion that you were coming home today and went
with Sister Maria to the Depot . . . Saw Mr. Haskins, Mr. Ewing,
Mr. Booker, Mat & Somerfield Dance and a good many others. I
told Somerfield I was mighty glad the substitute bill had passed and
he said he was ready and willing to go back into the army anytime
when all of the substitute men were called out, that he had paid for
his substitute two or three times by being at home this year and he
did not think the money ought to be refunded either. Mat looks very

serious on the subject . . . He has just got back from N. C. where he had been after his wife. He could not get within eighty miles of his wifes Mother's though, the Yankees had sent out two regiments of negroes from Norfolk and they had been to Mrs Whitby's and taken off all of her servants, horses cattle and everything else that they could carry away and were searching for him. . . .

Well now I must wish you a happy new year. This is the third new year that you have spent in the army and I hope it will be the last . . .

It is late and the baby keeps one awake nights so I think I had better retire. Good night – from your own
Mary 4

(ed: The Confederate Congress is repealing the substitute law and will now draft into the service those who have hired a substitute. The substitute will be kept in the service along with the draftee who had originally hired him. The desperate need for men has created these desperate measures. The legality of this bill will be upheld by the courts.) 5

(ed: Heavy snows in the winter of 1863–1864 created difficulty for many of the indigent families in Prince Edward County. Neighborhood groups hauled firewood and supplies to those in need.) 6

- - - - -

Orders appointing Captain Richard H. Watkins to an Inspection Board

HdQrs – Army of Northern Va
January 5th 1864

III Boards to be composed of three officers from each of the Brigades of the Cavalry Corps of this army are hereby appointed to meet at such time and place that may be indicated by Major Genl J. E. B. Stuart Comdg Corps whose duty it shall be to examine Regiments, Battallions & Companies &c of these respective commands and to ascertain there status whether as public or private. When after investigation, arms &c heretofore borne, on property Returned, are decided to be the property of the C. S. or of individual States ~ The Colonels of Regiments will [be] required to take them up and account for them, when in like manner the arms &c are decided to be legitimated private property ~ The Board will fix their value and report the names Regt & Company of claimant with the price of each article assures each board will forward its report with as little delay as possible to these Head Quarters.

The arms &c claimed as "Private" and recognized as such must not include those valued and borne on the muster-rolls at time of enlistment, these have been or are constructively paid for and must [be] reported as public property.

The Board will be composed as follows:
Capt P. Fontaine   Brigade Inspector   Wickhams
Capt W W Tebbs   Co K 2nd Va Cav   Brigade
Capt R. C Watkins   Co K 3rd Va Cav

By Commanding General Lee
(signed) R. H. Chilton
          AA General

For: Capt R. C. Watkins
        Co K 3rd Va Cav 7

(ed: General Samuel Cooper was the Adjutant & Inspector General of the Confederacy. Until 1864 the word haphazard would best describe the record keeping of the Confederate military departments. Finally, by 1864, General Cooper had the A. I. G. organized and had created standardized reports for most of his commands and departments. The monthly inspection reports (required of all commands) had a page for detailing Arms, Accoutrements, Ammunition, Horse Equipage, Clothing, & Camp Equipage totals and then asked for condition and deficiencies of same. This board, to which Captain R. H. Watkins is appointed,

apparently is charged with getting an accounting of weaponry prior to the January, 1864 Inspection Report.)

(ed: The orders for service on the board were written in error to Captain R. C. Watkins.)

- - - - -

Letter from Captain Richard Watkins to Mary Watkins

Camp near Charlottesville
Jany 12th 1864

My Own Dear Mary

I reached camp yesterday evening and hasten to let you know that the arduous march is over and I am still safe and sound. Have been marching in the mountains for thirty consecutive days through the severest weather that this country affords. Since leaving here the 11th Dec – have passed through Staunton, Lexington, Colliertown, Buchanan, Fincastle, Covington then almost to the Greenbriar White Sulphur, back again by the Hot Springs, Warm Springs, Jordan Springs in Rockbridge, Greenville, Staunton; then down the valley to Harrisonburg, New Market then across the mountains to Morefield, Petersburg, Burlington . . . then back again to Romney, Harrisonburg, Republic, Charlottesville. In all . . . at least 600 miles. The greatest part of the trip was made through snow & ice & sleet. The ice so smooth & glassy that often nearly the whole march of the day . . . had to be made on foot. We had not tents or shelter and I slept on the snow and under the snow. . . . Lived on hard bread & pork. Our regiment which started with 227 men and 23 officers returned with about 40 men & 4 officers the rest having fallen out on the way side some sick & others with disabled horses. . . . Well my application for a furlough has not yet returned but I hope . . . it will find its way back approved. . . . On returning to camp was greeted by your letters of 25th Dec & 1st Jany – and now sit in a tent with a chimney and a good warm fire happy in the reflection that you are well at home. On the night of 1st Janry at the very time you were writing I was making the most fearful march that I have ever conceived of. We had ascended the Alleghany Mountains one of the highest peaks along a narrow path used by scouts alone and never by citizens at all in the winter. Night overtook us on the top, the road on the North side was almost perpendicular & covered with ice & snow. Our horses could not be rode or even led but had to be turned loose and driven whilst we were slipping & falling & tumbling & grasping at trees & bushes & at men & horses. We reached the foot of the mountain. I hardly know how, my head swam & I felt like a drowning man. A biting freezing wind restored me to consciousness. I called loudly for my horse & Ned Price stopped him and gave me the reins, after marching a few miles further we went into camp for the night . . . Many were frost bitten on that night, some very seriously but how could I be with Mother's good warm gloves over my fingers and Patty's good visor over my ears. . . . Well, what did we accomplish. I fear very little for the sacrifice of men & horses: took about 100 prisoners and four or five hundred mules & horses and as many cattle. The counties of Hardy & Hampshire are under Yankee rule . . . The secessionists . . . are plundered by the Yankees and the union men by the rebels and then in addition to this is a large formidable band of robbers who style themselves Swamp Dragoons and plundered both sides. One old gentleman told me that they had robbed his house three times before his eyes of everything valuable . . .

Good evening to you now my precious one. Love and kisses to all. Will write again soon. Am very busy today Company work has been accumulating in my absence. . . . Good bye Yr Richard

(ed: Averell's objective was the Virginia and Tennessee Railroad at either Bonsack's Station in Botetourt County or Salem in Roanoke County. "At Salem the Federals destroyed miles of track, five bridges and the depot filled with railroad repair supplies, food stores, and leather goods.") 8

- - - - -

Captain R. H. Watkins – Request for Leave

Camp 3rd Va Cavalry
Janry 13th 1864

I most respectfully ask leave of absence from Camp for twenty days to visit my family in the County of Prince Edward. I have had no furlough of indulgence since February last. My 1st 2nd & Repl 2nd Lieutenant are all present for duty.

I have the honor to be
      R H Watkins Capt
      Co K 3 Va Cav

To: R H Chilton AAG
      ANV 9

(ed: Richard's request was approved on Jan. 15th 1864. On March 3, 1864 Richard will depart Farmville for Richmond to return to Co K of the 3rd Virginia Cavalry.)

- - - - -

Letter from Mary Watkins to Captain Richard Watkins

Linden Jan 17th

My Darling Husband

. . . I can not bear to think of the suffering and hardships you must have endured in that Averill campaign. I think those who went through with it all ought certainly to be promoted or if they prefer should be allowed the privilege of spending the remainder of the winter at home. Suppose you propose something of the sort to Gen Lee? Do you think he would treat it with contempt? . . .

Little Mary has two teeth and Emmie says is the smartest baby she ever heard of. She knows her name and answers when she is called . .

. One of her eyes is a good deal larger than the other and I am afraid will disfigure her. . . .

Tom burnt & planted last week. They are clearing and plowing now. Minnie is bothering me so I hardly know what I am writing . . . If I hear you are not coming home . . . will write again. Good bye. I want to see you so bad.
Your loving
Mary

- - - - -

Letter from Mary Watkins to Captain Richard Watkins

Sunday evening March 6th 1864

My Darling Husband

. . . I felt so disappointed when Mama got back from Farmville Friday to hear that you had been ordered to Richmond. I did not tell you good bye for good Thursday morning but fully expected to see you home again in a few days . . .

Emmie was right sick for two days . . . she sleeps with me now and I am right glad to have the company. . . . Mary has just cut two more teeth which accounts for her being so fretful for a few days past. She has been good as ever since she cut them.

I believe Mama has become entirely reconciled to [the] Government's taking her mules since she heard how the Yankees damaged Cousin Willie Walkers and says she could not believe anybody . . . as barbarous as Dahlgreen and his command. . . . There was an eloquent address from Gov. Vance to the North Carolinians in Saturdays *Enquirer* . . . I think from his speech that there must be a great deal of disloyalty among the North Carolinians.

. . . I must have my letter ready soon, ought to have sent it Monday. . . . All send love.

From your loving
Mary

(ed: The "Kilpatrick Raid" departed from the Union lines near Ely's Ford with a force of some 3,585 troopers to skirt Lee's army and attack Richmond. They departed on February 28ᵗʰ and at Spotsylvania 500 men under Col. Ulric Dahlgren split off to head a bit further west and cross the James upstream of Richmond and attack Rickmond from the west while Kilpatrick attacked from the north. Kilpatrick stalled in front of the Richmond defenses that were manned by old men, boys and government clerks. The cavalry of General Wade Hampton then arrived in his rear and drove him eastward across the Chickahominy toward the Pamunkey and Tunstall's Station. Dahlgren was unable to cross the James and pursue his goal of entering Richmond to free prisoners at Libby and Belle Isle prison camps. Dahlgren was killed when his force was attacked by the cavalry of Genl. Fitz Lee between the Pamunkey and the Mattaponi. Kilpatrick retreated down the peninsula to Yorktown. Instead of freeing prisoners, some 300 Union troopers were added to the prison population and they lost over 1000 horses. When the South learned that Kilpatrick's mission, included in a set of instructions found with Dahlgren, also included destroying bridges, burning the "hateful city of Richmond", and attempting to capture Jefferson Davis and other Rebel leaders, it sparked feelings and comments like those expressed by Mary Watkins.) 10

(ed: Inflation has almost doubled since November 21ˢᵗ. It now takes $30 Confederate to equal $1 U. S. The Confederate dollar is worth about 3 1/3 cents.) 11

‒ ‒ ‒ ‒ ‒

Richmond & Orange CoHo
March 8 to May 1, 1864

On March 10, 1864, General U. S. Grant is promoted to the rank of Lt. General and is given command of all Union armies. On April 17th General Grant cancels all exchanges of prisoners. This is a very unpopular move, both North and South, but General Grant realizes that the South cannot replace its lost manpower. This gives the North a huge advantage in a war of attrition.

General Banks invades Louisiana in a drive up the Red River. He is met and defeated in the battles of Sabine Crossroads and Pleasant Hill in early April. He retreats all the way to New Orleans. General Grant places General William Sherman in charge of the Union armies that will move against Atlanta and the Army of Tennessee. General Grant himself comes east to command overall operations against General Lee and the Army of Northern Virginia.

Richard writes Mary a note in early March to let her know he has deposited another $500 in their account to help her with paying taxes. They not only have their taxes to pay but also the 10% crop tithes to the government as crops are harvested and a 10% tithe, also in produce, to support indigent soldiers' families. In addition, the government impressment agents can drop in unannounced and impress additional grain and livestock. Many farmers hide a certain amount of grain to be sure they have seed for crops in the coming year.

Richard relates his efforts in Richmond looking for 200 pounds of rags and a hairbrush that Mary had requested. Prices are out of sight and selection is minimal. Richard receives orders to report to General Wickham in Orange, Virginia, to serve on a Board of Inquiry to fix the value of arms and equipage, for each soldier, and whether said arms and equipage are private or public property. This is being done for every soldier in every command. Richard really enjoys eating at "the General's table" since he has "a splendid cow . . . and 17 hens."

Mary writes that she is sending Purnall with another horse for Richard. However, when Purnall arrives Richard writes that the sorrel is in no better shape than the bay. Mrs. Dupuy is sending a box with some meat and bread to Richard and his messmates. Mary advises Richard that feed for the stock on the farms is running low and work horses have been breaking down. She also lets him know his mother is not doing well.

Inflation, failing farms, inadequate horses, rising tolls of dead and wounded, collapsing railroads, increasing desertions, and the lack of food and clothing for the troops all combine to paint a very bleak outlook for the Confederacy in the late spring of 1864.

Letter from Captain Richard Watkins to Mary Watkins

Cousin Barrett's Office
Richmond, Va
March 8ᵗʰ 1864

My Dear Dear Mary

We reached this place yesterday morning . . . Are now encamped on the Meadow Bridge Road about three miles from the city . . . we are still without tents . . . All seem gratified and rejoiced at the Exchange of Prisoners which is going on. Have not been able to learn yet whether Jacob Morton has been exchanged . . . Hear that the Yankees took every horse and mule that [Dr. Walker] had and six or eight of his negroes. Quite a severe loss especially as most of his horses are thorough-bred and very valuable.

. . . I deposited five hundred dollars additional for you to aid in paying taxes. After the 1ˢᵗ April will draw my pay in new issue and send you five hundred more . . . We will probably remain in Richmond a few weeks until a regular force for the protection of the city can be organized and then go back to Orange. . . .

Willie Dupuy, John Daniel and Jno Redd have just come in dripping with rain & each one with a broad smile on his face. Looking like soldiers indeed – Well good bye my own dear one. . . .
Yr own
Richard

(ed: In a note from Hanover Junction on March 13ᵗʰ Richards tells Mary that, "Like yourself . . . both of us have been considerably demoralized by my long, delightful furlough and . . . the prospect of [me] moving still further from you and going again to the Army of Northern Virginia as we are likely to do. . . .)

- - - - -

Letter from Mary Watkins to Captain Richard Watkins

Linden March 14th 1864

My dear Husband

... I am going to take advantage of your offer to get me some things in Richmond. In the first place I want some stamps, next I want about two hundred lbs. of rags from the tailors. I have taken a notion to have my room carpeted next winter ... Nannie wants a hair brush and a spool of black cotton will close my list. ...

It is past bedtime ... I suspect it will be raining tomorrow and I can write more ... Minnie asked me the other day what message you send her in your letter, sent his love I replied. I am much obliged to him she said very demurely. Goodnight
Your loving
Mary

- - - - -

Letter from Captain Richard Watkins to Mary Watkins

Camp near Richmond
March 17th 1864

My Darling Mary

Thanks again for another nice letter. I know you are the best wife in the world. ... Will go to town today and try to fill yr memorandum though tis very doubtful about the rags. Such things are in great demand I reckon. ... Am glad indeed to hear that the impressing agent has returned so many of the horses and mules. Would rather that he should have kept mine and returned both of mothers.

... Went down and inquired of Cousin Barrett about the chances of getting rags. He says the Government has contracted for all but he thinks that from a good Methodist friend of his he will be able to get as many as 200 pounds for you ... I then undertook to find a hairbrush and ... there is not one for sale today on Main Street. I then came to Broad and Powhatan ... where a few very indifferent ones could be found at $30 and $35 dollars apiece. ... I send two spools black cotton ... I sent no 9 & 10 as I suppose they are most generally used.

I send some stamps. If we remain here until after the 1st April will try to buy you some things not on yr memorandum. ... At present the prices are extravagent on account of the tax upon the old money. Our Quartermaster is owing me $500 or $600 dollars which I will not draw until 1st April. This money I have earned in the Army and I have a perfect right to spend it replenishing your wardrobe. ...

Good bye now darling. I love you more than ever. Kiss the children for me & tell them Papa wants to see them very very much. Much love to all. ...

I hope Mr Holt is doing well and relieving you of the care of the plantation. If he does not he is not accomplishing the main purpose for which I employed him. – Write to me every day. Goodbye Yr own Richard

- - - - -

Letter from Mary Watkins to Captain Richard Watkins

March 22nd 1864

My dear Husband

Purnall starts with your horse this evening and I will write a letter to send by him. ... Have given him a week's rations and $30 to pay his expenses. ... Little Mary is as delighted as I am with sunshine. She stays outdoors nearly all day and is as lively as a cricket ... Mr Baker came in the morning and told Mama that two of his horses had given out at the plow so she had to put her carriage horses in again.

I dread this summers campaign more than any we have ever had. I shall feel anxious and uneasy all the time. How I wish you were at home. . . .

Well I believe I will stop now. . . . Good bye from your own
Mary

- - - - -

Letter from Mary Watkins to Captain Richard Watkins

Linden March 24th 1864

My dear Husband

I have thought so much about you this cold, snowy weather. Hope you have comfortable tents with chimneys . . . Mama is going to send you a small box tomorrow, says she has nothing but meat and bread to put in it, but she thinks you will be glad for anything that will satisfy your hunger. . . .

My cold . . . and the children's colds are better . . . the children have all been exposed to the measles and it is about time for them to show some symptoms . . . if they are going to have it. . . .

(ed: Letter incomplete. Richard arrives unexpectedly for a couple of nights.)

- - - - -

Letter from Captain Richard Watkins to Mary Watkins

Richmond March 30th 64

My Darling Mary

I reached Richmond last evening in safety. The cars densely crowded and the rain pouring in torrents the whole way. . . . Well, on reaching Richmond found Jno Redd & Willy Dupuy waiting for me & glad enough to get sight of their boxes. . . . repaired to Cousin Barretts HeadQuarters and spent the night. This morning . . . chartered a wagon & took boxes to Camp. Had not been in camp 20 minutes when . . . I was delivered . . . with the compliments of Dr Walker & his lady . . . the nicest treat that I have ever seen in the Army. The nicest ham & bread & butter & cakes of various sorts . . . It was sent to Willy Dupuy & myself. . . . Just as I was congratulating myself on the high living . . . an order was handed me (BAH!) from Gen Fitz Lee to report in person alone to Gen. Wickham near Orange Courthouse for temporary duty as a member of a Board of Officers to . . . enquire into the right of property in all the arms in Wickham's Brigade. What is the consequence? Why simply tis our box is unopened & contents of the basket all to be turned over to the boys . . . again at Cousin Barretts HeadQuarters tonite to take the Central train at 6 o'clock AM tomorrow with a haversack containing a few biscuits and a small fraction of ham. . . .

How is my dear dear Ma. Oh how anxious I feel concerning her. . . . Please write me and have Patty to write me all about her condition. . . . Letter writing will do very well for all business . . . but it is a poor poor medium through which to communicate one's feeling to a sick mother. . . . Oh may a merciful God . . . restore her again to health and happiness. . . . Give much love to all . . . Good bye precious one – write often and still direct to Richmond.
Richard

- - - - -

Letter from Captain Richard Watkins to Mary Watkins

Hdqtrs Wickhams Brigade
near Orange Courthouse Apr 4th 64

My own Dear Mary

When I last wrote was about to leave Richmond for Genl Wickhams Headquarters . . . arrived here Thursday evening after a fatiguing ride on the Railroad (from Gordonsville in a Box Car) and still more tiresome march of two miles & a half from Orange CoHo carrying my baggage. The General recd me very cordially, gave me a seat at his table and . . . I began to feel almost at home. The business of the Board . . . is to ascertain the 'status' of all the arms and equipments of each officer and soldiers in the Brigade, whether they are private or public property: if private to fix a value and report it. All private arms & equipments in the Command are after that time to be considered public, the men to be paid the value assessed and hereafter to be held accountable for their loss or destruction. Of course we have a tedious job, but I hope to get through in five or six days and return to the Regiment, though I may possibly be here 8 or 10 days more. . . .

Since my arrival we have had every conceivable variety of bad weather, and the snow is now falling thick & fast – I am in a comfortable tent though with a plenty of good wheat straw & heavy blankets . . . Twould amuse you to see how the General is fixed. He has a splendid cow & a hen house with seventeen hens &c. So we have very nice egg bread butter & milk, nice ham, peas rice &c &c. Oh what a wide difference between the fare of a Genl & a private. – Tis two dark to write more & must close till tomorrow . . .

April 5th – Still hailing and raining. . . . "Capt – come to breakfast" says the General. Bless his dear old heart my appetite is as keen as a razor . . . we all sit with hats on eat fast & keep up a lively chat. The breakfast is soon over and I find myself again at the desk. . . . Good bye my precious one. Write to me every day. Kiss the children for me again & again.
Yr own
Richard

- - - - -

Letter from Mary Watkins to Captain Richard Watkins

Linden Apr. 11th 1864

My dear Husband

... What dreadful weather we have had for the crops. I am afraid there will not be half a crop made in this part of the country. Mama's feed for stock cattle and stock of all kinds is out and she has sent over today to borrow a load of tops from Mr Holt. Poor old Mr. Ned Dillon ... his whole family are sick with measles, he has no meat, but two barrels of corn, his horse has died, somebody has broken open his mill and stolen a bag of his meal, his oxen had given out for want of food and the poor old man came over to see if Mama could haul a stack of straw from Dick Scott's for him ...

April 12th. I have just received a note from Pattie saying that Mother is not so well. Uncle Aleck has just been for Dr Owen ... her appetite was very poor and she thought she could relish some fried chicken ...

Little Mary is enjoying the pleasant day. I heard her laughing just now ... She is just as good as can be ... I don't nurse her but twice a day now. ... Dabney Norval told Mr Holt that he would have to go before the <u>Board</u> again in a few days ... Mama advised Mr H to stay at home and attend to his business and let the "Board" alone until he was notified by the proper officers to appear before it. Mr Baker has already been notified. ... Good bye
Your loving
Mary

(ed: Each county has a board to evaluate residents who hold an exemption from military service. If deemed healthy and able to serve the board can cancel their exemption and they will be drafted into the service. The overseers at both Linden and Oldham could lose their exemptions.)

- - - - -

Letter from Captain Richard Watkins to Mary Watkins

Hdqrs Wickham's Brigade
April 12th 1864

My Precious Mary –

I would give anything in the world to see you this evening . . . I expect to return to the 3ʳᵈ Reg again, which is still near Richmond. My time has in some respects been very pleasantly spent here . . . Our camp is on the Montpelier Estate only a few hundred yards from the residence which is the most majestic and beautiful country residence that I have ever seen. It still bears the impressive character of Madison. . . .

Well the campaign will soon open and if the Yanks get to Richmond it will be over the bodies of many slain. I think Genl Lee is preparing to give Grant a warm reception. And the health and spirit of the Army is most excellent. . . . Hope to get back to my regiment in a day or two. . . Kiss my little girls often for me. Give a great deal of love to Ma & all at Mr Redds.
Yr own
Richard

— — — — —

Letter from Captain Richard Watkins to Mary Watkins

Hdqtrs Cousin Barrett
Richmond April 14ᵗʰ 64

My Precious Mary

Finished my work at Genl Wickhams . . . and came back to Richmond this evening to rejoin the Regt tomorrow. Regret to say that the Reg leaves for Fredericksburg tomorrow . . . Found Cousin Barrett quite well . . . told me to send you all his love . . . I will send you every bit of mine. I am in fine health and as homesick a poor fellow as you ever saw. . . . I dread the approaching campaign . . . No news at all in Richmond. Write to me often Darling and I will love you for it but the more. . . . Good night my Mary
Yr own
Richard

(ed: A small note from Richard dated the 17ᵗʰ of April, "Dear Mary – My bay horse is unfit for service & Mr Woolton goes home today after a fresh horse. Please let Purnall or some other of the servants bring my sorrel horse so that he can take my bay horse home. Let him come with Mr. Woolton. Good bye Yr own Richard")

- - - - -

Letter from Captain Richard Watkins to Mary Watkins

Orange CoHo
April 22ⁿᵈ 1864

My Precious Mary

...Just as we reached Guiney's Station about 20 miles from Fredbg recd from Genl Stuart an order to return to Orange CoHo and be present at the trial of our Col. Owen before a Court Martial for suffering some of the men of our regiment to go home after fresh horses without proper authority....I concluded that I was summoned as a witness ...A train of flat cars happened to be passing as I recd the order. I got ... aboard and in a few moments was enjoying a very airish ride back in the direction of Hanover Junction. . . . Found that I had been sent for to appear as counsel for Col ... found the Court was composed entirely of officers of inferior rank to the Col which is contrary to regulations . . . the trial is indefinitely postponed and I am out of the scrape ...

Tomorrow I go to Richmond and Monday to Fredericksburg. Am staying at present with a Mr. Hiden in a very fine brick house . . . Col. Owen and several of his Captains & Lieutenants . . . are with me. . . .

As to Mr. Holt, tell him for me that I sign no petition to keep any man out of the army who is able to do duty. I am truly glad that he is at my home, attending to my business and relieving you of a large share of your cares. But whenever he feels able to come to the Army or a properly constituted Medical Board decides that he is able I want him to "lay down the shovel & hoe" and come along like a man....Tell him if he has to come to the Army to commit his family to God as I have done with mine and he will certainly take care of them.

...Good bye now. I want to write more but tis growing dark – Much love & many Kisses.
Yr own
Richard

- - - - -

Letter from Captain Richard Watkins to Mary Watkins

Camp near Fredericksburg
April 28th 1864

My Darling Mary

Purnall came here two days ago and I thank you much for sending him . . . The horse though is in no better condition than the bay. Neither of them serviceable and I hardly know what to do. To buy another would cost $2000 . . . I have therefore determined to keep Purnall here as we are now getting corn enough and excellent grass, and by close attention to get them in better condition.

Purnall though is too valuable a boy to be exposed to all the evil influences of camp life and I would be glad if you could . . . dress up Andy and send him and I will send Purnall back. . . . send Andy by the first opportunity as Purnall has no clothes. I have been summoned this morning to appear before the Court Martial in Col. Owens case (as a witness this time). The court will sit at Milford Station.

Recd lately excellent letters from Nannie & Patty . . . will try to answer them as soon as possible.

Please tell Mr. Holt to prize my tobacco and send it to market. – Give love to all . . . Goodbye
Yr own
Richard

- - - - -

Letter from Mary Watkins to Captain Richard Watkins

Apr 29th 1864

My dear Husband

…Mama has gone to the Depot this evening, Sister Maria, Lavallette, Emmie, Minnie and Edna have walked down to see Mrs. Baker's <u>fine</u> <u>girl</u> and Little Mary and I have quiet possession of the house. . . . Have concluded to let Emmie go with Sister Maria [to Danville for a visit] and they will start tomorrow. . . . I believe the prospect of hearing Uncle Abner play on the violin . . . keeps her in the notion.

Received your letter this morning and was glad to hear that Purnall reached you safely. Archer Haskins is the only member of the Troop at home that I know of and am considering how to send Andy to you. How will it do to send him to Cousin Barrett . . . and get him to put him on the train to Fredericksburg writing you what day to meet him? Please write me immediately whether this will do . . .

I had rheumatism and head aches a good deal the first of this week but am better. . . . I am afraid you will think after awhile that I am made up of grunts and groans and old aching bones. Please now don't feel uneasy about me. My rheumatism don't generally last more than one or two days and I will write you if there is anything the matter with me.

Believe I will go to the Depot tomorrow and see Sister Maria and Emmie off. I really dread for them to go. We will be so lonesome. . . .

Good night
Mary

Apr 30th Emmie sends her love to Papa and says I must tell him goodbye she has gone with Auntie. Sister Maria sends her love to you.

(ed: This is the first of many visits to Danville by the Watkins girls. This will be an ongoing event in the childhood lives of all of Richard and Mary's girls.)

- - - - -

Letter from Captain Richard Watkins to Mary Watkins

Camp near Fredericksburg
May 1, 1864

My Darling Mary

I send Purnall home today. Am afraid that he is going to be sick. He appears quite unwell and seems to have some fever. Has probably taken cold from sleeping in the open air. Has been sleeping with Lee Redd's servant and says that he has slept warm, last night though … I took him in my tent made him a good bed and wrapped him in one of my blankets and I slept quite comfortably with my other blanket & overcoat. Since John Knight left us have been sleeping by myself.

My health and that of the Troop is excellent. Not a sick man amongst us. All quiet in front with occasional rumors of an advance of the Yankees. Active operations will doubtless soon begin. In the meantime I want to get Andy here. Please send him down at once to Cousin Barrett and he will send him to me. No time to write more at present. Give much love to all – I want to see you too bad.
Yr own
Richard

- - - - -

Spotsylvania to Richmond
May 5 to June 28, 1864

The spring campaigns open and the volume of killed and wounded soldiers is beyond belief. In Virginia there are huge battles at The Wilderness, Spotsylvania, and Cold Harbor. In Georgia the armies clash at Resaca, Adairsville, Cassville, Allatoona, Dallas, New Hope Church and Kennesaw Mountain. General Grant slips away from General Lee, crosses the James River and attacks Petersburg. General Hunter is leading a cavalry raid in the Shenandoah Valley destroying railroads, farms and mills.

On June 7th the Union Party nominates Abraham Lincoln and Andrew Johnson for President and Vice President of the United States.

Mary writes Richard on May 5th to advise that the corn is almost all planted and also two acres of sorghum. Minnie has gone fishing with Aunt Lettie and their little Mary is starting to crawl. On May 13th little Mary will be one year old. A big thunderstorm hit the night of May 24th and 13 hams were stolen from the smokehouse at Linden. In early June she forwards a letter from Mr. Holt with a farm report and late in the month typhoid fever is active in the neighborhood. Mary is sending Richard a pair of lead gray pants and is having a pair of boots made for $225. It bothers her to think of her husband being barefooted and that she can't help him.

"We are fighting every day" and yesterday had a terrific fight "holding a position until Longstreet's Corps could reach it." Richard is writing from Spotsylvania and the 3rd Virginia cavalry, fighting dismounted, has provided perhaps their finest day of service for the Army of Northern Virginia in holding this key crossroads against superior forces. In a letter written on June 14th Richard describes the battle at Trevilian Station against the cavalry of General Sheridan. Richard has another horse break down and picks up his correspondence with three excellent letters detailing action at Haws Shop, Cold Harbor and Bottom's Bridge protecting the right flank of Lee's army. In late June he describes chasing Sheridan and having four men from Co K wounded at the White House on the Pamunkey. He writes Mary with great concern about a Union raid in Prince Edward while the 3rd Virginia is chasing Sheridan to Trevilian Station. They are successful in preventing a junction between the forces of General Sheridan and General Hunter for operations against Lynchburg. Richard notes that since the start of campaigning in May he thinks the 3rd Virginia Cavalry has lost 25% of its men killed, wounded or missing.

The losses mount and there are no replacements. The Confederate reservoir of manpower is exhausted.

Letter from Mary Watkins to Captain Richard Watkins

Linden, May 5th 1864

My dear Husband

I am afraid you will think I am not so prompt . . . in sending Andy down, but the boy has worn out all of [his winter] clothes and I had to make him a new suit . . . and a pair of shoes . . . I will wait until Monday and get Cousin Barrett to forward him to Fredericksburg Tuesday (May 10th). Hope you will not be ordered off before this time. Mr. Ewing told me Monday that he was going down to see his boys this week and would take charge of Andy, but he has postponed his visit for a week or two now. Purnall reached here safely Monday . . .

I rode over home on Lizzie Leigh Monday . . . Mr. Holt said he thought he should finish planting corn in about two days . . . he has planted nearly two acres of sorghum. I must be on the look out for a mill to crush the cane. I told him you wanted the tobacco prized and sent to market . . . and he said he would attend to it. . . . I had no idea that I should miss Emmie so much, could not help crying when I bid her goodbye at the Depot. After the first train came down she got frightened at the whistle and put her arms around my neck with her eyes full of tears and said she wanted to go home with me. Sister Maria wrote that she stood the trip well . . . and full of fun . . . since she reached Danville. She and Uncle Abner were firm friends . . . Meat and bread seems to be in greater demand than anything else about here except horses and teams to work the crop. Mama's old carriage horses Bob and Jim died last week, they had been plowing all day and died at night within a few days of each other. Every few nights Uncle Hal comes for sage or pepper to drench a horse or mule that has given out during the day. . . .

I asked Minnie what I should tell Papa and she says "tell him I went with Aunt Lettie fishing and saw a little monkey lying on a rock, a great big little monkey with white under his neck and he was lying

just so." . . . have written just what Minnie told me. Lavallette says she can't imagine . . . but remembers Minnie telling her on the way home that she saw one. Mary is the sweetest, liveliest little puss you ever saw, she is beginning to crawl and can call . . . chicken or cat. Have come to the end of my paper before I knew it. Must write Cousin Barrett now.
Goodbye.
Your own
Mary

- - - - -

Letter from Mary Watkins to Captain Richard Watkins

Linden May 6th 1864

My darling Husband

I have felt real unhappy all day because I have not sent Andy . . . I saw in the paper this morning that they were expecting a battle very soon and I have felt uneasy and miserable all day . . . My candle went out Friday night while I was writing and I had to go to bed as there was no fire to light another by. Minnie went to church today for the first time in her life . . .

May 9th – I shall send Andy to the Depot this morning but doubt very much if he can go farther. There are a great many rumors afloat about Yankee raiders & they were reported to be six miles below Burkeville Junction Saturday and a good many men from this neighborhood went down there last night. . . .

Old Mr. McCormick spent the day here last week on his way to see Beverly who is in the Hospital in Farmville . . .

I am perfectly well now . . . I reckoned had taken a cold but am as well as ever now. . . . Wish I could have sent your boy to you before the battles commenced. Mama has begun to hurry me already though it

is only ten o'clock and the cars do not come until one. Good bye. I want to see you so much.
Your own
Mary

(ed: General Grant has launched his offensive against General Lee and as Mary writes her letters on May 5 & 6 the armies are engaged in the Battle of the Wilderness.)

- - - - -

Letter from Captain Richard Watkins to Mary Watkins

Camp near Spottsylvania CoHo
May 9th 1864

My Precious Mary

I have only time this morning to write you that I am well. We are fighting every day now, had a most terrific fight yesterday on foot against infantry, holding a position until Longstreets Corps could reach it. Am happy to say though that although many were killed & wounded in the Regiment and some taken prisoner, only one of my company recd a wound, John Baker was slightly wounded in the shoulder. It seems almost like a miracle. The bugle calls to horse and I must bid you good bye.

May God bless and protect you & our dear children . . . Accounts of the fighting done by our infantry is cheering but the issue of the battles is still undecided. Again good bye. Give love to all. I love you dearly.
Yr own
Richard

(ed: The cavalry troopers of General Fitz Lee and General Rosser had the job of holding the crossroads at Spotsylvania Courthouse until Longstreet's Corp, under the command of General Richard Anderson, could arrive. Greatly outnumbered, by the Union forces under General Sheridan and General Warren, the Confederate cavalry fought dismounted and held the

crossroads as the Confederate infantry, who marched through the night, came running to their support with no time to spare.) 1

- - - - -

Letter from Mary Watkins to Captain Richard Watkins

Linden
May 12th 1864

My darling Husband

I think of you all the time now and feel so anxious . . . I have not received a line from you since Purnall came home. . . . Uncle Joe and several gentlemen advised us not to send Andy, after he got to the Depot, so Mama brought him home . . .

We had a fine rain . . . which was very much needed. The grass and trees look so green and fresh now, and the wheat on Goodes Hill shows very prettily from the window. . . . The martins have taken possession of their houses in the yard and are chattering away at a great rate. . . . Emmie . . . well and very happy . . . I am so afraid something will happen to her or the Yankees will get the railroad so I can't get her home. We heard yesterday that they had possession of the South Side road and that Petersburg would probably fall into their hands and Mama wants to start right off for Emmie and bring her home Saturday. . . . these are certainly times that try mens souls.

. . . walked over home Monday evening. Everything looks so sweet and quiet over there. Mrs. Holt was . . . fixing to set up her loom. Lucy has a right fine girl born Monday morning. Mr. Holt finished planting corn last week and is weeding now.

Little Mary will be a year old tomorrow. Don't reckon I shall ever forget that day. . . . Wrote to you day before yesterday and have not much to write now. . . . Good bye. That your life and health may be spared is the constant prayer of

Your own
Mary

- - - - -

Letter from Captain Richard Watkins to Mary Watkins

Camp near Richmond
May 14th 1864 [letter dated April in error]

My Precious Mary

God in his infinite mercy still spares my life and that of every member of my Company. We have been steadily fighting against great odds for 8 or 9 days. Our brigade & the whole company has suffered greatly and it seems miraculous that our company has been so fortunate. We have been in all the fights & right along with the rest. John Baker, Frank Jenkins & Wm Woolton slightly wounded the rest not hurt at all. Wm Dupuy is certainly well too. We hear a rumor this morning that the Yankees are on the Danville road but hope tis not true. Whatever may happen Darling still trust implicitly in God & he will sustain & comfort & protect you. May his blessing be on you and our dear children & friends. Give much love to all. Would write more but have not time.
Yr own
Richard

(ed: With the constant action of the battles of the Wilderness and Spotsylvania, and the related cavalry movements, Richard is exhausted and makes dating mistakes on a couple of his letters. It is even possible that this letter was written on the 13th. John Baker was wounded at Spotsylvania and that confirms that May is the correct month.) 2

- - - - -

Letter from Captain Richard Watkins to Mary Watkins

near Hanover CoHo
May 21 1864

My Precious Mary

We are all still alive and well every member of the Troop. – No fighting since my last by our Brigade but the enemy is still threatening and contest is undecided.

John Knight reached us yesterday. Am very glad to have him with me as Haskins & Meredith are both at home sick. . . . Genl Lee & Grant still remain in the same positions and another great battle must ensue . . . I wish constantly that I could be with you but every man's services are now demanded in the Army. The crisis seems to have arrived. . . . It will be best not to send Andy till affairs become more settled. Write to me often & give a great deal of love to all the dear ones at home . – Our Army still in good spirits & confident of success. . . . Take good care of yourself now and I hope you will not be troubled again with rheumatism. Write me all about Ma & everybody at Mr. Redds. Has Nat been heard from lately. Heard that Wise's Brigade had been in Pr. Edward. – Good bye my dear dear one. I long to be with you again.
Yr own
Richard

(ed: There is no letter mentioning the death of General Stuart at Yellow Tavern. Perhaps a letter was written between his May 14th and May 21st letters and was lost.)

- - - - -

Letter from Mary Watkins to Captain Richard Watkins

Linden May 24th 1864

My darling Husband

It has been some time since I wrote you, but one or two of my letters were still in our P. O. a few days ago . . . May 25th . . . it is quite cool and pleasant this morning, very favorable weather for the wounded soldiers. We fixed a box last week to send to one of the Hospitals in Richmond . . . Mama and Aunt Sarah are going to send a box today. . . . Mrs. Foster . . . received a telegram that her husband was wounded . . . she started immediately to him, on her way to the Depot though she met a servant coming to tell her that he was dead. I don't believe I have ever felt as sorry for any one in my life . . . We had the severest storm here Monday night about nine o'clock that I ever saw. It thundered and lightened so that Lillie, Nannie and I put away our work . . . as soon as the storm was over I went into the porch to brush my teeth and thought the smoke house door looked . . . open. . . . We were all undressed but ran right out to see and found it even so. . . . Thirteen pieces of meat gone. We called up all the negro men . . . sent for Mr. Baker and began to track the rogues . . . by dark the next evening had recovered nine pieces of meat . . . what we recovered weighed 126 lbs. . . .

I go over home occasionally. They seem to be getting on right smoothly . . . I feel a great deal better to have some one over there though. Fancy has a pretty colt. Her other was a year old before this was born. Received a note from Pattie this morning she said Mother was coming down to see me soon. She had just heard from Bro Nat. He was well. 11 of his company were dead. My paper is out.
Your own
Mary

- - - - -

Letter from Captain Richard Watkins to Mary Watkins

Camp near Hanover CoHo
May 26th 1864

My own Dear Mary – I had just seated myself on a log to write you when your sweet little letter of the 12th was handed me. Oh tis so kind & good in you to continue to write when you do not hear from me. You must not think me forgetful . . . This is the fourth or fifth that I have written since Purnall left but . . . they seem not to have reached you. . . . Since my last which I hope you have now recd our

Brigade has done no fighting. At present though I am not with my company, they together with the greater portion of our Regiment went on a scout a few days since. My horse was in such bad condition the Col. told me that I need not go . . .

The Army of Northern Va as you have doubtless learned from the papers has fallen back behind the North Anna River, the greater part is said to be about Hanover Junction . . . Genl Lee knows what is best. His army has not yet been either routed or defeated, but I believe have had the advantage in every encounter with Grants forces – Genl Grant though seems to have maneuvered Genl Lee out of his position on the Rapidan after finding that he could not drive him from it. God will ultimately I trust grant us the victory.

. . . Hope the time is not far distant when I can be with you again. Give a great deal of love to everybody and write me again soon. I love you dearly. Good bye
Yr own
Richard

- - - - -

Letter from Captain Richard Watkins to Mary Watkins

Camp near Gaines' Mill
June 1, 1864

Darling – I am still well. Since my last we have been engaged in another severe fight with a loss to our company of one killed (Jas Wilson) and one severely wounded (Wm Binford) & two slightly wounded. James Wilson was an excellent boy . . . and I think a fine Christian. We sincerely regret his loss. This campaign is even more active than that of last year. We are going nearly all the time and almost every day are fighting . . . I thank you . . . for your last dated the 24th. . . . The bugle calls to horse again and I must close. Will write you again just as soon as I can find time. Much love to all. I love you oh too dearly. Good by
Yr

Richard

(ed: The casualties were suffered at the Battle of Haws Shop. Notes on the Co K roster, in the Richard Watkins collection, record Wilson, J. H. killed at Hawes Shop and Elliott, R. C. wounded at Hawes Shop. In Appendix One, Binford, Wm B. is shown as being wounded in the right ribs. There is no notation to indicate the name of the other slightly wounded soldier.)
3

- - - - -

Letter from Captain Richard Watkins to Mary Watkins

Camp near Gaines' Mill
June 1, 1864

My Precious Mary

I wrote you a short letter this morning but as Leigh Redd is going home and the Yanks are tolerably quiet . . . will write again. During the whole of the month of May we have been in a whirl. In the saddle at least sixteen hours a day watching, skirmishing, fighting. Of our Regiment about one fourth of those reported for duty the 1st of May have been killed wounded or captured. . . . The rest are well hearty in fine spirits and bountifully supplied with rations of excellent bacon and hard bread and plenty of ammunition. Genl. R. E. Lee has recd large reinforcements. His army . . . is well equipped, well fed in fine spirits & if Grant enters Richmond he will certainly display more skill and his troops more courage than I think they possess.

. . . Yesterday we were skirmishing with the enemy on the old battlefield of Gaines Mill but as the fight began to wax warm a portion of Beauregard's infantry came in and relieved us & the darkness of night relieved them. . . . we were carried into a fine clover field and have spent the day grazing our horses. Dr. Gaines farm is on the north of the Chickahominy. A beautiful place with a large proportion of low grounds. These are all in cultivation but the Yankee Raiders took all of the Dr's negroes . . . and all the operations of the farm are suspended. . . . The war seems to be increasing in intensity. The fights are more frequent & more deadly. . . . Tell [Sue] I wish she could see Willy Dupuy and Buck & Horace Booker in a fight. If she could see their coolness & composure and self possession she would be proud . . . I have not seen any better soldiers than these three . . .

In three more days comes my thirty ninth birthday . . . if I only had Leigh Redds horse detail & was a private instead of an officer – Ah! I don't know that at the present juncture of cav[alry] ops I ought to go home even if I were a private with an unserviceable horse. . . . This seems to be the crisis, the turning point of the war . . . But if all was quiet and Grant were not threatening Richmond would I not be too happy to eat a birthday dinner with you. . . . Give much love to Mother & all at home & kiss the children for me everyday.
Yr
Richard

- - - - -

Letter from Captain Richard Watkins to Mary Watkins

Camp near Bottoms Bridge
June 6th 1864

My Darling Mary

Since my last we have done very little fighting. Genl Grants forces made one assault upon Genl Lee's lines & were repulsed with heavy slaughter. . . . Our Brigade . . . have been acting as pioneers for the infantry. We keep on the extreme right of our army and as Grant shows a disposition to move in this direction we throw up entrenchments, hold them until our infantry arrives . . . move farther to the right upon another road and throw up earthworks again. The task is very laborious and the constant watching, fighting, working begins to make us all look a little care worn & haggard. The sick list is largely increased . . . Really tis so hard to get stationery away off here and keep it always at hand and tis so seldom an opportunity

[for] officers writing & of sending a letter off that I feel it my duty to send what few I write to you . . .

The Yanks went to Genl Wickhams in Hanover a few days ago took about 80 negroes, all of his horses, cattle &c his clothes almost everything that he & his family had and destroyed his furniture even breaking the locks off the doors.

No time to write more at present as the letters are about to be carried off. Good bye. I love you dearly – Give love to everybody & if Emmie has come write me what she says about Danville. Kiss our dear children for me. May God deal mercifully with you.
Yr own
Richard

(ed: Richard is making reference to the Battle of Cold Harbor when he notes, "repulsed with heavy slaughter." Exact casualty figures are varied but in less than one hour some 7,000 Union troops fell killed or wounded in front of the Confederate trenches. The Union officers and troops refused to launch two additional attacks that General Grant ordered.) 4

- - - - -

Letter from Mary Watkins to Captain Richard Watkins

Linden, June 10th 1864

My dear Husband

. . . Mama went to Danville yesterday for Emmie . . . I have had three right bad cases of dysentery to doctor since Mama went away and have been very successful. . . . Mrs. Mat Dance had just given [Pattie] a certain cure for dysentery. It proved so efficacious and is so simple that I am going to send it to you . . . "Take a little vinegar (about two teaspoons I used) put in as much salt as it will dissolve, pour a tablespoon of boiling water to it and as soon as it is cool enough drink a tablespoon full." You must remember this . . . it affords relief in a short time too. . . .

. . . We have not had a paper for two days and I begin to fear that Richmond is in danger. . . . It is getting late and as I am the housekeeper I have to rise early. I bid you goodnight.

June 11ᵗʰ – Isaac is about to start to the Depot . . . Mr. Holt sent a letter over here last night for me to direct to you. I suppose he has written you all about the crops. Liny and Mary Brown have been laid up for several weeks . . . Lizzie Lee is looking very well . . . Isaac is in a hurry to start and I must close.
Your own
Mary

- - - - -

Letter from Captain Richard Watkins to Mary Watkins

Near Frederick Hall, Louisa
May 14ᵗʰ 1864 [June 14, 1864]

My Dear Dear Mary – Some time has elapsed since my last was written but we have been on the march ever since and I have hardly had time to eat or wash my face. Sheridan with his raiding party started in the direction of Gordonsville. Our Brigade at the time was on the extreme right of our Army and was ordered in a great hurry to reinforce the cavalry on the left and the whole to go in pursuit. We overtook him at Louisa Court House and a very severe fight ensued lasting two days (last Saturday & Sunday). We were dismounted on both sides & fought as infantry and . . . we succeeded in repulsing him & taking about six hundred prisoners and killing & wounding a great many. He left a large number of his dead unburied on the field. Our loss in killed and wounded was quite heavy. God has signally blessed my company again. Although we held the most exposed position in the fight we sustained the slightest loss of any company in the regiment. None killed & only four wounded. Nat Thackston (one bone in wrist broken), [R. H.] Ragsdale (wounded in the head not serious), S. T. Woolton (ditto) and F. L. Elliott (slight wound in shoulder). All the rest well and ready to meet Sheridan again whenever he offers battle. Willie Dupuys horse is in bad condition and we have applied for a detail for him to get a fresh one. I hope to send this letter by him. Willy has rendered himself . . . well . . . there is not a better soldier in the Confederacy and the best of it is he is not aware of it at all. . . .

Well after Sheridan was drubbed he withdrew in the direction of Grant's Army and may possibly gather reinforcements and come at us again. We are at present quietly watching his movements.

Col. Carter was wounded in the hand & leg but we hope not dangerously. Amputation of neither will be necessary. We miss him very much. He is one of the bravest & most efficient cavalry officers that we have. The ladies of Louisa have been very kind & attentive to our wounded. All who were able to go have been sent to the Hospital in Gordonsville. I would give almost anything . . . to go with Willy when he gets his detail, but I am an officer and when my horse breaks down am presumed to have in my pocket $3000 to invest at once in another. A very strong presumption at present . . . Our fight near the Green Spring Country the most fertile portion of Louisa and very beautiful. But for the dusty conditions of the roads our marches would be . . . delightful for we are sufficiently near the mountains to get pure bracing air and the water is far better than in Hanover & below Richmond.

. . . please send me a clean pair of pants . . . My boots and pants are getting such bad condition that people actually begin to laugh at me. . . . Don't know what the Yanks would think if they should accidentally take me prisoner and discover that I am a Confederate officer. Perhaps twould be well to have my photograph taken . . . all covered with dust with my old slouch hat, ragged boots &c . . . Tis about time for us to mount again and I must close. Want to tell you a piece of news first strictly confidential which you must tell nobody but Emmie & Minnie. You you may tell little Mary too when she gets older. It is this. I love you with my whole heart and Emmie & Minnie & Mary according[ly]. Give a great deal of love to all &

especially to Ma whenever you see her ... Good bye now Precious –
May God continue to bless & protect you.
Yr own
Richard

(ed: The battle of Trevilian Station was fought on June 11 & 12 near Gordonsville, Virginia. Confederate cavalry under the command of General Wade Hampton, traveling with only 3 days rations, had won the race against General Sheridan who traveled with wagons and cattle. The initial day of fighting was a confused melee but the Confederate forces held the field and built a defensive line across the Virginia Central Railroad. On the second day they defeated the superior Union forces preventing them from destroying the railroad and from continuing west to join forces with Union General Hunter. Sheridan withdrew under cover of darkness and retreated eastward toward the North Anna River and the Army of the Potomac.

Unfortunately, Richard's positive outlook regarding Colonel Carter is incorrect and he will die from his wounds in the Gordonsville Hospital.)
5

- - - - -

Letter from Captain Richard Watkins to Mary Watkins

Near Bottoms Bridge
June 22nd 1864.

Well Darling – Here we are again. Have been all around Hanover, Louisa, Spottsylvania, Caroline, King William & New Kent after Sheridan, and have again turned up on the picket line. Today have the second day of rest since we left Fredericksburg the 1st May. And Oh how tired and dirty we are. I should be ashamed for you to see me ... Oh I am so tired and want to see you so bad but the campaign has not closed and a great deal of hard marching and fighting is yet before me. . . . Grant has thus far been foiled in all of his plans. Am sorry to say that in a skirmish yesterday four were wounded in my company but we have none seriously. – John Knight (flesh wound in thigh) Frank Penick (shot through shoulder) Hester Walton (in the hip) Chas. Clark (through calf of leg). All flesh wounds, some of them quite painful. God still spares my life ... Reckon you have seen Willy Dupuy and had a full account of our operations from him....

Tomorrow is your birthday. How am I to celebrate it. Well we have drawn today rations of sugar and coffee, good bacon and some nice crackers ... I can ... have a nice dinner and think of you all the time. ... or had I better get permission to go to Richmond and have a fine dinner with cake & ice cream at Pizzini's or Antoni's – If I could only meet you in Richmond ... and have such a dinner with you even if it cost me five hundred dollars ... You better not write me any more about Mother sending boxes to the Hospital in Richmond if you do not want me to report sick. Tis a great temptation I assure you. ... By the by on the day we started while marching in the dust between here and Richmond a gentleman ... held out his hand to me and to my surprise it was Dr. Beverly Watkins. He is surgeon or assistant surgeon in a North Carolina regiment. Had seen Nat only a few days before and reported him well. Beverly was looking very well indeed and I was glad to learn that he has been in the Army a long time. I like to find that all of your old beaux are doing their duty. ... Will close now for today ... Write me what Emmie has to say about Danville and give Bro Abner & Sister Maria ... many thanks for the kind care they take of her. With much love to all and many kisses to our children – I bid you my darling Goodbye.
Yr own
Richard

(ed: According to notes on the Co. K roster John Knight, and the others, suffered their wounds fighting with Sheridan's troopers near White House which was also called White House on the Pamunkey.) 6

- - - - -

Letter from Mary Watkins to Captain Richard Watkins

Linden June 25th 1864

My dear Husband

Little Mary has been very sick since I last wrote . . . much better today and if we can only get her along through July and August now I hope she will be raised. She was taken with croup . . . seems to be going off in her lungs, she coughs now as if she had the whooping cough. One day she laid in her cradle and dozed nearly all of the time . . . She has lived off of mint juleps for several days . . .

Cousin Ann received a stunning blow today. Her brother Willie was mortally wounded on the 27th of May and died two days afterwards . . . she listened so anxiously for tidings from him since Johnston has been fighting and looks in the papers . . . to see if Clebournes division was mentioned. About two weeks ago she told us at breakfast that she believed Will was wounded and had lost a leg. Said she waked up suddenly the night before . . . She received a letter from him the next day though which seemed to relieve her mind . . .

There is a great deal of sickness in the neighborhood this summer. Aunt Sarah Dupuy and Mollie Townes have the typhoid fever and there were several negroes sick . . . one boy about 12 years old died with it today . . . Mama has another case of consumption and one of pneumonia. . . . Jim Taylor has had the dyptheria very badly . . . Mrs. Holts baby has . . . pneumonia . . . Don't believe I have told you anything about Emmie since she came home. She talked a great deal for the first few days after she got home but has relapsed into her usual quiet habits now. . . . Seemed more delighted to see Mary than anything else, and the little darling knew her and held up her mouth two or three times to kiss her.

. . . I sent your pants to Richmond several weeks ago . . . Will send you another pair soon. Sister Sue sent me some cloth . . . it is lead colored flannel but I had them lined . . . I hope they will answer . . . Had almost despaired of getting you a pair of boots until Mr. Redd took it in hand. I sent to Farmville by Mr. Holt to get leather for a pair but the prices scared him . . . but Mr. Redd went there and

engaged Whitman to have a pair of good boots done . . . at $225. . . .
It almost made me sick to think that you were nearly barefooted and
I unable to help you. . . .

June 23rd. I had almost forgotten that this was my birthday . . . until
I went down to supper tonight and found a nice cake sitting before
my plate. . . . Paulina . . . had bought sugar to make me a cake and she
and Lavalette made it this evening. . . . really enjoyed it, wish you had
been here to eat it with me.

June 24th Willie Dupuy has come by to tell me that he is not going
today . . . Aunt Sarah is so sick . . . Drs. Owen and Eggleston are
both attending her and say that the next three or four days will be
the critical point with her . . . Little Mary is decidedly better . . . and
is playful again.

There is a rumor that the Yankees are near the Junction again. . . . the
telegraph line is out. . . . Will write again by Willie Dupuy and send
your boots. Must close now. Goodbye from
Your own
Mary

*(ed: Mint juleps are a sweet drink with a rum base. Because they are
so sweet and syrupy, medicine can be added quite easily and it can be
effective in hiding the taste. Mary may have just been putting a little rum
in a sweet drink to help Little Mary rest.)*

*(ed: Major General Patrick Cleburne's Division was in General Hardee's
Corp in the Army of Tennessee. During the time frame of May 25 to May
29 they were engaged in fighting at New Hope Church, Georgia.)*

- - - - -

Letter from Captain Richard Watkins to Mary Watkins

Camp near Richmond
June 28th 1864

My Precious Mary

The unpleasant intelligence reaches me through the papers that a raiding party of the enemy has been very near you. Perhaps at your own home and it may be that we have sustained some loss. Tis gratifying to know that their stay was only for a limited period. . . . I feel somewhat anxious to know to what extent our neighbors and ourselves have sustained damage and whether any have been subjected to insult or rudeness. . . . Our Division has chased and fought Sheridan until both parties seem to be exhausted . . . Thus far we have . . . repulsed him in his efforts to join Hunter at Lynchburg and again having whipped him badly last Friday and driven him under shelter of his gunboats. . . . I hope those of the Pr Edward troop who are at home sick . . . and those who are after fresh horses contributed to harass them during their stay.

. . . I succeeded in getting two hours leave . . . went to Richmond and equipped myself with a pair of new boots and found at Cousin Barretts a pair of nice clean pants and socks. Took a good bath & put on nice clean clothes and came back to camp feeling like a new man. . . . In the engagements we have had since Willy Dupuy left we have lost one killed (Joe Spencer) and five wounded but none mortally – Joe Spencer was a brave daring soldier, and was killed as we were charging a battery on foot, a grape shot striking him in the forehead. We do not fight now as cavalry but as infantry alone. After driving in the pickets we dismount & fight in regular infantry style. Of the two branches of service now I would greatly prefer the infantry – and am seriously fearful that I cannot afford much longer to keep myself mounted horses are selling so very high. Hope that Mother took the precaution to run her horses off before the Yankees reached Meherrin. . . . We are ordered to be in readiness to move again in an hour . . . We have plenty to talk about now since the Yanks have been to Pr Edw. . . . Good bye My Precious Mary. I am anxious beyond measure to see you again. Write to me very often. Give much love to all.
Yr own
Richard

(ed: Notes on the Co. K roster indicate Private J. C. Spencer, "killed in Chas. City.") 7

\- - - - -

Petersburg and Southside Operations
July 1 to August 15, 1864

In Georgia the Union forces under General Sherman have General Johnston backed up to the outskirts of Atlanta. On July 7th Johnston is forced into the defenses of Atlanta when the Union army crosses the Chattahoochee River. On July 17th command of the Army of Tennessee is given to General John B. Hood. He comes out of the defenses to attack the stronger Union forces and is defeated in the battles of Peachtree Creek, Atlanta and Ezra Church. In Virginia, General Lee sends General Early to the Shenandoah Valley to drive General Hunter from the Valley and create a diversion to perhaps draw General Grant away from Petersburg. Early moves rapidly north and crosses into Maryland on July 6th and threatens Washington but is turned back and is again in Virginia by July 14th. On August 7th Grant places General Phil Sheridan in command of Union forces in the Shenandoah with directions to clear the Valley of Confederate forces and to destroy the ability of the Valley to provide food for the Confederate forces.

Mary writes two marvelous letters describing the Union raids on their farms and the farms in Prince Edward County. At Oldham, five of their slaves were taken by force, six horses and all of their mules. Mary had not believed stories about the cruelty of Union forces but now thinks "there is nothing too mean for them to do, at least these Raiders." Only two colts have been left at Oldham. The raiders even steal their "plow gear" but they do not damage Richard's law library. The major concern is how they will bring in the crops. Mary mentions that they did not destroy the fields of corn. In a mid August letter Mary notes that Mrs. Watkins, Mr. Redd and others are loaning them horses and men on various days to help them bring in the corn crop. Things look bleak and Mary can "hardly think of next year."

Richard and the 3rd Virginia Cavalry are chasing the raiders and he writes, "I am alive & well & right side up!" They catch General Wilson and his raiders some 10 miles south of Petersburg and "Pitched into him & routed him completely captured all of his artillery . . . all of his wagons, all of his ambulances, about 400 or 500 negroes horses & mules." Among the captured negroes Richard found Purnall, Beverly and Clem from Oldham as well as some of his horses and one mule. He sends them back to Prince Edward with a detail going back for fresh mounts. He has Purnall take John Wesley, who has broken down again, back to the farm to regain his health.

Richard is hopeful that Early's raid will cause Grant to change his base away from Petersburg. Richard gets a final furlough in late July and will return to the command about August 15th.

Letter from Captain Richard Watkins to Mary Watkins

Jarralls Station Sussex County
July 1st 1864

Well Darling

I write a hundred letters this morning to let you know that I am alive & well & right side up! – We met Genl. Wilson with his raiders about 10 miles below Petersburg two days ago making his way back. Pitched into him & routed him completely captured all of his artillery 13 or 14 pieces, all of his wagons, all of his ambulances, about 400 or 500 negroes horses & mules, chased them about 20 miles and the whole country is strewed with guns & blankets & assorted clothing & negroes. – The most fearful sight which I have witnessed in the war was the confusion & terror of the poor negro women & children as we charged the Yankees through & over them. Little children one & two years old were strewn over the roads & fields, mounted horsemen were charging & fighting over them, the women rushing frantically about not knowing in what direction to go. To my surprise on yesterday after the fight was over whilst we were still pursuing the Yankees I came up with Purnall, Beverly, & Clem – and this morning return them with Mel Arvin & Sam Woolton who are going home after fresh horses. – I found also one of my mules. – Our loss I understand was considerable . . . Please write me about it. How many negroes are missing. These boys say that Frank, Shadrack, & Andy were with them, and I still have hopes of getting them as a large lot of negroes were sent off to Petersburg without affording me a chance to see them.

Have no chance to write more as the bugle has sounded to horse. Will write again soon. Cheer up and do not feel too much concern about the matter. All will be right some of these days. . . . Give love to all. Good bye. Yr own Richard

(ed: Jarrett's Station is on the Weldon Railroad "below Petersburg.")

- - - - -

Letter from Mary Watkins to Captain Richard Watkins

Linden July 1ˢᵗ 1864

My darling Husband

I wrote you last Friday morning and sent the letter with a pair of pants by one of your company. My letter had hardly got out of sight of the house before Charlie Redd rode up in considerable haste with news that the Yankees were at Meherrin. . . . I started Toby off with a note to Mr Holt to move into the house and take care of the horses. And then I set about hiding your papers . . . and whatever jewelry and articles of value I possessed. Whilst I was down in the woods by myself burying some papers the feeling came over me that they had been to our house and destroyed everything . . . Mr. Holt [was at Linden] on returning and . . . they had nearly ruined us . . . Toby got there just in time to find the house full of Yankees and all of our horses and mules and a good many of the negroes in their possession. They only left Fancy's two little colts. Mr. Holt said he with his hands were plowing . . . in that field next to Wardens when they came dashing up at full speed over fences . . . and called to the negroes to come along with them the negroes stood amazed for a little while when the Yankees commenced cursing and swearing and brandishing their sabers and guns and ordering them to unhitch the horses from the plow and ride them to the house. They seemed to be in a desperate hurry and Liny told them she could not walk so fast so they put her on a mule and made her ride down to the house . . . finally concluded to leave her with the rest of the women and children if they wanted to stay. The officer in command then went to the house burst the doors open also the drawers and your book cases and searched about in every place for gold and silver and papers. . . . Others stood guard over the negroes. They mounted Purnall (wasn't that mean), Beverly, Shadrack, Anderson, Clem and Frank on their horses and that is the last I ever heard of them. . . . Henry Brown and William they said they might remain with their wives . . . (they took only six horses and had no way of carrying more than six men.) Patrick they mounted on a mule before Anderson but as they were passing the cornhouse he rolled off and hid under it . . . Purnall was forced to go . . . he and Beverly evidently left with reluctance but were frightened half out of their senses when the Yankees were brandishing their sabres . . . I heard last night there were a good many horses at Drakes Branch retaken from the Yankees . . . [They] broke open both of Mama's stables and found no horses and left without doing further damage. They did not go to Uncle Joe's, Capt. Smith's, or any of the Redds . . . Received your letter yesterday and am so glad that your life and health are spared. . . . The Yankees did not touch our corn . . . Though they took all the plow gear. I never believed one half of what I had read and heard of the Yankees before but now I think there is nothing too mean for them to do, at least these Raiders. Mrs. Nolle had to endure them for 24 hours . . . Mrs. Owen . . . ran away from home whereupon the wretches took all of her and her childrens . . . clothes, ripped up all of her beds, broke up her earthenware and furniture, even destroyed her kitchen furniture, brought in negroe women and made them dress up in Mrs. Owens clothes . . . and then shot two of their broken down horses in her porch leaving them lying dead with their heads in her door. Some few fared better and some worse. . . . A great many negroes that they took came back to their masters in a few days . . . Well! there will be so many less to clothe and feed that is the straining point with me this year. If it wasn't for Purnall I should not care much for the others, but that was the unkindest cut of all taking Purnall, Fancy, Button & Lizzie Leigh. Lizzie was in fine order and right well again. . . . The weather has been so intensely hot and we have had so many sick ones here since Mama has been gone that I was rather afraid of contracting a fever by walking over there. . . . I don't know whether I told you of Fannies death. She was sick only five days with this terrible typhoid fever. Her baby followed her in a few days with the same disease. Little Mary is nearly well again and Emmies cold [is] better. . . . Good news . . . received yesterday that you had been to Richmond and got a pair of boots and some clean clothes, you don't know how badly I felt about you. . . . Mr. Holt is the only man that I heard of facing them when they came to a home . . . They took every one of Cousin Purnall Dickinson's horses and six of his men and his carriage too. They took Bro Wills shoes off his feet and carried off three of his horses and two men. . . . Intended to go over home this evening but it looked too threatening, did not rain much though, needing it very much.

Your own

Mary

(ed: Mrs. Emily H. Dupuy (Mary's mother) was not at Linden but is over at Falkland nursing Mrs. Joseph Dupuy (Aunt Sarah) who is near death. They felt fortunate that the Union raiders did not come to Falkland because they felt any excitement would probably have killed Aunt Sarah.)

(ed: It is interesting that the "unkindest cut of all" was the Yankee raiders taking "Purnall, Fancy, Button & Lizzie Leigh." Lizzie Leigh was filled out again and ready to be swapped with Richard's current horse before he breaks down. Purnall was listed first ahead of the three horses but he and the three horses are the most valuable property that they lost.)

- - - - -

Letter from Captain Richard Watkins to Mary Watkins

Camp near Petersburg
July 4th 1864

My own Dear Mary

Frank Womack came in two days ago and brought me yours of the 24th which had been given him by Willie Dupuy together with a pair of pants. I thank you much for them . . . if you have not already sent my boots do not send them as I have purchased a pair in Richmond. . . . [No] news of interest here since my last except the almost constant shelling of Petersburg. – This was the day fixed by Grant for his grand entry into Richmond. Hardly think he will get there. Feel quite anxious to hear what was the result of our loss to the raiders. Have a letter for Mr. Elbert Redd's that seven of our negroes left and that four has returned. Hope this may be true, for then with the three caught here we have them all again – The next question is what disposition must be made of them. I would like to consult Mr. Geo. Redd and Bro Edwin about this as there seems to be such an evident disposition on their part to get away by the Yankees but I have abundant proof to the contrary. I hear too that the Yanks entered the house and destroyed my library. Hope they did not get your tableware too. Upon the first intimation hereafter that the raiders are approaching it will be well for Mr. Holt to run the negroes & horses off for a few days . . . carry them into the interior. Cousin Wm Morton would be a good place, or any other place a little removed from the RR. [railroad] If Grant's army continues in the present position our cavalry will be subject to occasional raids and all the watchfulness conceivable on the part of our cavalry cannot prevent it. The way these things are accomplished is to get a few hours start when it is almost impossible to overtake them. The raiders have the additional advantage of getting fresh horses along the roadside which our cavalry have not. Our citizens ought to inaugurate a system of getting information so as to blockade the roads & get their property out of the way at least their negroes and horses. By blockading roads upon which the enemy is moving they would hinder his operations greatly.

I have sent in an application for ten days leave of absence I feel so anxious to see you and if possible to aid you . . . but fear that my application will not be granted. . . . I want to see you ah too much – Give a great deal of love to all . . . No time to write more. Kiss our dear little children for me. Good by
Yr own
Richard

- - - - -

Letter from Mary Watkins to Captain Richard Watkins

Linden, July 6th 1864

My dear Husband

... here it is only nine o'clock at night and I have just got the children to bed and everything quiet ... Mary is not well ... and Emmie is in very bad humor. Tonight I had to give her a good whipping before she went to sleep. Mama is still at Uncle Joes and I expect will be needed there several weeks longer. ...

July 7th Will now reply to your letter of the 4th July received yesterday. Wrote you a long letter on the 1st telling you of our losses but did not succeed in mailing until the 4th when I was in Farmville. Have been over home since and can tell you more about it. We lost every horse and mule ... Fancy's two youngest colts only left. The Yankees broke open the house, kicking out one panel to one of the doors ... They injured the two top drawers to the bookcase very much cutting and hacking them with their sabers ... they did not break open or injure in any way the bookcases where your law books were. ... I don't think they carried off ... any of your or my books ... I think Mr Holt told them he had the keys to the cellar and went with them into the new house. They tried the door to my china closet but concluded not to force it. I do not think the negroes were entirely to blame for going ... they were ordered ... to throw down their hoes, cut the horses from the plows and follow them. This they all did ... Mrs Holt says Purnall cried like a baby when they started from the house. ... Frank came home the day I was over there 1st July, said he got away from them while the fight was going on at Stoney Creek ... Purnall, Beverly and Clem you have seen ... Shadrick and Anderson are still missing. ... Rather have had the horses back then the negroes I believe. Mother has sent Uncle Aleck with her horses to plow for us a week. Cousin Polly sent two men, two horses & two plows for two days. Uncle Joe sent a mule for a week. Mr. George Redd, Capt. Smith and Mama will send as soon as they finish laying by corn. Good bye now. I must stop ...
Your own
Mary

July 9th Have kept this some time waiting for Willy Dupuy but his fathers family so sick don't know when he can go and have concluded to mail it. ...
MPW

- - - - -

Letter from Captain Richard Watkins to Mary Watkins

Camp near Petersburg
July 7th 1864

My Darling Mary

I want to see you too bad this bright beautiful morning. . . . Capt. Sam
McGeher is down here looking up lost negroes & horses, he leaves
this morning and I have a great mind to mount my old horse and go
home with him. . . . Why is he at liberty to go home to his family, to
ride about in search of his property, to go home and accumulate and
provide for his family: and I not allowed even ten days . . . I who have
already borne so much of the heat & thunder . . . Oh the inequity of
our legislation . . . The man who shirks his duty to his country is by
the laws of his country encouraged to shirk his duty. Whilst he who
shows an inclination to do what is right is . . . made to do all. War
is terrible enough of itself but when attended with such corruption
. . . the horror is inconceivable. . . . I am certainly in the right place,
exactly where I ought to be, but Sam McGeher ought to be here
too and all men of like character. Men who run away from their
homes and hide in the woods when the Yankees come, and wait for
their neighbors to attack the Yankees, risk their lives, & take back
his property and then ride up and claim it and carry it back . . . with
a smile of satisfaction on their faces, but with never a thought of
the soldier, & never a thought of their own duty. Oh, the skulker in
times like these, the fat, smooth face, smiling skulker.

Darling, what does friend Holt think of the Yanks: and what did
Mrs Holt say to them. Did she sass them any. . . . and how do Mr
Purnall & Mr Clem & Mr Beverly feel since their adventure. . . .
Darling I wish I could see you this morning I know you are looking
very pretty and sweet. . . .

Am so sorry to hear that Aunt Sarah is so sick. Hope though that
the crisis is past . . . Willy did right to remain with her . . . As to my

brother Nat although I reckon we are not more than seven miles apart, I have not heard a word from him since I came here and would not if allowed know where to look for him. He belongs to Wise's Brigade but I do not know what regiment. . . . News reached us last evening that Genl. Early is within a short distance of Baltimore . . . Hope he will create such a diversion as will render it necessary for Grant to change his base to the other side of the Potomac. I don't like his shelling of Petersburg. . . . I looked with all my eyes [when we marched through] for Mrs. Leavenworth's fine house but could not see it . . .

Well the 4th of July is past and Genl Grant has not taken his dinner in Richmond. By the by, how was the 4th spent in Pr Edward. . . . As usual I am writing a medley, jumping from one subject to another, but all such things are excusable in war when one has so little time to write letters. . . . Well when you all hear that the Yanks are coming again tell Mr Holt to take my negroe men & boys & horses and go off with two or three days rations some 10 or 15 or 20 miles from the Railroad and wait quietly until the storm blows over then return. . . . Don't show this letter to anybody . . . Tell [Mr. Holt] to make haste and cut my wheat, to hire someone to come & thresh it & send it to Richmond, for I understand Marse Bob Lee's boys want it, and I myself am getting tired eating corn bread. Good bye precious - . . . Am glad to hear that Hal Edmunds is still improving. Hope he will get entirely well yet and be happy with his dear Hatty. – What does Dr. Owen think of the Yanks and the state of the Country. Ha! Ha! Ha! I hear so many funny things way off down here in the pines. – Good bye My dear one
Yr Richard

(ed: Mary attended Mrs. Leavenworth's School for Girls in Petersburg, Virginia. Richard would visit Petersburg and call on Mary at Mrs. Leavenworth's during their courtship.)

- - - - -

Letter from Captain Richard Watkins to Mary Watkins

Camp near Petersburg
July 15th 1864

My Precious Mary

Just after my last letter I sent in an application for ten days leave of absence which was refused by Genl R E Lee, since then however we have been entirely idle. So that in reality I had as well been at home. In addition to this I have been quite sick ... It seems to be my regular summer cold ... Today I feel better ... I have no appetite and great repugnance to Camp fare but Leigh Redd ... kindly went out this morning and got me some nice buttermilk & biscuit which I have eaten with some relish. If I get any worse I will go to a Hospital & be transferred if possible to Farmville. ...

No news here. All sorts of sensational rumors and extravagant reports about Genl. Early's Maryland raid. ... but I very much fear that he will accomplish but little. Were he such a Genl as Stonewall Jackson would expect confidently to hear of the fall of Washington. ... Willy Dupuy has not yet returned and I feel much concern about Aunt Sarah ... We have received the sad news of Lt. Col. Carters death. On how our Regiment will miss him ... I can hardly conceive of a braver man ... Tis a sad loss to us.

I sent my bay horse, John Wesley, home by Purnall. Please tell Mr Holt to give hime every attention and fatten him as speedily as possible. ... Will write again in a few days. Good bye. Much love to all & many kisses to my children.
Yr own
Richard

- - - - -

Letter from Mary Watkins to Captain Richard Watkins

Linden July 15th 1864

My dear Husband

Mama came home from Uncle Joe's last Sunday with every symptom of fever and has been sick in bed ever since. . . . I expect she was just broken down with nursing and sitting up with the sick. Aunt Sarah is rather better . . . Willy Dupuy seems to feel very uneasy about staying at home so long but he is really needed there . . . I told Willie you said he did right to stay and it seemed to relieve him of some anxiety. . . . could hardly help laughing . . . the other day when I read your letter ordering Mr. Holt if the Yankees ever made a raid on this road again to run all the horses off from the railroad, when you did not have a horse or mule left. We have one mule, John Wesley, and two colts now and I reckon the Yanks will not get them if they give Mr. Holt an hour or two notice. They came upon us like a thief in the night the other time. You inquired if Mrs Holt sassed them any, she said she was scared out of seven years growth and I reckon had as little as possible to say to them. Mother has sent her horses over to plow another week . . . and Geo Redd sent two men and horses for several days. I think we can get the corn laid by and this years crop secured and I hardly allow myself to think of next year. . . .

Little Mary is much better and the other children are well except colds. . . . Minnie is very anxious to write you a letter and says that you must come home as soon as you can. I am not going to write you four pages of foolscap partly crossed this time. It looks like rain and I hope we will have some this evening. Need it badly. Well good bye for the present.
Your own
Mary

(ed: Richard got a furlough in late July and was home till about August 15th. He and Mr. Holt accomplished a lot of crop work on the farm, Aunt Sarah died on August 8th, and Captain Watkins departed mid-month with Willie Dupuy and Purnall Dickinson to rejoin the 3rd Virginia Cavalry.)

- - - - -

The Shenandoah Valley with Early
August 22, 1864 to March 14, 1865

Atlanta falls to Union forces on September 1st. General Grant keeps the pressure on General Lee at Petersburg, and keeps stretching the trenches westward, forcing Lee to keep thinning his defenses. General Sheridan is in the Valley against General Early and on September 19th soundly defeats the Confederate forces at Winchester. In October Sheridan drives Early up the Valley defeating him in a series of battles. November will find the Army of the Tennessee moving toward Franklin, Tennessee, and General Sherman begins his march toward Savannah and the Atlantic Ocean. Confederate forces are being driven back and defeated on all fronts. The end is near.

On November 8th Lincoln is re-elected winning the electoral college vote 212 – 21.

Richard writes to Mary from the Valley on August 30th that "Genl Early and Gen Sheridan amusing themselves running up and down the Valley." On September 8th he instructs Mary to have their "tobacco, wheat & corn sold" to pay for both the mules and the debt to Dick Hines. He notes that Atlanta has been lost. In his words, "the northern part of the Shenandoah is a wilderness." What he means is that the northern Valley is a desolate wasteland. Richard receives a letter from his brother Nat telling of the death of a newborn daughter, of too many skulkers and deserters, of continued ground taken by Grant, and of the hard losses by his company who have only 30 men present for duty. Richard's horse is wounded in the battle at Winchester and he buys another in Waynesboro. On October 10th Richard writes, "The Yankees are seriously endeavoring to starve us into submission. They are burning all the grain and mills . . ."

Mary, in a September 10th letter, notes that Andy has gotten back with the sorrel horse and then the horse died. They have only 5 pieces of meat left in the smokehouse at Oldham. She is unsure what the slaves are going to have for food. On the 27th Mary writes Richard that the papers have "nothing but bad news from Early, defeat, retreat, loss of men and artillery." Typhoid fever is prevailing again in Prince Edward County. In Mary's October 4th letter she explains that the wheat "will not make more than 130 bushels" and she has only enough sorghum for "about 12 gallons of molasses." Things are looking bleak at Oldham and Linden.

Richard is badly wounded in the left hand and wrist at Tom's Brook on October 9th. He will be evacuated to the Cavalry Hospital in Gordonsville and then will be transferred on to the General Hospital in Farmville. He will be granted disability leave on February 17, 1865, and will be retired to the invalid corps on March 14, 1865.

Letter from Mary Watkins to Captain Richard Watkins

Linden Aug 22ⁿᵈ 1864

My dear Husband

I suppose ere this you have reached your command and fallen very naturally into your old camp habits. Heard today that the gallant 3ʳᵈ was in Rappahannock County, moving up the Valley. Don't we wish the war was over . . . and every gallant Regiment . . . was marching toward home. . . . Mama and the girls went to Mt. Pleasant yesterday in the wagon and were caught in a tremendous rain. They looked like half drowned rats when they got home. Emmie and I congratulated ourselves frequently . . . that we had not gone. . . . We have had the greatest abundance of rain since you left. This has been more like an April than an August day. Mama and Mrs Baker went to the Depot this morning to barter for cards [cotton cards]. Mama succeeded in getting several pair with corn. I sent a pot of butter but could not get cards. . . . Dr. Owens had a hogshead of cider beat and put in the barn but it leaked out and wet the tobacco some. I have been busy all day cutting out pants for the men. Cut ten pairs while Mama was gone.

Aug 24ᵗʰ We had some excitement . . . rumor of another Yankee Raid . . . By the way, Capt. Halle is at home and says he has several horses and mules for sale over in Culpeper or Orange I believe it is. If your company is stationed there at any time perhaps you can . . . get some. Perhaps you had better write to him if you want them. . . . Cousin Ann [Dupuy] had heard twice from Cousin Johnny in the past week. He had a severe flesh wound in the thigh and several other wounds in different places . . . he suffered very much and had neuralgia in the head to contend with besides. Tell Willie Dupuy they are as well as usual at his house, the girls were at church Sunday. . . . My paper is nearly out and I must close.
Your own
Mary

(ed: Ann Dupuy lost two brothers during the war. John James will survive his wounds and will practice law in Tennessee following the war.)

- - - - -

Letter from Captain Richard Watkins to Mary Watkins

Camp near Smithfield
Jefferson County
Aug 30th 1864

My own Dear Mary

. . . I wrote you from reaching the vicinity of Martinsburg that our Regiment was in Maryland but it was a mistake. It merely went to the River at Williamsport fired a few shells across and returned. We are now between Charlestown & Winchester all well & much cheered by the good news from Petersburg in the papers of the 24th. And the *Richmond Examiner* has at last complimented the cavalry. . . . Truly we must be approaching peace. . . .

We are quite actively engaged here. Genl Early and Gen Sheridan amusing themselves running up & down the Valley. Early retreats to Strasburg hotly pursued by Sheridan. . . . Sheridan is back again across the Potomac. . . . The Valley is protected and a large quantity of wheat secured to the Confederacy.

Our trip from home here was as pleasant as could have been expected. . . . The third night we staid with Mr. Geo. Booker of Buckingham. He is a wealthy James River farmer, was formerly a member of our troop & compelled to leave from ill health. . . . he told me he had a very beautiful young cow which he wanted to make me a present of and I could either send for her now or he would after the end of the war have one in readiness for me. He has an improved breed of cattle and I think they are the prettiest I have ever seen. After leaving his home we got among strangers and the old Dutchmen of the Valley . . . Andy says he got mighty tired of light bread & apple butter. He bids fair to make a right good servant and I will soon be able to send him out to forage and he will then be of great help to me. He says I must write 'howdy' for him to all the folks at home and tell them he likes the Army very well thus far.

Now about home affairs. First and foremost If the Yankees ever come to Prince Edward again I beg of you most earnestly not to go over home or anywhere else to meet them. I do not want them ever to meet you or to see you. If they are inclined to burn our house, let them burn it. You cannot prevent it by being there and may subject yourself to gross insult. Please do not go near them if you can avoid it. . . . I have no serious apprehensions however of their getting to Meherrin again soon. Please tell Mr. Holt to hurry all that he can to get the oats & wheat seeded . . . Ask Bro Geo Redd to have all my wheat ground at his mill and sell so much as you think we can spare and pay the money to Dick Hines. Perhaps by taking a sample of my tobacco, Dick Hines might purchase that and cancel the debt. I am anxious to have it settled. No time to write more. Much love & many kisses to all at home . . .
Yr own
Richard

- - - - -

Letter from Captain Richard Watkins to Mary Watkins

Camp near Smithfield
Aug 31, 1864

My own Dear Mary

Wm & Horace Booker are about to start home and as I cannot suffer an opportunity to slip without letting you hear from me will drop a few lines . . . Our campaign is still an active one it seeming to be part of Genl Early's strategy to keep his troops constantly in motion. Last night our Regiment was sent to relieve another on picket. We entered a dark forest and halted for the night. The wind was cold and chilling and I as I threw my blanket down upon the damp ground many thoughts of the comforts of home came stealing or'e me. . . .

I send Andy home for fear that we may go over into Maryland or Penna – indeed we move about so much he cannot be of much service for the present. Please have made for him a warm pair of breeches & if possible a pair of shoes as I shall want him again when we get quiet in camp. John Redd has just reached us. All are well. Horace & Buck will give you all the news. Tell Mr Holt to write to me how he is getting on. Hope he is sowing oats & wheat rapidly.

Love & kisses to all, many kisses for our dear children. Excuse the poor letter but I have no more time at present. To God I commit you and our dear ones. Goodbye
Yr own
Richard

- - - - -

Letter from Mary Watkins to Captain Richard Watkins

Linden Sept 1ˢᵗ 1864

My darling Husband

It has been two weeks yesterday since you left home and I have not heard a word from you yet. . . . We are all jogging along as usual with a house full of company. Have several new cases of fever [typhoid] here and two at our house. Nelly got up and went to work the day after you left determined that she would not have the fever but she had to succumb to it in four or five days and has been quite sick ever since. I went over home monday and think William looks very much as if he had the fever . . . I sent him an emetic and he said he was better yesterday. Mr. Holt has succeded in getting a place at Mr. Carrington's . . . so you need not be uneasy about getting rid of him. Mr. Tom Anderson staid here night before last on his way to Farmville to sell some tobacco for Dr. Passmore, promised to call today and let me hear what he got for it. . . . Aunt Jane and Cousin Ann have gone to Uncle Joe's to stay with the girls while Uncle Joe has gone to Goochland . . .

Little Mary has been right sick for a week and looks considerably worsted. She is teething again I reckon. Emmie complains of headache every morning and I am a little uneasy for fear she will have the fever.

... went to Mt. Pleasant in the wagon sunday and had quite a rough ride ... The sermon we heard did not repay us for the ride. ... I think Mr. Beckham [the preacher] ought to be sent to the Lunatic asylum! ...

Sept 2nd No letter from you yet. What can be the matter? ... Cousin David Morton said there was a very good mule in Charlotte [County] which could be got for fifty bushels of wheat or 75 of corn and I told him if ... [he] thought it was fair he might get it ... Mr. Anderson did not get but sixty dollars for his tobacco and he expected $200. ... . I am in a hurry and must close.
Your own
Mary

- - - - -

Letter from Captain Richard Watkins to Mary Watkins

Camp near Winchester
Sep 8th 1864.

My very Dear Mary

Another of your good letters recd yesterday for which many thanks as usual. Am surprised that you have not received one or more of my letters. Have written three since I reached the army ... We are kept constantly on the march and our poor horses fare worse & look worse than ever before. My health excellent ... out here horses are so uncommonly high that I am thinking [again] of changing my branch of service. I cannot afford to buy cavalry horses ... You spoke of an offer to Cousin D. Morton of a mule for 75 bushels of corn. The same offer had been made before I left home ... and [I]

declined it. . . . I was offered a pair of excellent work horses a few days ago for one thousand dollars apiece but could not raise the money at the time. . . . Please ask Mr. Geo Redd to sell so much of my tobacco or wheat or corn as may be needed to pay for these various mules & would especially like Dick Hines to be paid as early as practicable. Am glad that Mr Holt has found so good a home. And Atlanta has fallen. Very well . . . we have had too many reverses during this long war to repine at that. Would amuse you to see the apparent unconcern manifested by our soldiers, "Well, Atlanta has gone up" and very little more said about it. They go on whistling and singing & cooking. Tis in reality though a right serious matter and I fear will result in a prolongation of the war. It certainly affords encouragement to the North to persevere. And will doubtless add to our privations both at home and in the army. . . . Changing the subject had I not better join the Richmond Howitzers. Can I afford to remain in the cavalry. Please give me your views on the subject in your next. Both of my horses are nearly broken down. Tis sad to see what a change the war has produced in this once beautiful Valley. From Strasburg to the Potomac a distance of nearly forty miles tis almost a wilderness and yet the armies continue to march over it and devastate. Hunter in his retreat undertook [to] lay the country entirely waste and would have succeeded had not his retreat been so hurried. He even burnt the wheat in shocks, and the dry hay in the fields. The best people have left the country. But it is so fertile it will not require many years after the war to recover itself. Well my horse is grazing and he has wandered so far that I will have to bring my letter to a close and go in search of him. . . . Wish I could be with you more and still hope for peace and a happy union with my family again. Give love to all.
Yr own
Richard

- - - - -

Letter from Captain Richard Watkins to Sgt. Nathaniel Watkins

Camp near Winchester
Sept 10th 1864

Dear Nat

A long time has transpired since we interchanged courtesies what say you to a renewal of acquaintance. Where are you? What doing? When about Petersburg I made several ineffectual efforts to see you and was informed always that you were down at the front; without being told at the front of what, or in which direction fronted. How do you like the war? What do you think of the fall of Atlanta? What of the nomination of McClellan? Why did you and Old Bob Lee allow Grant to get possession of the Weldon Road as soon as we left Reams? Is not that your best route home? Are not the Yankees between you and your Dulcinea? ... Do they put you in the trenches with the rest of the boys or do you just go in order that you may draw coffee ...?

We are having gay times over here ... Early has chased Sheridan and Sheridan has chased Early and Early has re-chased Sheridan & Sheridan Early until they have stopped from exhaustion and Wickhams Brigade has actually has three consecutive days of rest . . . How is the Ex Governor? Brig Gen Wise – Does he ever allude now to his gizzard foot & ebo skin administration. Have heard nothing from him for a long time. Would like to hear his views upon the subject of peace and a continuance of the war. And what he thinks of Old Bob Lee's present position. Do you all intend to hold Petersburg or will Old Bob allow himself to be flanked out of it as Hood was [flanked out of Atlanta]. . . I would like to be with you [and Nannie] in Pr Edward where Mary could also join in the conversation. I suppose you have heard how the Yankees served me. They took all of my mules and horses and the greatest part of my negroes. I recovered the negroes but mules & horses still in the vacation. Have had to incur great expense in replacing them and as a consequence entertain serious thoughts again of quitting the cavalry. Cavalry horse are enormously high. A good one cannot be bought for less than $2500 or $3000. . . .

How is sister Nannie and the little one. Always give her a great deal of love for me when you write ... Give my kindest regards to all the boys whom I know in your company and let me hear from you at your earliest convenience. It would disturb you to see the ravages of war on this beautiful valley [Shenandoah]. Our trials as Virginians have been great during this war but we must bear them as best we can . . .

Adieu – Yr Bro

Richard 1

- - - - -

Letter from Mary Watkins to Captain Richard Watkins

Linden, Sept. 10th 1864.

My dear Husband

I did not hear a word from you for three weeks after you left and then I received three letters at once. . . . Andy got back thursday, the old sorrel just held out to reach here and died the next day. Andy says he had to walk and lead him nearly all the way home. I went over home wednesday and found that . . . Cousin David Morton had got the mule . . . for 55 bushels of corn <u>and</u> 50 bushels of wheat . . . As there was a misunderstanding . . . about the price . . . Mr Redd advised me to send it straight back which I did . . . the sick are all improving at our house. Mr. Holt finished sowing oats thursday. Mr. Redd says his wheat is so full of smut and cheat he thinks we had better exchange with Mrs. Scott for seed. Sorghum is nearly ripe and I expect to go into the molasses business next week, have engaged a mill from Mr. Cliborne. I have only five or six pieces of meat left and can not with the utmost economy make it hold out until we kill hogs, so it is very well that we have molasses to fall back on or I reckon I should have to send the negroes to the Yankees. Emmie is well again but Minnie is right sick with sore throat and head ache . . .

Hal Edmunds was married last wednesday. You and I were invited and I believe I should have gone if the children had not been sick. I wrote Hal that he ought to have hurried up and had the wedding while you were at home.

. . . Cousin Johnny is improving, he was shot through both thighs and through the foot. . . . By the way what are they going to do with Willy! Uncle Joe feels very anxious about him. He heard soon after Willie left that Col. Owen had ordered the conscript officer to arrest him. So you are right in your prediction about Atlanta. I begin to think with you that Johnston is a great general. I did not see the *Examiner's* compliment to the cavalry. I would file the paper away if I could find it. Two infantry officers dined here yesterday and we had quite a warm discussion as to the comparative merits of Cavalry and Infantry. Nannie and I took up strongly for the cavalry and Lavallette to our great annoyance would side with the infantry.

A bee stung me on my right hand yesterday and holding the pen so long has made it right stiff and sore. This is the second letter I have written this morning. Goodbye.
Your own
Mary

(ed: No charges were filed against Pvt. Willie Dupuy for over staying his furlough during his mother's illness and death. Captain Watkins probably intervened with Col. Owen on Pvt. Dupuy's behalf.)

(ed: General Joseph E. Johnston had replaced General Braxton Bragg in command of the Army of Tennessee in early 1864. He managed the army well against General Sherman just as General Lee handled his army skillfully against General Grant. Both armies were on the defensive and needed to conserve irreplaceable manpower. General Johnston had poor personal relations with President Davis and eventually the President replaced Johnston with General John B. Hood. The fall of Atlanta, soon thereafter, was a huge loss to the Confederacy both as a manufacturing center and from a psychological perspective.)

- - - - -

Letter from Captain Richard Watkins to Mary Watkins

Camp near Newtown

Sep: 15th 1864

Another year has almost past My Mary and we are still apart . . . I am truly sorry to hear . . . that up to the 5th Sept you had recd no letter from me. Hope by this time they have reached you. . . .

We are still in this beautiful desolated Valley. So different now from what it was in the early part of the war but still beautiful and ever to continue so however much polluted by the tread of our cruel foe. The air is cool & bracing, all is quiet in front the army seems upon the eve of a move . . . we know not what. We . . . are on picket now and my squadron being in reserve gives me a little time to write. If I could only sit by you and talk . . . how much more pleasant it would be. . . . In your last you stated that Emmie and Minnie were complaining. I have felt much concern about them and hope that by this time the beautiful weather has restored them and that you all are all well . . . Would it not be well to wean Mary as soon as possible. If you could recover your flesh and strength before winter I doubt not you would be less subject to rheumatism than you were last winter. . . . Go to see Ma as often as possible and if you can, call to see Henry Edmunds & his bride for I understand that he has at length gained his prize and is doubtless in fine spirits. . . .

Tell him that if he will just put an end to the war you and I will attend him on his bridal tour either to Niagara Falls or to any other romantic place . . . I suppose Hal will hardly venture out of the Confederacy. . . . I wrote to Nat a few days ago and have not yet recd an answer. . . . We find the people in the Valley still loyal & true, I am agreeably surprised at this for a large majority of them are without slaves, very many never having owned them: and their habits and mode of living is though Yankee. They are the greatest people for apple butter in the world seem to live upon apples and milk and cold bread. From milk they make butter, cheese & smear-case and from apples apple butter, apple-sauce & apple pies and these with a little cold bread and wheat coffee constitute their meals. At the same time they have the largest quantity of fine fat hogs, some of the most beautiful I have ever seen, but you seldom find any bacon or pork on their tables. The girls are extremely coarse and many of them go barefooted as they do in Pennsylvania. It is all a source of merriment to our boys who go out foraging and "come in with various anecdotes of what they have seen and heard."

. . . Please tell Mr. Holt to write me at once what he has done & is doing. Has he finished sowing oats & wheat? Tell him not to cut his tobacco too early. Let it stand as long as possible. . . . To pay particular attention to the horses, hogs, cattle & sheep. And now good bye my Dear Precious one. I long to see you and our dear children & all at home. Write as often as possible.
Yr
Richard

- - - - -

Letter from Sgt. Nathaniel Watkins to Captain Richard Watkins

near Petersburg, Va
Sept 23rd, 1864

Dear Bro

Yours of the 10th was handed me a few days since as I reached camp from a three week furlough. When I reached home on the first I found a beautiful, healthy little baby girl of a week old to join in the welcome which Nannie & little Minnie had for me. We all enjoyed the little stranger for only a few days, for in another week, after three days of sickness & suffering, she was taken from us and we had to lay her by the side of our little . . . Charley. . . . When I came through Pr. Edward [on my return to Petersburg] I saw all of your little ones (just my number too) . . . I couldn't help feeling how highly blessed you and Sister Mary are . . . took dinner at Mrs. Dupuy's as I returned to the Depot Monday. Things looked very natural at the old place except the new house, a clearing you have made, & the fine young orchard you have coming on. I frequently thought of how happy we could be at our houses if we only could be permitted to live in peace. . . . I suppose the fall of Atlanta & the nomination of a War Democrat

315

by the Chicago Convention [are depressing]. . . . I found the country people very much down hearted . . . all feeling the "Confederacy gone up the spout." The great number of able bodied skulkers at home as detailed farmers & detailed anything else surprised me and I think is adding to this depression. . . . There have been few changes since you left Ream's [Station] except for occupation of the Weldon R.R. by the Enemy, which certainly annoys Old Bob [Genl. R. E. Lee] and myself a good deal; but . . . we can get along pretty well as matters stand provided Hampton will go around occasionally and capture a few thousand fat beeves . . . The Yankees seem very jubilant in the trenches & frequently ask "How we like Early" and rumors are reaching us of a great reverse at Winchester. . . . I see here . . . the frequent desertions of our men in the trenches to the enemy. The hard service I suppose is the principal cause . . . My old company has lost 16 killed, 17 wounded & 5 captured since we commenced fighting around P'burg – having averaged during the time about 30 men [available] for duty & counting on the muster rolls 107 men at the beginning of the fight. Our service since the 16th May has been almost constant & harder than any other brigade in Beauregard's army & our losses heavier. To have three or four men killed or wounded has been a daily occurrence for months. . . . I hope we will meet soon . . .

Your aff Bro

Nathaniel V. Watkins 2

(ed: Nat & Nancy (Nannie) have now lost two children. Only little Mildred (Minnie) has managed to survive. On his return from furlough he came through Prince Edward Cty. and visited the family. With the Weldon railroad being cut he needed to take a more western route to return to Petersburg.)

(ed: Nat also refers to General Wade Hampton's cavalry raid behind the Union lines where he captured almost 2500 head of cattle near City Point and herded them back to the Confederate line. Nat's unit, like others, is being winnowed down to mere shadows of themselves. The Confederacy will soon be drafting men from 16 to 55 as they scrape everywhere looking for bodies to shoulder rifles.)

- - - - -

Letter from Captain Richard Watkins to Mary Watkins

Waynesboro, Augusta
Sep 25th 1864 –

My own Dear Mary

You have doubtless recd tidings of the defeat of Genl Early in the Valley. He is retreating rapidly before the enemy and I fear will have to leave the whole Valley unprotected for present. At the battle of Winchester my horse was wounded and being broken down besides I applied for five days leave of absence to buy another and did not succeed until I reached this place. Expect to return to my command this evening. Am now at the home of Rev. William Richardson and simply write to let you know that I am well. All were well when I left the Company.
Good bye
Yr own
Richard

- - - - -

Letter from Mary Watkins to Captain Richard Watkins

Linden. Sept 27th 1864

My dear Husband

It seems a long time since I received a letter from you . . . The papers have nothing but bad news from Early, defeat, retreat, loss of men and artillery, I feel so anxious about you, believe this is the darkest hour of the war, everything seems to go wrong at home and aboard. . . . The children are preparing for bed and are making so much noise I can hardly hear myself think. Little Mary is in a great gale about a hog that she saw someone catch and put in the pen while we were at supper. . . . she is so excited . . . and tries to pull everybody into the porch to hear it squeal. Minnie is getting well again. I have cut her hair off today . . . She is very much gratified because she says her head looks like Emmie's now. Emmie is a real old woman. I wish you could have seen her this morning making feather flowers, she went out in the yard and picked up some feathers in her apron, got a pair of scissors and a box . . . smoothed out the feathers . . . stripped off the down and cut them in the shape of leaves and dropped them in the box. . . . I am trying to teach Emmie the sound of the letters now and find it right hard work.

Brother Nat was here last week. He had been home on a sick furlough looked pale and thin. Nannie [Nancy Daniel Watkins] had a girl just a week old when he got home, it only lived two or three weeks though. Sister Sue and Pattie spent the day here with Brother Nat. . . .

Nannie is right unwell today, has symptoms of fever. There are four new cases among the servants here and four at our house. Dennis, Jimmy, Ella and Lewis have it at our house now. Dennis and Lewis quite sick. [Typhoid] Fever seems to be prevailing to an alarming extent all through this country. Cousin Robert Smiths little daughter Watty is very ill with it. There is not the least hope of her recovery. Dick McCormick died last Thursday in Petersburg of fever . . .

Mr. Holt has put up the hogs, he finished sowing oats some time ago. . . . Mr. Redd set my mind to rest about the impressing agent. He told him that he knew the law on that subject and he was not to touch one grain of our wheat except the tithe so he eased off and carried his bags home empty. . . . I reckon Bragg has made all of the Quarter Masters and their agents draw in their horns a little. Now for the mule . . . Mr Dickinson . . . must insist on my standing to the bargain and paying 50 bushels of wheat and 55 of corn for the thing. He has written me two very gentlemanly letters on the subject and Cousin David Morton has written me one . . . and I received your letter saying you had refused this offer whilst at home, so I am just in a bother. Cousin D. says he will take the mule and settle with Dickinson after the war . . . I don't suppose Mr. Dickinson will agree to that though. I have just turned the whole matter over to Mr

Redd. He says it is too much to pay for the mule.... Oh dear! I wish the Yankees had let our horses alone or rather I wish they would all go home and attend to their own business and let us alone. Well I reckon you say why don't Mary shut up about the mule and bring in some more agreeable topics! But Sir my paper is most out and so is my candle but I will try and be more agreeable next time I write.... I reckon I have set up late enough tonight....
Adios
Your loving
Mary

P.S. Sept 28th Mr Holt brought 5 gal of our brandy home this morning. He has cleaned out the wheat and is sowing some of the same.... Mr. Redd thinks we will make about 140 bushels. We have put up 32 hogs, lost 3 since those negroes have camped at Forest Church cutting timber.
MPW

- - - - -

Letter from Captain Richard Watkins to Mary Watkins

Camp near Waynesboro
Sep: 29th 1864

My own Dear Mary

Our army has retired to this place and whilst we are grazing our horses will undertake to write you another short letter. Our duties at present are very arduous ... Your letter of the 1st has made me sad indeed. So long as you are cheerful & happy & our dear children are well I can bear up under our severe trials ... but when I hear that you are unhappy my resolution seems to be all gone. Perhaps it is wrong that I should thus love you better than I do my country....

Please ask Bro: Geo Redd to see to it that we do not suffer injustice at the hands of the impressing agent: that he do not take advantage of my absence and go beyond his authority. If the necessities of Genl

Lees Army are so great as to require the half of my crop and the crops of my neighbors I am willing and desirous that they have it . . . but it ought to be done legally and fairly. I hardly think the law would justify the impressing of my wheat under the circumstances . . . I have bought me a fresh horse. I know that I cannot afford it and would have sent in my resignation at once if the Army had been quiet and our affairs in better condition, but . . . I thought it better to go a little beyond my means than to be doing nothing in times like these when every man is needed in the field. . . . I could not bear going to the rear with an unserviceable horse . . . whilst my comrades were straining every nerve to save my country & my family. When the winter comes & puts a stop to active operations I will quietly withdraw from the cavalry and enter upon the next campaign in a different branch of the service.

Please write me again soon about Minnie . . . Tell her that Papa loves her and hopes she will soon be well again. If my wheat should not [have] been taken ask Mr Redd to have it ground at his mill as we will need offal this winter for our cattle & sheep. Ask Mr Holt to begin to fallow my hogs early as they fatten much more readily in warm weather. Twould be well to feed a little green corn to them. Ask him to have the apples gathered. . . . and to write me about the farm. Have not received a letter from him since I left. Has he finished sowing winter oats & wheat?

All the boys, are well, and God still mercifully spares our lives. . . . I saw Henry Watkins about a week ago & heard from him again yesterday. He is well. Give a great deal of love to Ma & Mother & all & write to me.
Yr own
Richard

- - - - -

Letter from Captain Richard Watkins to Mary Watkins

Camp near Bridgewater
15 miles below Staunton

Oct 5th 1864

Darling

. . . Your good letter of the 27th was recd two days ago and at the same time a long one from Nat bearing the sad tidings of the death of another little child. Oh would it not be an affliction if two of our little children should be taken from us in so short a time. . . . Almost every night [in the Valley] the whole sky is reddened with the glare from their burning houses & barns & mills. The Yankees are seriously endeavoring to starve us into submission. They are burning all the grain & all the mills within reach. The defeat of Early is the most serious disaster which Virginia has experienced during the war. Yet we hope to survive even that. The enemy is now retiring slowly before us and although we can hardly hope for a signal victory over him this Fall, yet we do hope to be able to hinder any further advance. The Valley however will be left a vast scene of desolation & suffering and the Government must look elsewhere for the supplies. Tis as you state, the darkest hour of the war. But a just God still rules and controls the affairs of Nations. . . .

I am sorry to hear we are losing our hogs. Just say to the negroes it is their only chance for meat for another year as I do not intend to buy meat and they are able to watch it and keep my hogs from being stolen. Am very glad to hear that Mr. Holt is seeding his oats & wheat. Please write me how much he has seeded and whether he has finished cutting tobacco & pulling fodder. I sincerely hope he will save a good lot of fodder as tis our only chance for long forage for the winter. – Let Mr Redd do what he thinks right about [the mule & Mr. Dickinson]. Tis however a little matter anyway. Good bye now. All well here. Write me again soon. I love you dearly.
Yr own
Richard

(ed: Bridgewater is north of Staunton but it is down the Shenandoah Valley as both branches of the Shenandoah river, and many of the

tributaries, flow northward toward Harpers Ferry. That is why Richard notes, "15 miles below Staunton.")

- - - - -

Letter from Mary Watkins to Captain Richard Watkins

Linden. Oct. 4th 1864

My dear Husband

Mr. Lee Redd will start back to the army tomorrow and I will write a short letter to send by him. Have not heard from you or any of your company in a long time . . . Minnie is well again and has fattened and looks better than she has for some time . . . Little Mary has fattened on molasses too she can't make a meal without it and it agrees with her first rate. . . . We had a molasses cake sunday and Nannie was saying . . . "I wish Brother could have some of this." Our sorghum turns out as I expected very badly, will make only about 4 cart loads of the corn and I reckon will make about twelve gallons of molasses. Mr. Holt was sent off to the army last week but his family are still [on the farm] . . . They did not give him half a day to make preparations on leaving. He came back from Farmville from the meeting of the board one evening and was ordered to report in Lynchburg the next day. . . . I let Uncle Joe have my sorghum mill after Mr. Holt left. . . . I am so glad you engaged Mr. Anderson for overseer another year. think you will save a great deal by it. . . . I have written [Mr. Dickinson] that we will deliver the wheat next week as soon as he sends the bags. I will go over and have it measured or get Mr. Booker to go. We will not make more than 130 bushels Mr. Redd says. . . . To our great surprise Watty Smith is mending nobody thought she would get well. Mama says she never knew anyone with her symptoms to recover. I must go and take up my molasses now or it will burn. . . . some of it is almost as light as honey. I just wish I had a hundred gallons of it. Don't know what I shall do to make the meat hold out . . .

The papers have just come and bring a report that the Copperheads have released and armed 8500 of our prisoners at Camp Chase. This is too good to believe ... Dinner is ready and I must say good bye. Wish you could sit down to the table with us and have a good dinner. Write to me as often as you can.
Your loving
Mary

(ed: Copperheads are a group of Confederate sympathizers in Ohio and Indiana. There has been no release and arming of Confederate prisoners from Camp Chase Prison in Columbus, Ohio.)

(ed: In the battle of Toms Brook, on October 9, 1864, Richard receives a " sabre thrust through the left hand and wrist, breaking the carpal bones and tearing sinews." Richard will be sent to the Cavalry Hospital in Gordonsville and then transferred on to the General Hospital in Farmville, Virginia, near his home.)

- - - - -

Captain R. H. Watkins – Certificate of Disability and 30 Days Leave

HeadQuarters
Department of Northern Virginia
17ᵗʰ Feby 1865

Special Order
    No. 45

VIII Leave absence upon Surgeons certificates of disability are granted the following named officers
                Capt. R. H. Watkins Co K 3ʳᵈ Va Cavalry
For thirty days

By command of Gen. R. E. Lee
        W W Taylor
            AA General

To: Comdg officer
    3 Va Cavalry
Through Genl Fitz Lee 3

- - - - -

Captain R. H. Watkins Certificate of Retirement to Invalid Corps

Army of the Confederate States
Medical Certificate to Retire Invalid Officer

Capt R. H. Watkins of the 3rd Va Cavalry Regiment, Wickhams Brigade, having appeared before the Board for exhamination, we do hereby certify that he is disabled . . . from Vert: Sclo: of carpal bones of the left hand, recd 9th Oct 1864 whilst in the line of duty: resulting in agglutination of the tendons & partial anclylosis [?] of wrist joint. Disability for field service permanent. We recommend that he be placed in the "Invalid Corps" & assigned to duty as an En Officer

Jas L White – Surgeon
H D Taliaferro – Surgeon
S C Smith – Asst Surgeon

Genl Hospital – Farmville, Va
March 14th 1865 4

(ed: Agglutination refers to adhesion. The sabre wound to his left hand and wrist tore sinew and damaged the carpal bones. Richard will have limited use of his left wrist for the remainder of his life. Richard's orders to the Invalid Corps are dated approximately 4 weeks before the Army of Northern Virginia will surrender at Appomattox.) 5

(ed: Dr. H. D. Taliaferro was formerly a surgeon in the United States Navy and was appointed the Head Surgeon and Director of the Farmville General Hospital when it opened in 1862. Dr. James L. White was the

Surgeon in charge of Division 3 and Richard must have been under his care.) 6

(ed: Since Richard has been wounded at Tom's Brook the value of Confederate currency has become almost pointless. On November 22, 1864 it took $42 Confederate to equal $1 U. S. By January 11, 1865 it took $60 and on March 5, 1865 it took $100 C. S. to equal $1 U. S. That means the Confederate dollar was worth one cent.) 7

- - - - -

After the Conflict

Richard is officially paroled in Danville, Virginia on May 21, 1865. He returns to Prince Edward County and, immediately thereafter, he and Mary move back to their farm and begin the task of rebuilding their lives. Reconstruction is a very difficult time in the former Confederate states. Richard and Mary have lost most of their livestock. They need to add horses, mules, chickens, goats and cows for the farm to prosper. The slaves are now free and they must decide which ones to hire as farm employees and how to pay them for their services. Richard and Mary are fortunate that they are not heavily in debt but if they could sell the farm they would be "free." Richard is gaining law cases but he is not getting paid. Some of their crops in the fall of 1865 are productive and others are a total failure. The year 1866 continues to offer challenges. Richard and Mary resolve all of the problems with the sale of the farm in the late summer of 1866.

The following five letters detail some of the changing challenges and conditions:

- - - - -

Letter from Pattie Watkins to Nathaniel Watkins

June 24, 1865

My own Dear Brother

... We have not been disturbed lately by the Yankees though we have a guard stationed at the Co House all the time. The negroes keep up a great commotion though getting their families together & some going off & some coming ... & some people driving them off so it is the common topic of conversation ... The wheat crop in this county is a complete failure. Mr R[edd] says he will make enough for seed & family flour. It was so poor last year that a good many people didn't sow any. Bro Dick will not cut his I hear. .. we have only been to see Bro Dick once since he moved home ... Sister Sue has a splendid garden & a good many fowls . . . Mr S[   ] says that [Andrew] Johnson makes a better president for the South than Lincoln would have made, as he knew the nature of the negro better . . .

Brother [Richard] sent off some of his negroes as he had nothing to feed them. John & Bet lost nearly everything & so Brother has to feed them & Hal out of what little he has left. The men around here have all taken the oath . . . Mr Booker has gotten rid of nearly half of his negroes . . . I could write you a book if I could just untangle it all. . . Ma says I must tell you that the vandals took every fowl Sister Maria had & only left Mollie one drake, one gander & three peacocks.
Your aff sister
Pattie 1

- - - - -

Letter from Richard Watkins to Nathaniel Watkins

Home
Aug 29ᵗʰ 1865

Dear Nat

. . . Was delighted on my return to find that Mr Redd had not suffered at all from the Yankees and that Ma [Mrs. Watkins] had not actually seen more than one or two. Everything at Mr Redd's goes on as if there had been no war. He has an excellent crop and is altogether one of the most remarkable men of the age. The equanimity of his temper seems not at all disturbed by anything that has happened. . . . The seasons have been very favorable for corn and I believe our Planters generally will make enough and have a little to spare. Mary & I moved home immediately on my return and considering all things have gotten along admirably. The Yanks had taken all of our meat excepting four pieces and all of our fowls except a goose and a peacock & they wouldn't mate. . . . We planted vegetables and soon had enough to furnish a much better table than I ever sat down to in camp. Now we are really at home. . . . Corn crop . . . promising at least

200 bushels with 25 stacks of oats. My wheat was an entire failure...
. Have had a prime fruit crop and Mary has quite a bountiful supply
of dried peaches & pears laid up. If you and Sister Nannie will come
over now you will find us in a condition to reciprocate your kindness
and hospitality ...

Ma recd a letter from Sister Ballantine a short time since ... Henry
had returned from India and was preaching in Marietta ... Anna
teaching school in Indiana & Lizzie teaching in Ohio. No further
news of interest. The Yanks have us completely subjugated. All of our
public places garrisoned with negro troops. And our people willing
to submit to any degree of debasement & degradation.

Farewell ... Mary joins me in much love to Sister Nannie & Little
Minnie.
Yr Bro
Richard 2

- - - - -

Letter from Richard Watkins to Nathaniel Watkins

Prince Edward, Va
Jan 25th 1866

Dear Nat

This letter paper is too small for my purpose. I feel like sitting ... and
having a long talk with you and Sister Nannie: I have been always
attached to you ... but ten fold more so since my last visit to North
Carolina. So warmly ... did you sympathize with me in those dark,
sad days – Gloom and sadness still rest heavily upon me for I see
nothing in store for our poor country but cruelty and oppression,
and when I look upon my little children, all well and cheerful and
happy ... What trials have they to encounter. ... I see that whilst a
majority of the Yanks, still wild with fanaticism & with the spirit of
the devil ... yet to one and another of their leaders there is a lucid
interval, for even Henry Ward Beecher in a public lecture declares

himself opposed to the execution of Pres. Davis & says that now is the time to heal & not to wound. Jim Lane of Kansas too can see no reason why men in Connecticut and Pennsylvania can advocate negro suffrage for the South & yet be unwilling to grant it in their own states. Tis a new era in Jim's life when he begins to cast about for reason & thinks of justice.

I have not yet learned to admire Andy Johnson or to regard him as a friend of the South. It is no easy matter for the leopard to change his spots . . . Johnson is devoid of principle and may at any moment throw his whole power and patronage on the side of the Radicals! . . .

Enough on politics . . . The freedmen do not work but still I have concluded to try them this year as I cannot sell and do not like to rent my plantation. Mother speaks of buying my interest in the DuPuy Estate. If so it will relieve me to a great extent of my indebtedness and if I can sell my plantation and accept of your offer both of us can be much more comfortable. Instead though of my selling and buying half of your land, would it not be better for you to sell and buy half of mine. I have quite enough house room for both of our families until times become easier and by this arrangement I could continue to practice law here where I am known. . . . We bring a good many suits but not a client has paid us a dollar yet. . . . with nothing to sell from my plantation and not a dollar coming in from my profession . . . I hardly know what I should do. . . .

I wish very much that we lived near enough to each other to visit more frequently. I want Sister Nannie & Little Minnie to get acquainted with my children . . . You must come to see us & bring your family & we will talk out the balance. . . . Mary joins me in love to you and yours.
Aff Yr Bro
Richard 3

(ed: Jim Lane has gone from being a leader of irregular Jayhawk forces in Kansas during the war to now being a member of Congress. Now the

Union version of Quantrill seeks justice and reason in asking why an amendment has not been passed, to the Constitution, freeing the slaves in the "Northern states?" It is a very good question.)

(ed: In the summer of 1866 Nathaniel and the family visited in Prince Edward County. Richard is fearful that he may lose his house from comments in an August 12 letter.)

- - - - -

Letter from Richard Watkins to Nathaniel Watkins

Prince Edward
August 25th 1866

Dear Nat

I sold my plantation a few days ago to Frank & George Redd jointly for $12000 and took in part payment your bond to Frank Redd. Please come over if possible as soon as you can and let us have a settlement and I will get you to substitute your bond in the place of mine to Patty . . . all well. Mary joins me in love to you. . . . "without money without clothes & without a home but better than slavery." Yr Bro
Richard (freedman) 4

- - - - -

Letter from Richard Watkins to Asa Watkins, his son

Pr Edward
Nov 9th, 88

My Dear Asa

We are in the midst of a dark rainy spell of weather and all of our surroundings appear gloomy. Last Monday evening Cous. Minnie Morton [daughter of Nathaniel & Nancy Watkins] sent over for Mama to see her little boy Henry who had been taken the day before with dysentery. Mama [Mary D. Watkins] went over & remained through the night & until Tuesday evening. Emmie [Emily Watkins Dupuy – Asa's sister] then went & took her place & remained until Wednesday evening when Mama again went & is there now this Friday morning. She wrote us yesterday afternoon that Dr. Eggleston pronounced the child better but that it was still quite sick & she would remain with it until this evening. We have heard nothing from it this morning & hope that it is still improving.

Sister Minnie [Asa's sister Mildred] has been quite unwell since Mama left but Sis has cured her & this morning she appears almost as well as usual.

The constant rain & freshets have prevented my gathering my poor crop of corn the poorest I have ever made and it seems as if the rogues will carry it all off in bags. They actually go into the field & shuck out a pile & leave the shucks. They get then into the public road or into the creek, & we cannot track them.

In addition to all the bad weather & bad health & bad conduct we learn that Harrison is elected President and that the Radicals are to rule the country another four years.

After all however, we can fall back upon Old D' Smith's comforting remark at the time of Lee's surrender that "God Rules" & rejoice in that.

Good bye Yr aff Papa 5

(ed: Asa is in Granville County, North Carolina attending the classical boarding school run by Nathaniel Watkins. Asa studied under Nathaniel in 1888 and 1889. Richard is less than pleased that Benjamin Harrison has been elected as the 23rd President of the United States.)

- - - - -

Richard and Mary move to a farm in the Hampden District of Prince Edward County. He will practice law and farm here until 1895 when records show they move to Farmville and open the law offices of Watkins, Watkins and Brock.

In 1868 a fourth daughter, Virginia, arrives. Sometime shortly after the 1870 census, in a span of less than 14 days, both Mary P. and Virginia die of diphtheria. On a much brighter note, Asa D. Watkins is born on March 14, 1873 at "Cottage Farm."

Richard is very active in civic affairs. He serves as an Elder in both the Briery and Farmville Presbyterian Churches. In 1867 he is involved, with many other citizens, in forming the Conservative Democratic Party to try to elect locals to various government posts and oust the carpetbaggers. Richard will serve several terms in the Virginia House of Delegates. The panic of 1893 brought financial crisis to Virginia. On August 1, 1893, The Commercial Savings Bank of Farmville is the first bank in Virginia to fail. Richard is appointed receiver. The Farmville Herald *on August 5th reported that the bank had "$50,000 of liabilities and assets at 60% of that number." Richard disburses a final 2% payment to depositors in September of 1898. 6*

Asa graduates from Hampden-Sydney in 1894, from Harvard in 1900 with an AB in English, from Union Theological Seminary in 1903 and in 1918 is the head of the English Department at Hampden-Sydney.

In 1901 Minnie (Mildred) and her infant son both die of pneumonia shortly after his birth. Minnie is 40 years of age.

Richard dies on July 5, 1905, at the age of 80 years and one month. Richard is buried in the Westview Cemetery in Farmville. Richard's brother Nathaniel passed away in 1899. His sister Pattie will survive him and die in 1922 at the age of 88.

Mary passes away on June 4, 1921, at the age of 82 years and 11 months. She is buried beside Richard in the Westview Cemetery in Farmville. Mary is survived by her daughter Emily and her son Asa.

In 1929, eight years after Mary passed away, Emily and Asa donate all of the letters in Mary's trunk to the Virginia Historical Society.

In 1932 Asa will pass away at the age of 59.

Hal Edmunds, despite all of his medical problems during the war, will live to be 88 years old. His son, Richard Watkins Edmunds, will precede him in death by four years.

Nathaniel and Nannie Watkins will have another son and name him Richard Henry Watkins. They will be survived by two daughters and Richard Henry of Mississippi.

Emmie (Emily) is the final surviving child. She married Edward Dupuy and they had three children. They lived in Worsham, in Prince Edward County, their entire adult lives. Emily died in 1939 or shortly thereafter. She is buried in the Dupuy family plot at Linden. She is buried beside her husband. She was survived by her children Mary, Richard and Lawrence.
7

POSTSCRIPT

On the evening of December 28, 2009 I received an e-mail from Richard Watkins. I was unsure if this was a late Christmas present or if perhaps Rod Serling was joining me for an episode of *The Twilight Zone*. Richard Watkins had died in 1905 and there were no indications in the files at the Virginia Historical Society or with the Prince Edward Historical Society that anyone in the direct Watkins line existed beyond Richard and Mary's only son Asa. Dead men don't send e-mails. It turns out that great-grandsons do.

I opened the email and it stated, "While doing research on my relative, Richard Henry Watkins, I found references to your new book. I believe the Richard Henry Watkins that I am looking for is the one your book is about . . . My father was Asa Dupuy Watkins, Jr., his father was Asa Dupuy Watkins . . . I may be able to provide more information about the family. My aunt, Julia Day Watkins (Richard and Mary's grand-daughter), is still alive and a wealth of information." Then Richard asked me if I could confirm how his grandfather died. Asa, who was the head of the English department at Hampden-Sydney, had shoveled snow and then walked to the campus post office with his daughter Julia Day Watkins. On the way home he began walking slower and slower, kept bending over, and was having trouble breathing. He and Julia got to their house, Asa rested on the sofa, then walked into the next room, fell down and died. Confirmation that Richard and Mary's son Asa was indeed his grandfather elicited the one word response, "Eureka!"

Richard Dupuy Watkins has introduced me to Julia Day Watkins as well as great grand-daughters, great-great grandsons, and assorted other relatives. They have all been most generous in sharing their portions of the family history. The pictures and additional letters that have been added in this revised edition are all from the personal collection of Richard Dupuy Watkins.

It turns out that Richard and Mary's children had 6 children that reached adulthood. Asa had two, Minnie had one, and Emmie had three. This varies considerably from all the notes and records that were available when I published the first edition. The family has been able to help me correct the record and *Boots & Kisses* has given them an intimate, personal history of their great-grandparents during the War. They did not know that Asa and Emmie had made a donation of more than 300 letters to the Virginia Historical Society in 1929. I am sure some comments had been made, by Asa and Emmie, but verbal history has a difficult time moving forward through the generations.

"Linden" which was the home of Asa and Emily Dupuy no longer survives. Neither does "Oldham" which was Richard and Mary's home during the war. There were two "Lindens" in Prince Edward County and the one that is located near Briery Creek, a short distance south of Worsham, exists and is currently being restored. It was purchased by a Mr. Watson during the war. The Dupuy "Linden" was further south and east and on the southeastern side of the Bush River.

Briery Presbyterian Church, which was dedicated to God in 1858, still stands and is virtually identical to the way it looked in the 1860s. Mr. William Earl Thompson, the retired Presbyterian minister at Hampden-Sydney, gave me a tour of the college campus and told me stories that related to Asa Watkins during his years at the college. Then he directed me to Briery Presbyterian which is located, on the southern edge of Prince Edward County, only a few miles from the location of "Oldham" and "Linden." When you look at the pictures of the church you will note the dual front doors. The church is shaped like a "T" and the front doors are at the center of the top of the "T." The pulpit is between the two doors directly in front of the center window. The congregation was seated in front of the pulpit and occupied what would be the base of the "T." Anyone who arrived late for services had to enter one of the two front doors, facing the entire congregation, directly under the minister and the pulpit. The two seating areas to the sides, in the top part of the "T", were reserved: one for Negros and one for nursing mothers. Reverend Thompson said he often "imagines the little Calvinist boys straining their necks to peer into the "nursing mothers" section."

On more than one occasion it has been my distinct privilege to visit with Julia Day Watkins at her home in North Carolina. Those visits were a true portal back in time. She knew Asa and Emmie and lived the first two decades of her life mostly in Prince Edward County. I treasure those visits and our correspondence.

There is no doubt in my mind that I received a late Christmas present on December 28, 2009. Thank you Richard, and thank you for allowing me to share your family history.

ACKNOWLEDGEMENTS

The "Richard H. Watkins Collection" is housed at the Virginia Historical Society in Richmond, Virginia. It is a superb research facility. I would like to thank E. Lee Shepard, Director of Manuscripts and Archives, for permission to transcribe and edit the marvelous letters of Richard and Mary Watkins. I also thank Katherine Wilkins, Greg Hansard, and Sarah Bouchey for all of their assistance in bringing me files, answering questions, and even assisting with the deciphering of "difficult to read" words and phrases. Lastly, the pleasure of being allowed to work with over 300 of the original letters is almost beyond words to express. Over time, and there was a lot of time, Richard and Mary became my friends and their letters seemed to gain the power to transport me into their lives and time.

The Earl Greg Swem Library, on the campus of The College of William and Mary in Williamsburg, Virginia, houses the "Nathaniel V. Watkins Collection." To have a second collection of family letters dominated by letters from Richard's brother Nathaniel, and his sister Pattie, created a resource for adding complimentary correspondence to the story. I would like to thank Susan Riggs, of the Special Collections Research Center, for permission to transcribe and quote selections from their collection. I also thank Chandi Singer, Bea Hardy, and the rest of the staff for their assistance in shuttling folders and mining their archive.

Thank you to the United Daughters of the Confederacy in Richmond, Virginia, for the use of your microfilm files containing the service records of Confederate soldiers. Hilda Bradberry must have wondered why she needed to give me refresher courses, during each visit, in how to feed the microfilm into the machines. Hilda didn't initially grasp the depth of my mechanical aptitude. Thanks for your assistance and good humor. It is always a pleasure to use your wonderful reseach facility.

Tom Nanzig wrote the *3rd Virginia Cavalry* as part of the Virginia Regimental Series and edited *The Civil War Memories of a Virginia Cavalryman – Lt. Robert T. Hubard, Jr.* Lt Hubard served, as a staff officer, in the 3rd Virginia Cavalry. I utilized roster research Tom had in the *3rd Virginia Cavalry* and added information from the service record microfilm at the United Daughters of the Confederacy, the handwritten roster in the *Richard H. Watkins Collection*, and a few confirming notes from Richard's letters to create the Company K roster in Appendix 1. Tom's two publications served as great primers and sources of key information and insight into the 3rd Virginia Cavalry. Tom, it was a pleasure meeting you at the Virginia Historical Society early in 2008. It is wonderful to visit with someone with a deep interest in the soldiers of the regiment and with another individual who is drawn to the letters of Richard H. Watkins.

The two fine works by Tom - the 1982 publication of the Private William Corson's letters, *My Dear Jennie. A Collection of Love Letters from a Confederate Soldier. . .*, edited by Blake Corson - and now this collection of letters, when combined, offer a compelling overview of a Confederate regiment from the perspectives of a staff officer, a private, and a company captain and his wife.

Proofreading remains a thankless task. It is impossible to catch all the errors and the project seems to be never ending. I have personally proofed the text so often that I look at the same mistake multiple times and just cannot see it. My wife Jan, of course, is my major proofreader and also my major source of support and encouragement. I am forever grateful. Thanks to Bobbe Redding, Chuck Redding, Martha Barnett and George Barnett for your sharp eyes and all of your helpful suggestions.

To the members of the James City Cavalry Camp #2095, of the Sons of Confederate Veterans, my thanks for your help proofreading Richard and Mary's letters. The James City Cavalry was originally Company I of the 3rd Virginia Cavalry until they were transferred to the 5th Virginia Cavalry in May of 1862. I would like to specifically thank Bill and Wendy Blizzard, Fred Boelt, William M. Harrison,

Ken Parsons, David and Sherron Ware, and Don Woolridge for all of their notes and suggestions.

My sincere appreciation to Eric J. Wittenberg, noted authority on Confederate and Union cavalry, for calling my attention to the May 14, 1864 letter from Richard being dated in error. Richard is exhausted and should have dated this letter in June since he is describing the battle at Trevilian Station which took place on June 11 and 12 of 1864.

Thanks to Neal Wixson, editor of *Echoes from the Boys of Company H* which is a history of Company H of the 100th New York Volunteer Infantry told through the letters and diaries of nine of their members. Neal's work was published in 2009. I appreciate his proofreading, comments, suggestions and support of my project.

I would be remiss if I did not thank Amelia Barnett (www. luckybugdesigns.com) for her assistance with the photographic section and also her design and layout of the bookmarks I provide when I am at booksignings and book talks.

The final expressions of appreciation go to Richard and Mary Watkins for saving their letters and to Emily Watkins Dupuy and Asa Watkins for donating the letters to the Virginia Historical Society. They left us a rare gift.

APPENDIX 1

Roster of Company K – 3ʳᵈ Virginia Cavalry
"The Prince Edward Dragoons"

Allen, Daniel J.: enlisted 6/24/61, Pr. Ed. CH, Age 49, Private, Cpl.; wounded 5/62; Chimborazo Hosp. 5/26/62, admitted to Farmville General 5/28/62, still shown at Farmville 6/14/62; Re-enlisted 7/5/62 for $50 bounty; provost guard duty 7-8/63 in Fredericksburg; shown AWOL 4/64; discharged 6/24/64.

Allen, H. A.: enlisted 4/7/62 with a $50 bounty for 3 years; 7/29/64 shown in Wayside Hospital (General Hospital #9), Richmond; nfr. (no further record).

Anderson, Charles B.: enlisted 3/9/63, Culpeper CH, Private, paroled 4/65.

Anderson, Charles W.: enlisted 7/16/64, age 18, Private, transferred from Pr. Edward Reserves 7/16/64; paroled 4/65.

Anderson, Frank C.: enlisted 3/13/62, age 21, Richmond, Private; hospitalized 5/15 to 6/30/62 at Farmville General; 12/1/62 admitted to Farmville General with rheumatism; 3/25/63 still shown at Farmville; 6/9/63 at Farmville General with heart disease; Farmville General Hosp. 12/64 (rheumatism), died after 1918.

Anderson, Henry T.: enlisted 6/24/61, Pr. Edward, Private, 8/1/64 requisition for 2 horseshoes and nails for a barefooted horse; nfr.

Armistead, Drury L.: enlisted 6/24/61, Pr. Ed. CH, Private; 6/31/61 5 days leave; detached 4/62 as orderly for Genl. Joe Johnston; wounded 10/1/63 at Raccoon Ford in arm; Farmville General 10 & 11/63; 5-22-64 horse detail 15 days & 6-64 absent with leave to procure horse; 6/9 to 6/17/64 at Farmville General with diarrhea acute; horse killed 8/16/64 at Front Royal and CSA reimbursed $3000; paroled Farmville 4/65.

Arvin, Mellborne L.: enlisted 6/24/61, Private; Age 20; 7/5/62 re-enlisted for $50 bounty; 6/64 on leave to procure horse; 7/14 to 8/21/64 at Farmville General Hospital; captured 11/12/64 at Ninevah, Virginia; prisoner at Point Lookout 12/18/64; exchanged 2/10/65, nfr (no further record).

Baker, James A.: enlisted 6/24/61, Pr. Ed. CH, Private; hospitalized 5-7/62 at Farmville Gen. Hospital (fever); 7/5/62 re-enlisted for $50 bounty; promoted 7/63, Cpl; wounded 5/8/64 at Spotsylvania; wounded 8/16/64 at Front Royal; paroled 4/23/65.

Baker, John W.: enlisted 3/12/62, age 31, farmer, Richmond, Private; wounded 5/6/64 at Todd's Tavern in right shoulder; admitted to Chimborazo #2 5/9/64; wounded 8/64 in Shenandoah Valley in the head; 8/13/64 admitted to Farmville General; 8/23/64 furloughed for 60 days with sabre wound to scalp; paroled 4/23/65.

Bell, James A.: enlisted 6/24/61, Pr. Ed. CH, Private; promoted 4/62 Lieutenant; 7/5/62 re-enlisted for $50 bounty; resigned 10/20/62 (rheumatism).

Berkeley, Peyton R.: enlisted 6/24/61, Pr. Ed. CH, age 57, Lieutenant; 4/26/62 Captain; resigned 11/1/62 (health).

Berkeley, Robert Blair: enlisted 6/24/61, Pr. Ed. CH, Sgt.; transferred 11/24/62 to 54th Virginia Infantry as steward.

Berkeley, William R.: enlisted 8/12/63, Fredericksburg, Private; detached 9/63 to 10/64 as clerk to Gen. J. E. B. Stuart; hospitalized 10/64 to 3/65 (diarrhea), paroled 4/27/65.

Binford, William A.: enlisted 1/20/64, Pr. Ed. CH, Private; wounded 5/28/64 at Haw's Shop in the right side 3" below right nipple exiting between 7th & 8th rib in back; 5/29/64 Jackson Hospital, Richmond; 6/3/64 Farmville General Hospital; 6/17/65 furloughed for 30 days from hospital; absent 6/64 to 1/65 recovering from wound; paroled 4/9/65 at Appomattox.

Bondurant, Clifford A.: enlisted 3/1/63, Culpeper CH, Private; wounded 3/17/63 at Kelly's Ford in the right leg; 3/23/63 Gordonsville Hospital; 3/24/63 General Hospital #9, Richmond; 7/1/64 horse detail for 13 days; paroled 4/20/65 at Burkeville.

Bondurant, John J.: enlisted 6/24/61, Pr. Ed. CH, Private, 36, farmer, 6', florid compl., dark hair, blue eyes; hospitalized 5/18 to 7/31/62 at Farmville General (typhoid fever); discharged 10/62; paroled 4/65.

Bondurant, Samuel J.: enlisted 6/24/61, Private; detached 12/61 as orderly for Colonel Winston; 7/5/62 re-enlisted for $50 bounty; 10/63 granted leave to procure horse; hospitalized 12/28/63 Charlottesville General; 12/30/63 transferred to Lynchburg; 9/15/64 requisition for 4 horseshoes; nfr.

Bondurant, Samuel W.: enlisted 3/18/62, Yorktown, Private, age 21; furnished substitute 11/1/62 (John Skelly – 36 years old).

Booker, George: enlisted 9/3/61, Buckingham CH, Private, age 32; absent sick 11/61 to 3/62, nfr.

Booker, James Horace: enlisted 2/19/64 at Camp Lee, Virginia (draft), Private; hospitalized at Farmville General 2/26 to 3/6/65 (scabies); 3/13/65 returned to duty; nfr. Died 7/7/1902, age 86, buried Hollywood Cem.

Booker, William D.: enlisted 3/14/63, Culpeper CH, Private; horse killed 3/17/63 at Kelly's Ford. Died 1921.

Bragg, Alexander A.: Private; paroled 4/9/65 at Appomattox.

Bragg, Antelicus A.: enlisted 6/24/61, Pr. Ed. CH, Private; detached 10/61 as orderly to Gen. John Magruder; 7/5/62 re-enlisted for $50 bounty; Farmville General Hospital 3/14 to 6/13/63 with dysentery; promoted 7/63 Sgt.; 1/3/65 granted horse detail for 23 days;

1/11/65 to 2/28/65 Farmville General Hospital; paroled 4/20/65 at Burkeville.

Brooks, John William: enlisted 3/15/64, Richmond, Private; 11/9/64 requisition for 4 horseshoes; 11/25/64 Farmville General Hospital; paroled 4/65 Burkeville.

Brooks, Thomas G.: enlisted 8/8/64, Private; hospitalized 1/65 Farmville General; 1/31/65 furloughed 60 days at home; 4/4/65 Wayside Hospital, Farmville (rheumatism), paroled 4/26/65 Farmville.

Bruce, Samuel A.: enlisted 5/1/62, Richmond, Private; hospitalized 12/63 with diarrhea Farmville General; 3/12 to 3/22/64 with bronchitis Farmville General; 10/3/64 requisitioned 4 horseshoes; Farmville General 10/4 to 10/20/64 with fever, nfr.

Bruce, William A.: enlisted 5/16/62, Richmond, Private; 2/21/63 horse detail 15 days; 7-8/63 headquarters orderly; 9/27/64 requisition for 4 horseshoes; nfr.

Carter, Samuel: enlisted 6/24/61, Pr. Ed. CH, Private; absent sick 6-10/61, "never officially mustered into service," nfr.

Chaffin, John T.: enlisted 7/20/64, Private; paroled 4/65 Farmville.

Christian, B.: Private; absent sick 2/62, nfr.

Clark, Charles E.: enlisted 1/20/64, Pr. Ed. CH, Private, Age 32, farmer; wounded 6/21/64 at White House in the right leg below knee [calf]; 6/22/64 admitted Chimborazo #1; 6/25/64 furloughed 40 days from Chimborazo #2; 8/16 furloughed 40 days from Farmville General Hospital; 11/18/64 granted 14 day leave on horse detail; 12/2/64 requisition for 4 horseshoes; paroled 4/9/65 at Appomattox.

Crafton, W. C.: Private; wounded 11/64, hospitalized 11/25/64 to 12/31/64 Farmville General; nfr.

Crafton, William T.: enlisted 3/10/62, Pr. Ed. CH, Private, Age 42; horse killed 11/12/64 at Cedar Creek; paroled 4/65 Farmville.

Cralle, Alexander Brand: enlisted 6/24/61, Pr. Ed. CH, Private, Cpl., Age 22; present 7/62; 7/5/62 re-enlisted for $50 bounty; nfr.

Cunningham, John Robert: enlisted 6/24/61, Pr. Ed. CH, Private, Age 23, sheriff, 5'10", blue eyes, lt. hair, fair complexion; discharged 8/22/61, re-enlisted 3/18/62; wounded 3/17/63 at Kelly's Ford gunshot in abdomen; admitted Farmville General 5/30/63; ball still retained in abdomen 8/26/63; detailed 9/26/63 to the medical department – purveyors with the Surgeon General in Richmond till June, 1864; from November, 1863 thru March, 1864 detached to Medical Purveyors, Depot 5, Atlanta, Georgia; Farmville General Hospital with diarrhea 5/21/64; retired to the invalid corps 6/64; 7/29/64 ordered to Pamplin Depot, Appomattox County as the tithe gatherer; discharged 3/9/65 when elected a civil officer; nfr.

Cunningham, R. N.: Private.

Dalby, Richard W.: enlisted 6/24/61, Pr. Ed. CH, Private, Cpl.; wounded 11/6/61 gunshot wound in right leg; 5/64 Farmville

General Hospital with rheumatism; detached as mounted guard in Pr. Ed. County; discharged 11/64.

Daniel, John Moncure: enlisted 9/10/63, Fredericksburg, Private, Age 18, b. 8/14/45; present 8/64, nfr. (listed on hand written roster in Watkins papers as John W.)

Davis, R. E.: Private. Hospitalized 2/24/64 at General Hospital #9; 2/25/64 at Chimborazo; 4/13/64 shown in Chimborazo #1 with syphilis; transferred 5/5/64 to Farmville General; nfr.

Dickinson, John P.: enlisted 6/24/61, Pr. Ed. CH, Private, Age 19; detached 10/61 as an orderly with Col. Colquitt at Yorktown; detached 1/18/62 as an orderly for Col. Noland; 7/5/62 re-enlisted for $50 bounty; 6/64 absent sick; 7/9/64 to 8/18/64 General Hospital Farmville; paroled 4/65 Farmville.

Dickinson, Robert M.: enlisted 6/24/61, Pr. Ed. CH, Private, Age 21, Lawyer, 5' 10", blue eyes, dark hair, fair complexion; detached 10/61 as orderly for Gen. Magruder; discharged 5/6/62 to accept commission in army.

Dupuy, William Purnell: enlisted 5/12/63, Culpeper CH, Private, b. 1845; wounded 10/19/63 at Buckland Mills with gunshot to head (fleshwound); 10/24/63 admitted to Chimborazo #1; 10/27/63 30 day furlough from Chimborazo #1; 11/26/63 Farmville General; 12/18/63 still present at Farmville General; 6/64 leave to procure horse; wounded 10/9/64 at Tom's Brook; paroled 4/65 Farmville; d. 1904.

Edmunds, Henry Watkins: enlisted 8/25/62, Brandy Station, Private; wounded 3/17/63 at Kelly's Ford canister shot fractured left ribs; 5/2/63 admitted to Robinson Hospital, Richmond; 5/28/63 admitted to Farmville General; bullet entered under left nipple exited between ribs 4 & 5 in back, fracturing both, frequent loss of bone material, blood, & body matter accompanied with irregular fevers; retired 7/26/64, paroled 4/26/65; Buried in Westview Cem., Farmville.

Elliott, Francis Lillas: enlisted 6/24/61, Pr. Ed. CH, Private; hospitalized 4/6/62 at Chimborazo #3 with cystitis and debilitis; 5/12/62 transferred to Farmville General; 7/5/62 re-enlisted for $50 bounty; 8/19/62 returned to duty; horse killed 11/4/62 at Upperville; hospitalized 7/29/64 Petersburg General with fever; returned to duty 8/13/64; nfr.

Elliott, John A.: Private; hospitalized 12/30/64 Farmville General, nfr.

Elliott, Robert C.: enlisted 6/24/61, Pr. Ed. CH, farmer, Private; Sgt. 7/63; 7/5/62 re-enlisted for $50 bounty; 7/30/63 to 8/31/63 at Farmville General with rheumatism; 10/63 leave to procure horse; [wounded 5/26/64 at Haw's Shop]; 6/26/64 admitted to Chimborazo #4 with tibula of right leg fractured; mortally wounded at St. Mary's Church gunshot fracture of the right leg and died of wounds at Chimborazo 7/6/64; Personal effects document noting "$80.85 and various sundrie."

Evans, William W.: enlisted 6/24/61, Pr. Ed. CH, Age 39; Private; 7/5/62 re-enlisted for $50 bounty; October, 1863 furlough; 7/5 to 7/12/64 at Farmville General with dibilitis; wounded 8/16/64 at Front Royal (head wound); 8/23/64 to 11/21/64 at Farmville General with head wound; 1/3/65 at Farmville General with cystitis; paroled 4/65 Farmville General Hospital.

Ewing, John J.: enlisted 8/1/62, Hanover CH, Private; 10/63 leave to procure horse; 6/23/64 Farmville General Hospital with debilities; returned to duty 8/16/64 from Wayside Hospital of Farmville; paroled 4/21/65 Burkeville.

Ewing, William W. H.: enlisted 8/25/62, Brandy Station, Private; 10/63 leave to procure horse; bugler at HQ 5/64; wounded 8/23 to 8/31/64 at Farmville General with wound in left arm; paroled 4/25/65.

Faulkner, Alexander H.: enlisted 6/24/61, Pr. Ed. CH, Private, farmer, 5' 8", yellow eyes, dark hair, fair complexion; detached 10/26/61 as orderly to Gen. Raines; 11/22/61 sick furlough; discharged 10/8/62 (bladder stone and chronic rheumatism).

Flournoy, Charles: enlisted 9/10/61, Pr. Ed. CH, Private; 7/5/62 re-enlisted for $50 bounty; detached 4/64 to bale hay; transferred 5/64 to the Richmond Howitzers.

Flournoy, John J.: enlisted 6/24/61, Pr. Ed. CH, Private, Age 23, hotel keeper, 5' 9", blue eyes, sandy hair, fair complexion; on extra duty with QM Dept. 8/1/61; sick furlough 1/1/62; 5/28/62 to 6/7/62 Farmville General Hospital with diarrhea; 7/5/62 re-enlisted for $50 bounty; wounded 1862; 10/4 to 10/10/62 at Clopton Hospital in Richmond; 1/19/63 at Farmville General Hospital with deafness being considered for discharge; discharged 2/23/63.

Flournoy, Thomas: enlisted 2/18/63, Culpeper, Private; 8/63 leave to procure horse; detached 4/64 as wagoner; absent sick 6-8/64; nfr.

Foster, George: enlisted 8/10/64, Richmond, Private (drafted); hospitalized at Farmville General with pneumonia 3/16/65; paroled Farmville 4/24/65.

Foster, William Rowland: enlisted 3/12/62, Richmond, Private, Age 25, b. 1833; absent sick 3-8/64 with pleurisy, rheumatism, debilitis; absent sick 10/64 to 3/65 debilitis; paroled 5/2/65; d. 1909.

Fowlkes, George G.: enlisted 6/24/61, Pr. Ed. CH, Private; discharged 10/30/61.

Fowlkes, George W.: enlisted 6/24/61, Pr. Ed. CH, Private Age 26, wheelwright, 5' 10", blue eyes, light hair, fair complexion; 1/6/62 to 2/28/62 sick furlough; declined to re-enlist 4/62; re-enlisted 7/5/62 for $50 bounty; nfr.

Fowlkes, James D.: enlisted 3/12/62, Richmond, Private, Age 18; paroled 4/9/65 at Appomattox.

Fraver, James: Private; paroled 5/8/65.

Garrett, Lafayette J.: enlisted 3/16/62, Pr. Edward, Private; detached 10/62 to 12/64 as teamster to Brigade; paroled 4/23/65 Farmville; d. after 1903 in state asylum.

Gilliam, Charles: Private; present 7/64, no earlier records, 2/10/65 admitted to General Hospital #9, Richmond; paroled 4/9/65 Appomattox.

Guthrie, James Henry: enlisted 3/12/62, Richmond, Private, Age 19; 5/18/62 to 6/23/62 at Farmville General Hospital; 4/3/63 to 4/19/63 leave to procure horse; admitted 7/18/64 to Chimborazo #1 with dysentery; paroled 4/65 Farmville.

Harvey, Thomas J.: enlisted 6/24/61, Pr. Ed. CH, Private, Age 42, farmer, 5' 11", blue eyes, dark hair, florid complexion; sick furlough home 2/13/62; hospitalized 5/18 to 6/15/62 Farmville General Hospital; discharged 9/30/62 over age.

Harvey, William T.: enlisted 6/24/61, Pr. Edward, Private, Age 38, 1/7/62 to 1/31/62 detached special service; 7/5/62 re-enlisted for $50 bounty; promoted QM Sgt. and detached 8/62 to QM department; POW 4/65 Burkeville; Paroled 4/23/65 Burkeville.

Haskins, Archer Alexander: enlisted 6/24/61, Pr. Ed., Private, Age 21, b. 11/4/39; 4/6/62 absent sick; 7/5/62 re-enlisted for $50 bounty; 2nd Lieutenant 10/20/62; 4/6/64 admitted General Hospital #4 Richmond; 4/11/64 re-admitted with fever, 30 day sick furlough 4/13/64; paroled 4/65 Farmville; d. 6/4/1910 Meherrin, Va.

Haskins, Thomas E.: enlisted 7/9/62, Hanover CH, Sgt.; 10/63 leave to procure horse; 6/26/64 to 7/14/64 absent sick at Chimborazo #3 with dysentery; present 8/64, nfr.

Hill, _____: Private; absent sick 12/61, nfr.

Holladay, John Zachary: Private, Age 16; Sgt; detached 3-10/64 forage master in Ordnance Reserve; 6/64 at General Hospital #9, Richmond with rheumatism; nfr.

Hunt, A. J.: Private; admitted 6/17/64 to General Hospital #9; 6/18/64 transferred to Chimborazo; nfr.

Hunt, George: enlisted 3/12/62, Richmond, Private, Age 25, 5' 11", blue eyes, light hair, fair complexion; hospitalized 12/2/62 at Chimborazo #3; 12/15/62 transferred to Farmville General with rheumatism; 5/18/62 admitted at Farmville; 3/26/63 returned to duty; captured Williamsport, MD 7/5/63; POW 7/63 to 6/19/65 at Fort Delaware Prison, DE; paroled 6/26/65 at Ft. Delaware.

Hunt, John C.: enlisted 3/12/62, Richmond, Private, Age 34; detached as a courier for General Kemper; mortally wounded 7/3/63 at Gettysburg, captured and died 7/3/63 Gettysburg.

Ivins, W. W.: Private; hospitalized 7/5/64 to 11/15/64 at Farmville General Hospital with diarrhea and debilitis; nfr.

Jeffress, Edward Hudson: enlisted 6/24/61, Pr. Ed., Private, b. 1840; 7/5/62 re-enlisted for $50 bounty; hospitalized at Chimborazo #3 and Farmville General from 10/62 to 8/64 with chronic rheumatism and atrophy of the musculature in the right leg; retired 9/64; d. 1904.

Jenkins, Benjamin Franklin: enlisted 12/10/61, Bethel, Private, Age 20; 4/6 to 4/26/62 at Chimborazo #3 with burnt eyes; 7/5/62 re-enlisted for $50 bounty; 4/10/63 detailed to bale hay; wounded 7/3/63 at Gettysburg when shot in the left side, developed gangrene; 7/12/63 admitted to Charlottesville Hospital; 7/23/63 to General Hospital #1 – Richmond; 6/13 to 6/15/64 Stuart Hospital – Richmond with ulcers; paroled 4/30/65 Burkeville.

Jenkins, John: enlisted 2/1/64, Pr. Ed., Private (drafted); 5/31/64 General Hospital #9 Richmond; 6/1/64 Chimborazo – Richmond; Wayside Hospital and Farmville General in Farmville from 8/5/64 to 11/28/64 with diarrhea; returned to duty 11/28/64; 2/3/65 23 days leave to procure horse; paroled 4/65 Farmville.

Johnson, Harvey: discharged 1862.

Johnson, Napoleon B.: enlisted 6/24/61, Pr. Ed. CH, Private, Age 24, overseer, 6' 1", blue eyes, flaxen hair, fair complexion; detached 7-9/61 as hospital steward; discharged 9/4/61 with a hernia.

Kent, John: "Irish Conscript", Pvt., captured 7/17/63 at Gaines Crossroads; POW 7/31/63 to 1/20/64 at Point Lookout Prison, Maryland; paroled 1/21/64 at Point Lookout to join the U. S. Army; enlisted U. S. Army 1/29/64.

Knight, John Hughes: enlisted 6/24/61, Pr. Ed., Sgt., b. 10/25/29; 7/5/62 re-enlisted for unspecified bounty; Lieutenant 10/20/62; 10/1/62 admitted to Farmville General with debilities; 10/11/62 given private quarters at Farmville; 12/8/62 released; 12/21/62 re-admitted to Farmville with debilities; 2/20/63 released; 6/18/63 Farmville General with intermittant fever; 8/12/63 released; 4/64 absent as judge in courts martial; wounded 6/28/64 at Stony Creek Depot in the thigh [RHW letter of 6/22/64 notes Lt. Knight getting wounded in thigh 6/21 at White House]; 6/22/64 to 6/30/64 General Hospital #4 – Richmond with gun shot to thigh; 6/30/64 to 9/2/64 at Farmville General; 9/2/64 returned to duty; horse killed

10/13/64 at Cedar Creek; promoted to Captain 3/65; paroled 4/9/65 Appomattox; buried Westview Cem., Farmville.

Ligon, James G.: enlisted 6/24/61, Pr. Ed., Private; d. 6/19/62 in General Hospital at Farmville from diarrhea.

Ligon, Richard V.: enlisted 1/20/64, Pr. Ed., Private; 6/64 leave to procure horse; paroled 4/9/65 Appomattox.

Lincoln, George: Private; captured 1/3/63 POW at Old Capital Prison, Washington City

Lockett, Edmond S.: enlisted 4/1/62, Richmond, Private; 8/2/62 Chimborazo #1 with typhoid; 8/8/62 transferred to Farmville General; 9/2//62 returned to duty; 3/4/63 Farmville General with bronchitis; 11/8/63 General Hospital #9 with diarrhea; 11/9/63 admittted to Chimborazo #1; 11/13/63 admitted Farmville General with bronchitis; 3/22/64 returned to duty; 10/21 to 11/12/64 Farmville General with bronchitis; paroled 4/9/65 Appomattox.

Martin, Charles: enlisted 6/24/61, Pr. Ed., Private, Age 44, b. 4/26/17; detached 8/61 to 3/62 to Quartermaster Department; discharged 1862; d. 3/10/98 in Danville, VA

Meredith, Henry T.: enlisted 6/24/61, Pr. Ed., Private; 5/7 to 5/21/62 Farmville General with dysentery; promoted to Sgt. 7/62; 7/5/62 re-enlisted for $50 bounty; captured 9/15/62 at Boonsboro, MD; POW 9-10/62 exchanged 10/17/62; promoted to Lieutenant 12/23/62; 6/3/63 Farmville General with nephritis; 7/22/63 returned to duty; 12/2/63 Farmville General; 5/17/64 admitted Farmville General with chronic diarrhea with emaciation and dibility; 6/1/64 40 days leave from Farmville General; paroled 4/9/65 Appomattox.

Miller, Richard A.: enlisted 4/1/62, Richmond, Private; absent sick 11/62 to 3/64 with typhoid fever; hospitalized 6/17 to 7/22/64 at Farmville General with fever remittens and hemorrhoids; 7/22/64 60 day furlough to recover from typhoid fever and debilitis; paroled 4/24/65 Burkeville.

Miller, W. M.: Private; captured 7/4/63 at Gettysburg; POW 7-9/63 at Fort McHenry, MD, Fort Delaware and Fort Columbus; 9-11/63 at Point Lookout Prison, MD; hospitalized 11/63 and transferred to Hammond General Hospital as a POW; nfr.

Moore, Abner F.: enlisted 6/24/61, Pr. Ed., Private; transferred 8/20/61 to the 18th Virginia Infantry.

Morton, William H.: enlisted 10/2/63, Welford's Farm, Private; hospitalized 2/65 with scabies; paroled 5/18/65 Danville.

Moseley, Charles R.: Private; d. 8/6/1923 buried Hollywood Cem., Richmond.

Nicholas, George: Private (substitute); deserted 12/28/62 near Fairfax Court House, Va. during Stuart's Christmas raid.

Penick, Frank J.: enlisted 3/17/62, Pr. Ed., Private, Age 26, farmer; 5/62 Chimborazo #2 – Richmond with Haemoptysis; 6/3/62 transferred to Lynchburg; 8/21/62 admitted to Farmville General with rheumatism; 11/22/62 at Farmville General Hospital; 2/20/63 clothing issue at Farmville General; 3/3/63 re-admitted to Farmville General; 4/14/63 returned to regiment; 4/21/63 arrived regiment & signed by "Watkins"; captured 7/3/63 at Gettysburg; POW 7/63 at Fort Delaware Prison, DE; exchanged 7/31/63; hospitalized 8/2/63-10/21/63 at Farmville General with debilitis; 5/22/64 horse detail for 7 days by Genl. F. Lee; 5/31/64 Farmville General; wounded 6/21/64 at White House in the right breast [shoulder]; 6/22/64 General Hosp. #2 – Richmond furloughed 40 days, age noted at 29; 8/9/64 Farmville General – ball entrance near second rib of right side. Exit near external edge of Scapula furloughed 30 more days; 10/25/64 Charlottesville General with acute bronchitis, furloughed 30 days by Surg. J. L. Cabell. 11/22/64 Farmville General retained for further treatment; 11/24/64 Wayside General in Farmville for bronchitis released to private quarters 12/19/64 to 1/2/65 with periodic checks at Farmville General; 1/3/65 to 4/3/65 still on leave Farmville General; paroled 4/65 Farmville.

Penick, Lavalette M.: enlisted 3/17/62, Pr. Ed., Cpl, Pvt., Age 30; discharged 8/7/62 with a lung illness; 9/3/62 General Hosp. #21 – Richmond with consumption; detached 4/63 as a wagoner; 8/30/63 still detached a wagoner; 1/31/64 paid $90 for clothing; 2/29/64 paid $48; 4/1/64 detached duty with Captain White; detached 7/21/64 to 8/17/64 as wagoner with regiment; 8/64 detached duty with Major Paxton in Lynchburg; 8/30/64 to 9/20/64 Farmville General; paroled 4/24/65 Farmville.

Price, Edward N.: enlisted 6/24/61, Pr. Ed., Pvt., Sgt.; Age 34, 4/30/62 paid $64; 7/5/62 re-enlisted for $50 bounty; detached 7/63 to 7/64 as an orderly at cavalry HQ; 8/23/64 admitted Farmville General with a fistulous opening to the left of the rectum caused by an old abscess recently aggravated on buttocks – 30 days furlough; 9/27/64 still furloughed; 10/28/64 same; 12/6/64 retained for treatment by Dr. Taliaferro; 12/21/64 returned to duty from Farmville General; nfr.

Ragsdale, Bracy Hester: enlisted 7/15/62, White House, substitute for A. B. Cralle, Private; wounded 5/6/64; 2/10/65 to 3/5/65 at Chimborazo #4 with gonorrhea; deserted 4/65 at Fort Powhatan; paroled and of oath of allegiance 4/12/65 Washington, D. C; transportation provided to Suffolk.

Redd, Charles E.: enlisted 6/24/61, Pr. Ed., Private, Age 30; hospitalized 5/28/62 at Chimborazo #3; transferred to Farmville General 6/3/62 with hepatitis; 7/5/62 re-enlisted for a $50 bounty; 7/19/62 returned to duty; discharged 9/6/62 when he furnished a substitute.

Redd, Francis Dabney: enlisted 6/24/61, Pr. Ed., Lieutenant, Age 36, b. 1825; 7/31/61 $90 pay; 9/30/61 receipt for $90 pay for 1 months service; 12/61 15 day furlough; 1/62 on leave to visit sick wife; resigned 4/24/62; service expires 6/24/62; d. 5/11/1900.

Redd, John A.: enlisted 6/24/61, Pr. Ed., Private, Age 25; 7/5/62 re-enlists for $50 bounty; hospitalized 518/62 -7/28/62 Farmville General with nephritis; 5/27/63 -7/22/63 Farmville General with nephritis; present 8/64; nfr.

Redd, John H.: Private; present 8/64; nfr.

Redd, John Wesley: Private; hospitalized 9/6/64 to 1/9/65 at Farmville General with typhoid fever; d. 9/6/1923 at age 78 in Richmond; buried in Hollywood Cem.

Redd, Joseph T.: enlisted 6/24/61, Pr. Ed., Private, Age 36; 7/31/61 5 days leave; hospitalized 5/7/62 -7/23/62 Farmville General; 8/31/62 paid $187.40 for clothing; discharged 9/23/62.

Redd, Robert Leigh: enlisted 6/24/61, Pr. Ed., Private, Age 31; 7/61 on extra duty in QM department as forage master; 7/5/62 re-enlisted for $50 bounty; 8/63 leave for fresh horse; present 8/64; nfr.

Richardson, John D.: enlisted 5/25/62, White House, Private, substitute for C. E. Redd; 8/63 leave for fresh horse; 4/6/64 duty at Wayside Receiving Hospital – Richmond; 6/64 leave to procure serviceable horse; nfr.

Richardson, William M.: enlisted 4/30/62, Richmond, Private; paroled 4/65 Burkeville.

Rowlett, James Chap: enlisted 3/3/62, Private, age 19; hospitalized Farmville General 12/63 to 4/64 with pneumonia and 6-9/64 with chronic bronchitis and 12/64 to 3/65 with bronchitis & debilitis; wounded 4/1/65 at Five Forks; nfr.

Rowlett, Junius C.: enlisted 5/1/62, Richmond, Private; horse killed 3/17/64 at Kelly's Ford; present 8/64; wounded 8/16/64 at Front Royal and had a leg amputated.

Rowlett, Samuel S.: enlisted 7/6/64, Richmond, Private; hospitalized 1-3/65; paroled 4/9/65 Appomattox.

Scott, Edward A.: enlisted 6/24/61, Pr. Ed., Private; present 10/61; killed in action in 1861 on picket duty near Newport News, VA.

Scott, Francis H.: enlisted 6/24/61, Pr. Ed., Sgt., Age 29; 3/18/62 to 4/18/62 sick furlough; demoted to private 7/62; hospitalized 1-5/63 with a bladder disorder; detached 5/63 as a hospital guard; detached 10/63 to QM Dept., Capt. Mayre in Farmville till 8/64; nfr.

Scott, Lafayette: enlisted 6/24/61, Pr. Ed., Private, Age 23: 5/14/62 Chimborazo #4 admitted and transferred to Dinwiddie Hospital with measles; 7/5/62 re-enlisted for $50 bounty; wounded 3/17/63 at Kelly's Ford with a gunshot wound to right leg; hospitalized 3/63 – 12/63; 12/5/63 Farmville General recovering GSW right leg recd in March abcess recently formed loss of specula bone. Recently in private residence in Keysville, Charlotte Cty – not in hospital; 6/64 transferred to 1st Engineer Corps; hospitalized 8/64; nfr.

Skelly, John: enlisted 11/62, Upperville, Private, substitute for S. W. Bondurant; arrested 5/62 while assigned to Stuart's Horse Artillery; AWOL 7/24/63; nfr.

Spencer, Charles B.: enlisted 2/15/64, Pr. Ed., Private; 5/31/64 diarrhea; 6/13/64 Farmville General returned to duty; paroled 4/27/65 Farmville.

Spencer, Joseph C.: enlisted 3/12/62, Richmond, Private, Age 17; 10/63 on leave to procure horse; killed in action 6/24/64 at St. Mary's Church.

Spencer, Nathan Bell: enlisted 6/24/61, Pr. Ed., Private, Age 24, b. 3/13/37; absent sick 6/62 and 10/63; 7/5/62 re-enlisted for $50 bounty; paroled 4/24/65 Farmville; d. 6/14/1919 Redlands, CA; buried Hillside Cem.

Starling, S. A.: Private; paroled 5/10/65 Danville.

Stokes, Richard Cralle: enlisted 6/24/61; Pr. Ed., Lieutenant, Age 33; 9/61 absent sick; resigned 4/25/62.

Sublette, P. B.: nfr.

Thackston, Nathaniel: enlisted 10/1/62, Charlestown, VA, Private; captured 7/5/63 at Waterloo, MD; Transferred from Ft. Delaware to hospital 7-8/63 in Chester, PA; exchanged 8/17/63; 8/29/63 Farmville General with debilities & typhoid fever to 10/63; 10/63 leave to procure horse; wounded 6/12/64 at Trevillian Station with a fractured right forearm; 6/13/64 Charlottesville General; 7/11/64 60 day furlough; 9/16/64 Farmville General – GSW right forearm with a fractured radius and partial anchylosis of wrist joint – ordered to regiment; 10/18/64 Farmville General w/ arm problems 60 day furlough; nfr.

Thornton, John Thurston: enlisted 6/24/61, Pr. Ed., Captain, Age 32, b. 1829, lawyer; detached 8/30/61 ordered to Fort Smith, Arkansas but no evidence of transfer; present 1/62; 2/7/62 furlough; promoted to Lt. Colonel 4/62; killed in action at Sharpsburg, MD on 9/17/62.

Todd, Albert H.: enlisted 3/12/62, Richmond, Private, Age 23; 8/63 leave to get fresh horse; present 8/64; d 1-17-1930 in Talladega, Alabama.

Trueheart, William C.: enlisted 3/12/62, Richmond, Private, Age 21, b. 8/8/40; 8/63 detailed provost guard at Culpeper CH; present 8/64; d. 4/2/1872 in Stanford, Kentucky.

Venable, Andrew Reid: enlisted 3/17/62, Pr. Ed., Private, Age 31; discharged 2/25/63; appointed Captain / Asst. Quartermaster.

Venable, Charles W.: enlisted 5/2/64, Pr. Ed., Private; 3/6/65 Farmville General with scabies; 3/8/65 furloughed to private residence; nfr.

Walton, John F.: enlisted 6/24/61, Pr. Ed., Private, b. 1839; detached 3/62 as orderly to Col. Goode; 7/5/62 re-enlisted for $50 bounty; detached 9/63 to 10/64 QM Department at Gordonsville; 9/20/63 admitted Farmville General with remittent fever; 10/6/63 Farmville General chronic diarrhea, bronchitis furloughed 30 days to Green Bay, PE Cty; 12/4/63 Farmville General with tonsillitis, furlough extended at home of W. B. Richard; 12/31/63 pay voucher for $144.13; 6/8/64 pay voucher for $96.13; 7/15/64 7 days leave from hospital; 7/22/64 Farmville General – here 4 weeks with diarrhea, emaciation and debility; 8/31/64 muster roll shows at QM Dept. at Gordonsville Cavalry Hospital; paroled 4/65 Farmville.

Walton, John J.: Private.

Walton, Lucius D.: enlisted 6/24/61, Private, Age 18, b. 1843; Sgt.; 7/5/62 re-enlisted for $50 bounty; 5/16/63 $12.75 for rations while on leave 28 Sep to 15 Oct 62 to procure a fresh horse; 8/63 leave for fresh horse; 11/30/63 Farmville General with scabies and catarra; 6/17/64 Farmville General with debility – ordered to hospital for treatment; 6/20/64 to 8/1/64 Farmville General with debilitis; 12/31/64 to 3/4/65 Farmville General; 3/4/65 returned to duty from Farmville General; paroled 4/9/65 Appomattox; d. 1901.

Walton, Robert H.: enlisted 6/24/61, Pr. Ed., Farmer, Private; 5/14/62 Chimborazo #4 with measles – returned to regiment 5/18/62; 7/5/62 re-enlisted for $50 bounty; promoted to Cpl. 7/63; wounded 6/16/64 with gunshot to the right hip [RHW letter of 6/22/64 notes Cpt. Walton getting wounded 6/21 at White House]; 6/22/64 Chimborazo #2; 6/28/64 60 day furlough to Farmville; 10/7/64 Farmville General released for return to regiment; nfr.

Watkins, Richard Henry: enlisted 6/24/61, Pr. Ed., Private, b. 6/4/1825; Age 36; lawyer and farmer; detached 7/4/61 to Commissary Department; elected 2nd Lieutenant 4/25/62; promoted to 1st Lieutenant 4/27/62; promoted to Captain 10/23/62; wounded

10/31/62 with a saber cut to the head in skirmish near Aldie and lost horse to Union cavalry; 2/25/63 thrown from horse at Hartwood Church and horse led Union cavalry from the field; horse killed 3/17/63 at Kelly's Ford; 8/25/63 to 9/4/63 Farmville General with debilitis; horse wounded 9/19/64 at Winchester; 10/9/64 wounded at Tom's Brook with a saber wound to left hand and wrist; hospitalized 10/64 to 2/65 at Gordonsville Cavalry Hospital and Farmville General Hospital; 2/65 Disability Leave; 3/14/65 transfer approved to Invalid Corps; 3/31/65 transfer effective to Invalid Corps; paroled 5/12/65 Danville, VA; practiced law in Pr. Edward County and Farmville and farmed; senior partner in the firm of Watkins, Watkins and Brock of Farmville; d 7/8/1905; buried at Westview Cem., Farmville.

West, George Marcus: enlisted 5/3/64, Hamilton's Crossing, Private; paroled 4/65 Farmville.

Wiley, Oscar: enlisted 6/24/61, Pr. Ed., Private; discharged 10/18/61.

Williams, John C.: enlisted 6/24/61, Pr. Ed., Private; detached 1-3/62 orderly to Col. Ward; 7/5/62 re-enlisted for $50 bounty; detached 7-10/63 at camp for disabled horses in Albemarle; 10/63 leave to procure fresh horse; 11/3/63 Farmville General with neuralgia caused by disease of prostate gland; 1/26/64 Farmville General admitted with cystitis; 4/11/64 admitted to Charlottesville General Hosp; 4/25/64 admitted to Farmville with neuralgia; 4/27/64 Farmville General 60 day furlough; 7/5/64 Farmville General with debilitis – 60 day furlough; 9/2/64 extended 60 days; 11/1/64 Farmville General put on light duty; 11/2/64 to 1/12/65 Farmville General with chronic cystitis; 3/24/65 transferred to Battery Garnett – James River defenses; nfr.

Wilson, James H.: enlisted 5/1/62, Richmond, Private; 1/1/63 clothing receipt; captured 6/17/63 at Aldie; POW 6/63 at Old Capital Prison in Washington City; exchanged 6/25/63; 8/17/63 absent sick; 12/29/63 Farmville General with scrofillas of lymph glands; killed in action 5/28/64 at Haw's Shop.

Womack, Adam C.: enlisted 3/17/62, Pr. Ed., Private, Age 22; 5/26/62 Chimborazo #1 with fever and diarrhea; 5/28/62 transferred

& admitted Farmville General; 6/23/62 returned to duty; 10/63 leave to procure horse; paroled 4/65 Farmville.

Womack, Archer W.: enlisted 6/24/61, Pr. Ed and re-enlisted 9/15/63 Richmond, Private, Age 36; detached 1-2/62 Company Quartermaster; 3/62 leave to get a fresh horse; discharged 9/23/62; hospitalized 7/64 to 1/65 with a fractures of both right leg bones 2 ½" above right ankle in a fall from a horse; age reported as 37 in 7/64 hospital form; nfr.

Womack, David Gaires: enlisted 10/10/62, Charlestown, Private; paroled 4/23/65; d. 1870.

Womack, Eugene: enlisted 4/1/63, Culpeper, Private; 3/11/64 Farmville General with scabies – returned to duty 4/15/64; wounded 6/28/64 in the right side of the neck; 7/1/64 Wayside Receiving Hospital transfer to Chimborazo #3; 7/2/64 Chimborazo #3 with debilitis and GSW right side neck – 30 day furlough effective 7/7/64; killed in action 10/9/64 at Tom's Brook.

Womack, Frank L.: enlisted 9/20/63, Vidiersville, Private; present 8/64; nfr.

Womack, William D.: enlisted 6/24/61, Pr. Ed., Private, Age 22; 7/5/62 re-enlisted for $50 bounty; 7/28/62 to 9/19/62 Farmville General; 11/10/62 Chimborazo #3 with cystitis; 1/23/63 Farmville General deserted from hospital; 9/8/63 to 11/17/63 Farmville General with debilitis; 4/13/64 Gen. Receiving Hosp. #9; 4/14/64 admitted Chimborazo #2 with pneumonia; 4/18/64 transferred to Petersburg; 4/22/64 admitted Farmville General; deserted twice from hospital on 5/18 (returned on 20th) and 6/24; 8/21/64 General Receiving Hosp. #9 –Richmond; 8/22/64 received Chimborazo; 9/6/64 clothing issue at Howards Grove Hospital – Richmond; 12/12/64 transfer to Charlotte County for care; 12/13/64 clothing issue at Chimborazo Hospital; paroled 4/65 Farmville.

Wootten, Samuel Taylor: enlisted 5/1/62, Richmond, Private; wounded 6/12/64 at Trevillian Station; paroled 4/9/65 Appomattox.

Wootten, William B.: enlisted 12/2/63, Troyman's Mills, Private; 5/31/64 Chimborazo #9 – Richmond; 6/64 absent sick; present 8/64; nfr. 1

APPENDIX 2

U. S. Census Reports – Richard Watkins & family

- - - - -

1860

Schedule 1. – Free Inhabitants in _____ in the County of Prince Edward, State of Virginia, enumerated by me on the 11 day of July, 1860. Frederick B. McRobert Asst. Marshall

Post Office – Moore's Oridinary

Name	Age	Sex	Occupation	Real Estate	Personal Prop.
Richard H. Watkins	35	M	Lawyer	$10,000	$25,000
Mary P.	21	F			
Emily D.	1	F			
John Daniel	23	M	Overseer	$ 5,000 1	

- - - - -

1860

Schedule 2 – United State Cenus, Slave Schedules: In the County of Prince Edward, State of Virginia, enumerated by me on the 11 day of July, 1860. F. B. McRobert, A. M.

Richard Watkins – Owner:
69M, 55F, 49F, 40F, 45M, 27M, 25M, 24M, 21M, 20M, 19F, 17F, 17F, 14F, 14M, 14M, 13M, 12M, 12M, 10M, 10M, 8F, 8F, 3F, 3F, 10/12M, 5/12F. (27 total slaves). 2

- - - - -

1870

Page No. 47
Schedule 1 – Inhabitants in Hampden Township, in the County of Prince Edward, State of Virginia, enumerated by me on the 22 day of August 1870.
Post Office – Farmville, Va H. R. Hooper – Asst. Marshall

Name	Age	Sex	Race	Occupation	Real Estate	Personal	Born
Watkins, Richard H.	45	M	W	Lawyer/ Farmer	$10,000	$1,000	Va
Mary P.	31	F	W	Keeping House			Va
Emily D.	11	F	W				Va
Mildred S.	9	F	W				Va
Mary P.	7	F	W				Va
Virginia	2	F	W				Va 3

- - - - -

1880

Page No. 13   A
Supervisor's Dist. No. 2   312
Enumerator Dist. No. 191

Schedule 1. – Inhabitants in part of Hampden District, in the County of Prince Edward, State of Virginia, enumerated by me on the 12 day of June, 1880.

Frederick B. McRobert
Enumerator

Name	Sex	Age	Relation	Occupation
Watkins, Richard H.	M	55		Farmer
Mary P.	F	41	wife	Keeping House
Emily D.	F	20	daughter	w/o occupation
Mildred S.	F	19	daughter	w/o occupation
Asa D.	M	7	son	student 4

- - - - -

(ed: In the "1850 Census of Prince Edward County – Including Slave Schedule," Wm. F. Anderson, editor; Farmville, 1999: I was unable to find a listing for Richard H. Watkins on the "Slave Schedule." Richard is only shown with $200 worth of real estate. At age 25 he did not own any slaves. In the same census report I did find Henry & Mildred Watkins, his parents, listed with a total of 52 slaves. I was unable to find Mildred on the 1860 report but I would surmise that her slave holdings had increased.) 5

- - - - -

U. S. Census Reports – Emily H. Dupuy & family

1850

Schedule 1. – Free Inhabitants in _____ in the County of Pr. Edward, State of Virginia, enumerated by me, on the 9th day of Sept. 1850.
Jms. H. Dupuy
Asst. Marshall

Name	Age	Sex	Real Estate	Where Born
Emily H. Dupuy	38	F	18,900	Mass
Mary P.	11	F		Va
Maria	9	F		Va
Lavilett	7	F		Va
Nannie	5	F		Va
Emily	3	F		Va
Lucinda Howe	64	F		Mass
Anna Whitaker	41	F		Mass
Margaret Arvin	18	F		Lunenburg, Va
Mary B. Jones	15	F		Lunenburg
Frances	13	F		Lunenburg
Lucy Woodson	14	F		Lunenburg
Emily Bowman	16	F		Lunenburg
Emma Dupuy	11	F		Lunenburg 6

- - - - -

1850

Schedule 2 – United States Census, Slave Schedules: In the County of Prince Edward, State of Virginia, enumerated by me on the 9th day of September. J. H. Dupuy, A. M.

E. H. Dupuy – Owner:
52F, 48F, 46M, 43F, 41F, 39M, 36M, 32M, 28F, 27F, 26F, 24M, 29M, 42F, 38F, 33M, 36M, 28F, 53M, 58M, 23M, 21F, 60F, 63M, 20M, 18F, 16F, 15F, 16F, 15M, 14F, 9F, 13M, 11M, 11M, 9F, 8F, 8M, 8M, 8F, 7M, 6M, 6M, 6F, 5F, 5F, 4F, 3F, 2F, 2M, 1F, 1F, 1M, 50M. (54 slaves). 7

- - - - -

1860

Page No. 23
Schedule 1 – Free Inhabitants in _____, in the County of Prince Edward, State of Virginia, enumerated by me, on the 12 day of July 1860.
Post Office – Moore's Ordinary F. B. McRobert – Asst. Marshall

Name	Age	Sex	Real Estate	Personal Prop.	Born
E. H. Dupuy	48	F	$35,000	$53,500	Mass
Maria L.	19	F			Va
Eliza L.	17	F			Va
Nannie L.	15	F			Va
Lucinda H.	14	F			Va
Ann H. Whittaker	51	F			Mass
Wm. Whittaker	12	M			Va 8

- - - - -

1860

Schedule 2 – United States Census, Slave Schedules: In the County of Prince Edward, State of Virginia, enumerated by me, on the 12 day of July, 1860. F. B. McRobert, A. M.

E. H. Dupuy – Owner:
70M, 68M, 49F, 56M, 49M, 60M, 40M, 44M, 40M, 34M, 33M, 30M, 25M, 22M, 21M, 18M, 17M, 17M, 11M, 11M, 8M, 8M, 6M, 6M, 6M, 6M, 6M, 4M, 4M, 3M, 2M, 48M.

68F, 58F, 58F, 54F, 53F, 48F, 37F, 38F, 36F, 32F, 28F, 27F, 26F, 24F, 21F, 19F, 18F, 18F, 15F, 15F, 14F, 13F, 13F, 12F, 11F, 9F, 8F, 8F, 8F, 8F, 7F, 5F, 5F, 3F, 3F, 3F, 1F, 1/2F, 4/12F, 2/12F, 1/12F, 3F, 8F. (32 males slaves and 43 female slaves = 75 slaves). 9

- - - - -

Appendix 3

McKinney & Dupuy – Butter & Lard Sales Payment

Sale of Butter & Lard on acct Richd H Watkins Esq
1861   by
                                              McKinney & Dupuy

Decr 16	W H Benson	1 Pot Butter	$ 9.20
	..	1 Tub Lard	13.44
	Mrs Motley	1 Tub Lard	11.69
	..	1 Tin Lard	9.44
	J. F. Reynault	1 Bucket Lard	4.81
	Mrs Mosby	1 Bucket Lard	8.12

		$ 56.70
Charges		
Freight .93 drayage to & from office	.50	1.43
(Comm 2 ½ % on $56.70	1.42	2.85
Cash		$ 53.85

McKinney Dupuy
Richmond Decr 16, 1861

Mrs R H Watkins
    Madam
    Above we hand you [____] sales of butter & lard at the highest prices we could obtain net proceeds $53.85 to Mr Watkins credit. A few days before the net of your consignment butter sold as high as 50 cents, but in consequence of recent large receipts prices are down and today it is being offered prime quality at 40 c.

We are at a loss to know what to do about buying salt, for you & your Mother – we had hoped that before this [_____] from the salt works in Va would have caused it to decline, but the supply from that source has ceased entirely & there is very little in market. Liverpool sacks are held at $25 per Sack a small lot of Ground alum can be had at $20 per sack & [_____] put up in bags of about 100 lbs at $10. Will you and your mother be pleased to give us further instructions about buying.

The butter pot, tin & buckets shall be sent to the Depot tomorrow to go up the next day. We hope Mrs Dupuy recd the sugar & Molassas, bill of which please find enclosed for her.

> Most Respy
> McKinney Dupuy 1

My very best love to you all
BD

Appendix 4

John J. Flournoy letter of February 24, 1862

- - - - -

Letter from Private John J. Flournoy to Private Richard H. Watkins

Pr Ed Co Ho Febr 24, 62

Cousin Dick

I write you a few lines on a subject that much concerns me, I heard the other day from a number of our company that Charles Redd, Charles Crawley and yourself were trying to raise a company of cavalry for F. D. Redd. I think I can give you almost positive assurance, as far as the present company is concerned you are their choice for Captain, in the event that Capt. Thornton no longer desires command of that Company. I want to urge you to hold on in the Co and at the proper time declare yourself a candidate, that is if you intend to reenlist. Old Berkeley [Lt. Peyton R. Berkeley] is Electioneering with all his might and so is Frank Redd neither of whom I want to be Captain of that Co, not that I do not like them personally, but a good many agree with me they are not fit for leaders.

John Knight, William Evans, Big Harvey _____, Wm Womack, Red Spencer, Chas Flournoy, Hester Walton, and I think John Walton and Mell Arvin, and I believe George Fowlkes, Daniel Allen, Fayette Scott, & myself and I believe others that I do not now remember are all anxious I believe for your election. When I come down I will find out and let you know. We are going to try and put Stokes [2nd Lt. Stokes] in the ranks, if we can get him to reenlist.

I expect to be down the 7th March and I wish you to tell Andrew Venable to meet me in Yorktown with my horse. The weather is bad that I have not been farther from home than Farmville. I was at John Knights yesterday. I think he certainly has camp fever, Dr. Dillon attends him regularly, he was able to sit up a little, _____ is mending. Give my regard to all my friends.

Yours truly

John J. Flournoy 1

Appendix 5

McKinney, Dupuy & Archer – Tobacco Sales Receipt

- - - - -

Sale of R. H. Watkins Tobacco in Richmond on June 19 & 25, 1863

Sales of 7 Hhds Tobacco on Acct Capt R. H. Watkins, by
McKinney, Dupuy & Archer

1863

June 19	Gilmour	Dib	RHW	142.1148	26	$298.48
	White	..	..	142.2356	15	188.40
	..	..	..	142.1308	18	235.44
	Gilmour	..	..	142.1117	25	278.00
	Morton	..	..	142.1620	31	440.20
	Jones	..	..	142.1344	45	604.80
25	Harris		..	145.1260	23	289.80

		2335.12
Charges		
Freight of 52.47 [_____]	120.47	
Comm[ission] 2 ½%	53.38	178.85
Net pro[ceeds] cash		2156.27

McKinney, Dupuy & Archer
Richmond June 26th 1863

Capt R H Watkins
    Dear Sir, Above we hand [___] sales of 7 hhds [hogsheads] of tob: net proceeds $2156.27 to your credit subject to your orders. –

We fear you will be disappointed in the sale of This tob. as we know you were offered more for it than it sold for, but while it was all sound & in pretty fair order, still it was rather an indifferent crop, and we did the very best we could for you.

Very Truly Yours,

McKinney, Dupuy & Archer 1

Notes

Formation of the 3rd Virginia Cavalry

1. Nanzig, Thomas P., *3rd Virginia Cavalry*, Lynchburg, 1989, p. 1-14, 52:
   Sifakis, Stewart; *Compendium of Confederate Armies – Virginia*, New York, 1992, p. 105-107.

Camp Ashland

1. Slabaugh, Arlie; *Confederate States Paper Money*, Iola, 2000, p22-31 (Hereafter cited as Slabaugh).
2. *The Richard Watkins Letters* – Mss1 W3272a, Section 1, Folder 3 (1861 Letters). Manuscripts Collection, Virginia Historical Society, Richmond, Virginia. (Hereafter cited as RHW Letters).
3. RHW Letters, Section 1, Folder 1.
4. RHW Letters, Section 1, Folder 2.
5. Ibid #4.
6. Ibid #4.
7. RHW Letters, Section 1, Folder 4, synopsis notes p. 30.

Yorktown

1. Slabaugh, p. 32-46.
2. RHW Letters, Mss1 W3272a 193 handwritten 3rd Virginia Cavalry muster roll with notations (Hereafter cited as RHW Muster Roll).
3. Bradshaw, Herbert C., *History of Prince Edward County*, Richmond, 1955, p. 388 (Hereafter cited as Bradshaw).
4. RHW Letters, Section 1, Folder 1.
5. Foote, Shelby *The Civil War a Narrative*, New York, 1958, Vol. 1, p. 138-139 and 160-163 (Hereafter cited as Foote).
6. RHW Letters, Mss1 W3272a, Section 1, Folder 4 (1862 Letters).

7. Nanzig, Thomas P., *The Civil War Memories of a Virginia Cavalryman – Lt. Robert T. Hubard, Jr.*, Tuscaloosa, 2007, p.243 (Hereafter cited as Hubard):
Toalson, Jeff; *No Soap, No Pay, Diarrhea, Dysentery & Desertion*, Lincoln, 2006, p. 45 and p. 57.
8. Bradshaw, p.387.
9. RHW Letters, Section 1, Folder 1.
10. Ibid #9.
11. Yearns, W. B. & Barrett, J. G., editors; *North Carolina Civil War Documentary*, Chapel Hill, 2002, p. 145 (Hereafter cited as NCCWDOC).
12. Schaadt, Mark; *Civil War Medicine*, Quincy, 1998, p. 85:
Heimlich, J. *What Your Doctor Won't Tell You*, New York, 1990, p. 54.
13. DeVinne, Pamela, editor; *American Heritage Dictionary*, Boston, 1976, p. 1017 (Hereafter cited as AHD).
14. RHW Letters, Section 1, Folder 1.

Williamsburg & Seven Pines

1. *Nathaniel V. Watkins Letters* 39.1 – W32, Box 1, Folder 2, Special Collections Research Center, Swem Library, College of William and Mary, Williamsburg, Virginia (Hereafter cited as NVW Letters).
2. Bradshaw, p 386.
3. Bradshaw, H. C., *History of Farmville 1798-1948*, Farmville, 1994, p. 315 (Hereafter cited as Farmville).
4. NVW Letters, Box 1, Folder 3.

Richmond

1. NVW Letters, Box 1, Folder 3.
2. AHD, p. 178.
3. AHD, p. 1079.
4. RHW Letters, Mss1 W3272a 15, Folder 1.
5. NVW Letters, Box 1, Folder 3.
6. RHW Letters, W3286a194.
7. AHD, p. 935, 1355 & 605.

Sharpsburg & Chambersburg

1. Priest, J. N., *Antietam – The Soldier's Story*, Shippensburg, 1989, p. 331 & 343.
2. NVW Letters, Box 1, Folder 3.
3. *The Confederate Soldier in the Civil War*, Fairfax Press, undated, p. 112.
4. AHD, p. 363.
5. RHW Letters, Box 1, Folder 2.
6. NVW Letters, Box 1, Folder 4.
7. AHD, p. 738.
8. NVW Letters, Box 1, Folder 4.
9. Foote, Vol. 1, p. 540-541, p. 704-710; Vol. 2 p. 120-121.
10. NVW Letters, Box 1, Folder 5.

The Winter of Lost Horses

1. Slabaugh, p. 54-58.
2. Jones, J. B., *A Rebel War Clerk's Diary*, 2 vols., New York, 1935, by date (Hereafter cited as RWCD).
3. RHW Letters, W3286a 78.
4. RHW Letters, W3272a 356.
5. NVW Letters, Box 1, Folder 6.
6. RHW Letters, 3272a 24, Folder 2.
7. NVW Letters, Box 1, Folder 6.
8. Hubard, p. 67.
9. RHW Letters, Mss1 3272a, Section 1, Folder 5 (1863 Letters).
10. AHD, p. 1310.
11. NVW Letters, Box 1, Folder 8.
12. AHD, p. 815.
13. NVW Letters, Box 1, Folder 9.
14. Ibid #12.
15. Ibid #12.
16. AHD, p. 1380 & 247.

Chancellorsville

1. Slabaugh, p. 59-64.
2. NCCWDOC, p. 184 and photo inscription p. 154.
3. RWCD, by date.
4. AHD, p. 1310.

5. AHD, p. 399.
6. Foote, Vol. 2, p. 314.
7. RHW Letters, Section 1, Folder 7.

Gettysburg
1. NVW Letters, Box 1, Folder 2.
2. RHW Letters, Section 1, Folder 2.
3. Ibid. #2.
4. NVW Letters, Box 1, Folder 2.
5. *Civil War Times Illustrated*, Gettysburg, Vol. 2, #4, *The Cavalry Invasion of the North*, Glenn Tucker, p.28 (Hereafter cited as CWTI).
6. *CWTI*, Gettysburg, Vol. 2, #4, *The Aftermath of Gettysburg*, Robert D. Hoffsommer, p. 49.
7. AHD, p. 1103.

The Rapidan Line to Bristoe Station
1. RWDC, by date.
2. Bradshaw, p. 390.
3. RHW Letters, Section 1, Folder 2.
4. Foote, Vol. 2, p. 792-795.
5. RHW Muster Roll (also see Appendix 1).
6. RWCD, by date.

Pursuit of Averell
1. Slabaugh, p. 65-71.
2. Marshall, Nancy H.; *The Night Before Christmas, A Descriptive Bibliography . . .* ; New Castle, 2002, p xx-xxiv.
3. RWCD, by date.
4. RHW Letters, Mss1 W3272a, Section 1, Folder 6 (1864 Letters).
5. NCCWDOC, p. 148-154.
6. Bradshaw, p. 387.
7. RHW Letters, W3272a 357-358.
8. Hubard, p. 265.
9. RHW Letters, W3286a41.
10. Foote, Vol. 2, p. 907-917.
11. RWCD, by date.

Spotsylvania to Richmond

1. Dowdey, Clifford; *Lee's Last Campaign*, New York, 1960, p. 183-193 (Hereafter cited as Dowdy).
2. RHW Muster Roll (also see Appendix 1).
3. RHW Muster Roll (also see Appendix 1).
4. Dowdy, p. 286-300.
5. Foote, Vol. 3, p. 308-311.
6. RHW Muster Roll (also see Appendix 1).
7. Ibid. #6.

The Shenandoah Valley with Early

1. NVW Letters, Box 2, Folder 2.
2. RHW Letters, Section 1, Folder 7
3. RHW Letters, W3272a 357-358.
4. RHW Letters, W3272a 359.
5. AHD, p. 87.
6. Farmville, p. 392.
7. RWCD, by date.

After the Conflict

1. NVW Letters, Box 2, Folder 5.
2. Ibid. #1.
3. Ibid. #1.
4. Ibid. #1.
5. Personal collection of Richard Dupuy Watkins, Lake Luzerne, New York.
6. Farmville, p. 647, 531 & 532, 419, & 115.
7. RHW Letters, W3268a 580 – 601.

Appendix 1

1. Nanzig, Thomas P., *3rd Virginia Cavalry*, Lynchburg, 1989, p. 94-136:
   3rd Virginia Cavalry, Co. K Muster Roll, RHW Letters, Mss1 W3286a 193:
   Microfilm Files of *Compiled Service Records Confederate - Virginia*, United Daughters of the Confederacy, Richmond, Virginia, Micro Copy 324, Rolls 25 – 37.

Appendix 2

1. Ancestry.com 1860 Federal Census, Roll M653-1371, p. 874, Image 271.

2. Microfilm Records of U. S. Census, Slave Schedules, Mss10, No. 383, Reel 11, p.27, Collection of the Virginia Historical Society.

3. Ancestry.com 1870 Federal Census, Roll M593-1673, p. 100, Image 200.

4. Ancestry.com & Church of Jesus Christ of Latter-day Saints, 1880 U. S. Federal Census, Roll 79-1384, FHF 1255384, p. 312.1000.

5. Anderson, Wm. F. (Jr.), *1850 Census of Prince Edward County, Virginia*, Farmville, 1999, p. 88.

6. Ancestry.com 1850 Federal Census, Roll M452-970, p. 39, Image 80.

7. Ibid. #5, p.77.

8. Ancestry.com 1860 Federal Census, Roll M653-1371, p. 825, Image 272.

9. Ibid. #2, p. 29.

Appendix 3

1. Personal collection of Richard Dupuy Watkins, Lake Luzerne, New York.

Appendix 4

1. Personal collection of Richard Dupuy Watkins, Lake Luzerne, New York.

Appendix 5

1. Personal collection of Richard Dupuy Watkins, Lake Luzerne, New York.

Biographical Index

96, 105, 122, 132, 151, 157, 159, 163, 164, 169, 239, 247, 267, 271, 275, 285, 328

Dupuy, Nannie – 13, 37, 60, 72, 96, 116, 131, 142, 161, 170, 197, 277, 313, 322

Dupuy, Purnall – 61, 108, 113, 147, 160

Dupuy, Sarah – 286, 287, 296, 299-302

Dupuy, William – 75, 201, 231

Dupuy, Willie – 161, 165, 169, 181-184, 197, 203, 209, 228-230, 275, 280, 283, 285, 287, 288, 296-298, 301, 302, 305, 313

Dupuy, William H. – 170, 191, 286

Early, Jubal (Genl.) – 300, 301, 306, 307, 311, 316-317, 321

Edmunds, Henry (Hal) – 20, 21, 22, 67, 116, 122-125, 129, 130, 136-138, 140, 143, 151, 161, 167, 168, 169, 173-179, 181, 183-185, 190, 199, 300, 312, 314, 334

Eggleston (Aunt) – 116

Eggleston (Dr.) – 109, 146, 165, 287

Elliott, R. C. – 279

Ewell, Richard (Genl.) – 201, 224

Ewing, Henry – 18, 123, 130, 161, 201, 228, 243

Ewing, John – 130, 161, 218, 219, 228, 243, 247, 271

Ewing (Mrs.) – 18, 247, 271

Fitzgerald, Pat – 133

Flournoy, Charles – 49, 94, 147, 369

Flournoy, John J. – 49, 50, 140, 369

Flournoy, Tom – 169

Flowers (Mr.) – 162, 169, 184

Floyd (Genl.) – 65, 70

Fontaine, P. (Capt.) – 249

Foster, James – 222

Foster (Mrs.) – 277

Gaines (Dr.) – 279

Gibboney, Robert – 222

Grant, U. S. (Genl.) – 272, 276, 278-281, 284, 297, 300,

Goodall (Mrs.) – 121

Goode (Mr.) – 116

Hardy (Mr.) – 132

Hart, George – 204

Haskins, Archer – 17, 27, 125, 129, 130, 136, 151, 161, 166, 199, 201, 231, 243, 267, 276

Haskins (Mr.) – 18, 96, 108, 139, 161, 174, 247

Haskins, Tom – 13, 18, 99, 110, 130, 139, 184, 186, 201, 227, 243

Hill, A. P. (Genl.) – 132, 224-226

Hill, D. H. (Genl.) – 133

Hines, Dick – 307, 310

Hines, Sam – 188

Hines, Tom – 89, 188

*(ed: Woolton – Wootten: The U. S.
Census and the CSA Military
Records record as Wootten and
all of Mary and Richard's letters
spell as Woolton.)*

Subject Index

Ipecac – 45, 76
Laudanum – 47, 73
Lobelia – 136, 137, 184
Morphine – 175
Mustard plaster – 45
Opium – 76
Snake oil root – 197

Military Units:
Amelia Company – 11
Central Guard – 20, 70, 188
Charlotte Troop – 6, 123, 131
Cumberland Troop – 6, 11, 44
Dinwiddie Cavalry – 48
Farmville Guards – 137
Halifax Troop – 6, 169
Hampton's Legion – 168, 169, 184
Henrico Company – 11
King & Queen Artillery – 75, 93-95, 99, 224
Longstreet's Crop – 273
Lunenburg Troop – 6, 11
Meagher's Irish Brigade – 209
Mecklingburg Troop – 11, 35, 205
Merherrin Grays – 72
Mississippi Troope – 16
New Kent Troop – 19, 31
Nottoway Dragoons – 75, 231
Pickett's Division – 205
Prince George Troop – 75
Richmond Howitzers – 48, 310
Virginia Rangers – 11
1st North Carolina Infantry – 42
1st South Carolina Regiment – 184

3rd Arkansas Mounted Rifles – 196
4th Tennessee - 180
5th Virginia – 128
6th New York Cavalry – 161
8th Alabama Infantry – 42, 48
16th Massachusetts – 41
18th Virginia – 81, 137

Negroes:
Births – 274
Blankets for winter – 128, 134, 182, 217, 218-222, 226, 228, 231, 234-237
Deaths – 25, 61, 74, 131, 197, 207, 286, 293
Delivering horse to 3rd Va. – 125, 135, 138, 175, 259, 265, 266, 271
Dowry – 159, 160-163
Drafted as workers for fortifications – 146, 163, 189, 222
Escorting Mary between farms – 123, 141
Exchange/Trading of – 31, 162
Foodstuff to send Richard – 57
Garden crops (personal) – 244
General health – 165
General welfare – 47, 268
Hiring – 58
Hiring out (renting) – 162
Marriage – 31
Medical care – 24, 73, 197
Mixing groups of slaves – 229
On the battlefield – 293
Post war – 327, 328, 330

Recovered from the Yanks –
293-298, 311
Runaways – 83
Selling – 155, 163
Servant for Richard at the front
– 126, 127, 129, 162, 164, 266,
267, 271, 272, 274, 276, 277,
306, 307, 308, 312
Servants with Prince Edward
Troop – 36, 116, 125, 266, 268
Shirting cloth – 67
Shoes – 36, 45, 271, 308
Singing – 230
Soldiers – 248, 329
Suffrage – 330
Taken in Union raid – 257, 281,
293, 294-297, 311
Tacking thieves – 277
Winter clothing – 37, 40, 182,
216-220, 224, 237, 244, 271
Without an overseer – 210, 233

Political Comment:
Atlanta (fall of) – 310, 311, 313,
315
Conditions in Richmond – 110,
259
Condition of the army – 206,
264, 276, 279
Darkest Hour of the War - 321
Duration of the war – 34, 77,
99, 109, 159, 162, 175, 185,
204, 211
England joining the conflict –
53-55
European recognition – 22, 41,
142

French ministers – 78
Mason and Slidell Affair – 53,
54
Negro suffrage – 330
"Our Southern Confederacy" –
69, 78
Peace talks – 143
President Davis (execution) –
330
President Harrison - 332
President Johnson – 328, 330
President Lincoln – 17, 22, 142,
143, 196, 328
Republican convention – 315
Secretary of War – 70
Southern rights – 169
Yankee comments – 54-55,
329-330

Prison Camps:
Fort Delaware – 106, 191
Camp Chase – 169, 170, 182,
192, 323

Religion:
Chaplain – 49, 60, 81, 90, 221
Church Elders – 108
Church services (military) – 8,
9, 14, 49, 60, 64, 217, 219
Church services (home) 49, 50,
73, 104, 272, 305, 307
Communion – 108
Funeral Services – 50
Presbyterian Church (Briery) –
111

CPSIA information can be obtained at www.ICGtesting.com
Printed in the USA
LVOW042031181212

312270LV00002B/423/P